UNEASY REUNIONS

NICOLE DEJONG NEWENDORP

Uneasy Reunions

Immigration, Citizenship, and Family Life in Post-1997 Hong Kong

STANFORD UNIVERSITY PRESS

STANFORD, CALIFORNIA

Stanford University Press
Stanford, California

Printed in the United States of America on acid-free, archival-quality paper

Library of Congress Cataloging-in-Publication Data

Newendorp, Nicole.
   Uneasy reunions : immigration, citizenship, and family life in post-1997
Hong Kong / Nicole Newendorp.
      p. cm.
   Includes bibliographical references and index.
   ISBN 978-0-8047-5813-0 (cloth : alk. paper)
   1. Hong Kong (China)—Emigration and immigration—Social aspects.
2. Hong Kong (China)—Emigration and immigration—Government policy.
3. Immigrants—Family relationships—China—Hong Kong. I. Title.
JV8758.N49 2008
305.9'06912095125—dc22

                                                              2007044938

Typeset by Thompson Type in 10/14 Janson.

Contents

Acknowledgments

I am greatly indebted to a number of people and institutions without whose help this book could not have been written. Foremost, I want to thank the employees of the social service center in Sham Shui Po, Hong Kong, with whose help I conducted the bulk of the research for this book. These individuals generously (and literally!) made space for me in their cramped office and in their busy work lives from May 2001 through June 2002 and made every effort to accommodate any needs or requests that I had then or have had since. Likewise, I remain extremely grateful to the mainland Chinese immigrant women and children who shared aspects of their lives with me, thus enabling me to gain understanding about how they experienced their transitions from mainland Chinese to Hong Kong life. My discussions about these individuals in this book simply do not convey the extreme enjoyment that I experienced through my daily interactions and conversations with them. Furthermore, I hope that I have not in any way betrayed the trust they placed in me with the details of their everyday lives.

Rubie Watson, my dissertation supervisor at Harvard University's Department of Anthropology, has for the past twelve years consistently given her dedicated attention and interest to my research and writing projects. It is difficult for me to express the full range of gratitude that I feel for this ongoing support. I greatly value the encouragement and guidance that she has provided throughout this time, without which my work on this project would have faltered long ago. James L. "Woody" Watson and Michael Herzfeld, the other members of my faculty committee, have also contributed immensely to the successful completion of this book. Additional faculty mentors at Harvard who served as important influences in the development of my intellectual interests in the formative stages of this project include Stanley Tambiah, Sally Falk Moore, and the late Begoña Aretxaga. A number of colleagues in the department, particularly Manduhai Buyandelger, Michelle Tisdel Flikke, Vanessa Fong, Erica James, Pilar Montalvo, Sisa DeJesus, Young-a Park, and Sonja Plesset, provided unflagging comradeship and essential critical commentary on my work while I was a graduate student. I remain extremely grateful to all of these members, past and present, of Harvard's Department of Anthropology.

A number of institutions provided the financial and logistical support that enabled me to conduct the research for this book in Hong Kong. Substantial funding for the project was provided by a research grant from the National Science Foundation (BCS-0090244). The Blakemore Foundation and the United States Department of Education Foreign Language and Area Studies (FLAS) Program provided generous financial support that enabled me to spend one full year studying intermediate and advanced-level Cantonese at the Chinese University of Hong Kong's Yale-in-China Language Center from August 2000 through July 2001. I am also indebted both to Dr. Elisabeth Sinn at Hong Kong University's Centre of Asian Studies, where I was affiliated from August 2000 through July 2001, and to Professor Tan Chee Bing at the Chinese University of Hong Kong's Department of Anthropology, where I was affiliated from August 2001 through July 2002. Their personal and institutional help enabled my access to Hong Kong researchers, libraries, and academic support, without which I could not have completed this project. During the final stages of writing and editing my dissertation based on this research, I was supported by a Graduate Society Dissertation Completion Fellowship from Harvard University.

While conducting research in Hong Kong, I relied on a number of professionals and academics for information, help, and advice. In particular, I would like to thank Nelson Chow, Ernest Chui, Leo Goodstadt, Juanita Ho Kit-mui, Tim Ko, Agnes Ku, Viki Wai-ki Li, Iris Liu, Tik-sang Liu, Maria Tam, Gordon Mathews, Joseph Bosco, Cora Man, Janet Scott, Aihe Wang, and Stephen Yau for their support and encouragement of my research.

I also owe many thanks to a number of individuals in Cambridge, Massachusetts, who have contributed to my ability to complete this book. I would like to thank Anya Bernstein, Director of Studies at Harvard University's Committee on Degrees in Social Studies, for her flexible approach to faculty management that has allowed me to forge a balance between my professional life and my family life. Without her understanding and support, I could not have found time to complete this manuscript while also teaching, advising, and raising two young children. I am also grateful to have had the opportunity to engage with the excellent students and faculty members in social studies, with whom I have shared many conversations on subjects related to this book. In particular, I would like to thank Ajantha Subramanian, who first suggested that I might frame my book in terms of "migration across political difference," and Mae Bunagan and Currun Singh, students whose senior honors theses touched on similar topics and with whom I spent many hours discussing various aspects of immigration, citizenship, and belonging in the United States and in France. I am also extremely grateful to a number of individuals who have read and provided critical commentary on drafts of this manuscript. My work has benefited substantially from close readings of the entire manuscript provided by Vanessa Fong, Sonja Plesset, Tulasi Srinivas, Rubie Watson, and Andrea Yang. I also thank Erica James, Manduhai Buyandelger, Elanah Uretsky, and Catherine Geanuracos for providing important feedback on selected chapters. Laura J. Miller and Kimberly DaCosta, as members of my writing group, have provided weekly commentary on my work for the past year. Their careful readings and thoughtful comments have been particularly important in enabling me to finish this book. Sonja Plesset and Jason Ur provided last minute advice in selecting and formatting photographs to go along with the text. Asya Troychansky helped with checking citations quoted in the text.

A number of friends and family members in both the United States and in Hong Kong also provided crucial support for my research and writing over the past ten years. In Hong Kong, I would particularly like to thank Jacqui Hutchings, Patrick Condon, Bobby Mohseni, and Bellyann Tamayo for providing friendship, places to stay, and child care. In the United States, I would like to thank my family, including Laurie Newendorp, Terry Newendorp, Kathryn Lindquist, Ken Newendorp, Taylor Newendorp, and Kate Murphy, for their unfailing encouragement over many years.

At Stanford University Press, I am extremely indebted to Muriel Bell for the consistent support and expert editorial advice that she has offered me throughout the process of revising and publishing this book. The final version of this manuscript has also benefited greatly from the extremely helpful comments provided by Sara L. Friedman and one anonymous reviewer. I would also like to thank Kirsten Oster and Joa Suarez for their patience and enthusiasm in dealing with my many questions and concerns throughout the publishing process.

Finally, I owe a special thank you to my husband David, who has provided daily encouragement for my research interests and professional life throughout my graduate school and postgraduate career. More so than anyone else, I could not have completed this book without his help. My sons, Zeke and Gabriel, who have lived with this project for their entire lives, were especially patient as I worked to complete the final version of the manuscript. Zeke has been an invaluable research assistant in all my Hong Kong-based fieldwork, and I find inspiration on a daily basis from Gabriel's optimism and zest for life. My most constant sources of support throughout this long, difficult, and rewarding project, David, Zeke, and Gabriel have all contributed in their own important ways to the final result.

UNEASY REUNIONS

ONE

Split-Families, Reunited Families, and Political Difference

It was late morning on a weekday in 2002, and I stood waiting on the street outside exit C of the Sham Shui Po MTR station. The MTR is Hong Kong's subway system—with sleek, ultramodern cars that arrive in each station no less frequently than every minute during rush hour and every four minutes at other times. I had been in Hong Kong long enough that I took for granted the clean, fast-paced, and orderly convenience of the MTR; nor did I pay particular attention to the sharp contrast between the MTR's environment and that of the neighborhood where my fieldsite was located in one of Hong Kong's poorest residential areas. The street—like most streets in Hong Kong—was crowded, but not with the fashionably dressed young business people seen in many other parts of the city. Instead, homeless people and gaunt women pushing carts of garbage mingled with mainland immigrants and the elderly, rummaging through the piles of cast-off pots, pans, electronic equipment, and other salvaged household goods heaped on blankets along both sides of the street. Behind the blankets a number of small shops opened directly onto the street: a pet food store, with small bamboo cages of goldfinches hanging in the doorway, and a noodle shop, where patrons eating breakfasts of steaming rice porridge, fried dough, and round, fat noodles sat at the rickety tables that spilled out onto the sidewalk. The old buildings that housed these shops were dingy and gray, and despite being short by Hong Kong standards—only five or six stories like most housing built in the 1950s and 1960s—they nonetheless effectively blocked out the sun on the street below.

A-Chun, my informant, was late for our meeting. As I checked the time on my cell phone, it rang. "Where are you?" asked A-Chun. "I'm at exit 'C,'" I replied. "So am I," she said. A few seconds later, she was by my side. She and I had been waiting on opposite sides of the street for over ten minutes, each thinking that the other had not yet arrived. We hadn't been able to see each other because the structure of the MTR exit had blocked our views. When she reached me, though, she was laughing. She explained why. The first time she had visited her husband in Hong Kong, when she was heavily pregnant with her second daughter almost nine years earlier, she and her husband had waited for each other at the same exit, walking around and around in circles, without meeting. Because neither of them had known exactly what time she would arrive in Hong Kong from mainland China, neither knew that the other was already there. When they finally found each other, they realized they had both been waiting, across the street from each other, for almost an hour. Having told me this story, A-Chun, still giggling, held me gently by the arm and steered me toward the tenement building where she had been living with her family of five in one 80 square foot room for the past year, since she and her children had all legally immigrated to Hong Kong from the mainland.

A-Chun is from a rural part of southeast mainland China only a few hours away from the border with Hong Kong. Although she and her Hong Kong husband got married in 1990, before her recent immigration to Hong Kong, she had continued to live in her home village on the mainland while waiting for the legal documentation that would enable her to move across the border to live with her husband. During this time, she was only able to visit Hong Kong once—at which time she gave birth to her second daughter. In this respect, A-Chun and her husband's split-family life was not unusual. Hundreds of thousands of mainland Chinese residents, who are

Figure 1.1 Sham Shui Po (January 2005)

already eligible for the legal right to live in Hong Kong, have waited up to or exceeding ten years in order to rejoin their immediate family members in Hong Kong, and tens of thousands are still waiting.

Since 1995, the People's Republic of China (PRC) and Hong Kong governments have allowed 55,000 mainland Chinese citizens to immigrate to Hong Kong legally each year. Ninety-eight percent of these immigrants come to Hong Kong for the purpose of family reunion, and the majority—over 85 percent—are the wives and nonadult children of local Hong Kong men. Because of the strict enforcement of immigration quotas, most mainland Chinese wives and children have waited, on average, between five and ten years to join their husbands and fathers in Hong Kong. Since all

Hong Kong and Vicinity

Map 1.1   Hong Kong and Vicinity, showing the border with mainland China and the railway line between Hong Kong and Guangzhou, the capital city of Guangdong Province

applications for immigration are processed independently, these fathers, mothers, and their individual children experience many years living as split-families in various combinations of nuclear and extended family households on the mainland and in Hong Kong. Separation, as A-Chun told me, is not easy on family life:

> It was like this: my older daughter already got her one-way permit [to immigrate to Hong Kong from the mainland] in 1996. But there was no one

[in Hong Kong] to take care of her, so I took her back to the mainland with me to go to kindergarten there—she was only three years old. Then, well, my younger daughter was born in Hong Kong, but I also took care of her on the mainland. Finally, in 2000, [the children] came to Hong Kong to take advantage of going to school in Hong Kong. At that time, I [knew that I would get my one-way permit to immigrate soon, and so I applied for] a visitor's permit and came with them. A few months later I got my one-way permit—and we could all stay in Hong Kong.

It wasn't that I really wanted to live separately, but I had chosen this path—this path to Hong Kong—so we had to live separately . . . [My husband] would come to visit once a month—until finally the expressway was built, and then the last two years he was able to come every week . . . Before I had kids, I didn't care one way or the other. But after I had the children, the time [waiting for him to come] seemed so long.

It was a bitter and difficult life . . . At the beginning when [the children] were little, my mother helped me look after them. Later when they were older and went to kindergarten, I had to do everything myself . . . So, to be separated, it's not that great. It's better for the family to be together . . . Sometimes, you'll feel sick, but the kids are loud, they wake you up, and you can't rest. Or sometimes this one has a fever, that one has a fever— in the middle of the night you have to take them up to the doctor just by yourself . . . [My husband] was always very worried about the children. If I told him that one of the kids had a fever, he would call at least several more times during the night. I had to tell him that he shouldn't call so often . . . , that he was wasting money.

During the decade that A-Chun waited to join her husband in Hong Kong, mainland China's "late" socialist economy experienced dramatic growth, resulting in mainlanders' increased access to consumer goods and other amenities associated with a "modern" lifestyle. Transportation and communication infrastructures were significantly improved, with one result being that Hong Kong husbands could visit their mainland wives more frequently, and phone calls during times that they were apart became more affordable. In Hong Kong, on the other hand, the previously booming economy was ravaged during the 1997 Asian financial crisis. Businesses folded, restaurants closed, and property prices plunged, leaving many middle-class home owners saddled with mortgages worth more than the value of their properties (Yoon 2002). Another recession followed in 2002, when the jobless rate reached an all time high of 7.4 percent, and more people were receiving welfare assistance than ever before (Yoon 2002:43). During the spring and early summer of 2002, local newscasts featured almost nightly stories of Hong Kong businesses and restaurants that had folded overnight, with no notice or warning given to the luckless employees who, in most cases, were owed thousands of dollars of back wages in addition to being newly unemployed. Newspaper articles even reported the abandonment of many Chinese "second wives" of Hong Kong men, who no longer had the resources to support their mistresses on the other side of the border. As a result, when A-Chun finally did migrate legally across the Hong Kong/mainland Chinese border, she—along with other migrant wives and children who had waited for years to make this move—experienced sharp downward mobility. In their squalid tenement housing in Sham Shui Po and other low-cost residential areas, immigrants like A-Chun and her children had little access to the comfortable, glittering, and "modern" city that they had imagined from afar. Furthermore, they faced significant stigmatization, discrimination, and marginalization from the Hong Kong population at large.

Migration for the purpose of family reunion is one the most common forms of contemporary migration flows, comprising over two-thirds of all migration to the United States and the European Union (Kofman 2004). In most cases, countries do enforce a period of waiting of one year or longer for the entrance of family members, and these wait periods are often significantly longer for immigrants than for citizens (ibid.). In this way, the situation of Hong Kong husbands and their wives, who live for long periods as split-families on both sides of the Hong Kong/mainland border, is not unusual.

What makes these long waits for family reunification in the Hong Kong context surprising is that Hong Kong husbands and their mainland wives and children have shared one official nationality—that of the PRC—since Hong Kong reverted to mainland Chinese sovereignty on July 1, 1997. In other words, these long waits take place to cross an internal, rather than an international, border. Furthermore, these two groups of Chinese citizens have similar ethnic backgrounds, speak the same languages, and share a long historical and cultural past in addition to living in increasingly interconnected and fast-changing worlds in which mass consumption and capital accumulation are the norm. Nonetheless, mainland resident and Hong Kong resident PRC citizens have vastly different access to rights, including, in particular, the right of movement to cross the Hong Kong/mainland border.

I investigated the experiences of family reunion in the mainland/Hong Kong context through eighteen consecutive months of research that I conducted in Hong Kong from January 2001 through June 2002. The data that I collected through this period of fieldwork were also supplemented by shorter research trips in 1997, 1998, 2005, and 2007, along with twelve months of advanced level Cantonese language training in 2000 and 2001. My data collection focused on trying to understand how mainland Chinese wives' immigration experiences were affected by their long waits to gain entrance to Hong Kong, along with how they were taught to become "Hong Kong people" once there. In particular, I was forced to account for the many everyday struggles that they encountered in adapting to their new lives in Hong Kong's vibrant urban metropolis—despite the many similarities that they shared with Hong Kong people. I also sought to understand what was behind the antagonism toward them by many Hong Kong officials and other residents.

My conversations with migrants reflected the many anxieties they experienced because of their long waits to become legal Hong Kong residents, as well as their concerns about the well-being of children and parents left on the mainland, disputes with Hong Kong in-laws over living arrangements, and conflicts between personal aspirations and the demands of employers, social workers, and Hong Kong officials. As a result, in this book, I follow these immigrant women—women like A-Chun—through the paths that they took: from their marriages to Hong Kong men and their long waits on the mainland to the downward mobility and familial struggles that they experienced once in Hong Kong, where, because of these difficulties, they sought help from Hong Kong social workers and other government officials. These social workers and officials hoped to aid wives' adjustment to Hong Kong life by educating them in the qualities of civility idealized in Hong Kong discourses of belonging.

Overall, I argue here that mainland women's experiences of family reunion in Hong Kong are anxiety provoking—not only because of the everyday difficulties involved with living together in a new environment after long years of separation—but also because their migration for the purpose of family reunion requires a move across political difference. By political difference, I mean that both mainland immigrants and Hong Kong people, as individuals but also as members of larger social groups, have been socialized with different expectations of privileges and goals for relating both to the state and also to society around them. These differences find both discursive and actual expression in the cultural and social landscapes that immigrants encounter in their everyday interactions with Hong Kong people, thereby engaging migrants in new possibilities of action and behavior but concomitantly engendering struggles and complications in their adjustment processes overall. The effects of mainland wives' moves across political difference extend beyond the legal-political realm into the social realm, and, in the case of family reunion migration, into the domestic sphere and family life, because the roles that individual family members (as citizens) are expected to play, and the values that they should hold and pass on—as mothers, in particular, but also as wives and daughters-in-law, are also constructed through interaction with the discursive realm of difference. Moreover, these everyday interactions among immigrants and Hong Kong people (including family members, social workers, government officials, and employers) expose the many rifts that exist in the social imaginary of "belonging" in Hong Kong.

Throughout this ethnography, I define immigration as the journey (and concomitant hopes, accomplishments, and struggles) over localized processes of membership and inclusion. As a result, this book is as much about the Hong Kong discourses articulating the imagined qualities desired of citizen residents as it is about the migrants themselves.

One Country, Two Borders

Hong Kong, a dynamic and vibrantly cosmopolitan city on the Southeast China coast, is situated on a series of small islands and one tiny peninsula that connects with China's Guangdong Province. Hong Kong's tall hills of lush green parkland jut sharply out of the surrounding ocean waters, providing a striking backdrop for the immensely tall skyscrapers that seem precariously perched over the city's famous harbor. Of its 6.99 million residents in 2006, approximately 95 percent were classified as "ethnic Chinese"

Figure 1.2   Hong Kong's glittering skyscrapers
(January 2007)

(Census and Statistics Department 2002). China initially ceded Victoria Island (modern day Hong Kong Island) to the British in 1841 after China's defeat in the Opium War. In 1860, the Kowloon Peninsula was also ceded to British control, followed by the ninety-nine-year lease of Hong Kong's "New Territories" to the British in 1898. On July 1, 1997, after more than 150 years of British colonial rule, the colony was returned to mainland Chinese sovereignty as the Hong Kong Special Administrative Region (HKSAR) of the PRC.

Hong Kong has always enjoyed a unique historical and geographic relationship with China and with its neighboring province of Guangdong in particular. Strong family and economic ties between residents of Hong Kong and Guangdong have meant that in all but a few periods of the twentieth century—namely, the Japanese occupation of Southern China and

Hong Kong during World War II and during the height of the Cultural Revolution—there have always been significant movements of people from China into Hong Kong and vice versa (Kwok and Ames 1995:17). These complex historical, economic, and familial linkages between Hong Kong and the rest of Southeast China have long facilitated the practice of Hong Kong men marrying mainland women (Lang and Smart 2002).[1] Although political barriers provided a formidable deterrent to this form of marriage during the heyday of the PRC's socialist period, mainland China's economic liberalization over the past two decades has paved the way for the renewal of economic and social ties between Hong Kong and neighboring areas of Southeast China. As a result, such marriages have once again become common and are on the rise. In 1996, 2,215 Hong Kong men registered marriages with mainland women; by 2006, that number had jumped to 18,000—more than one-third of all marriages recorded by Hong Kong men that year (Connolly and Wong 2/23/07).

Strictly speaking, Hong Kong people are historically, culturally, and ethnically very closely "related" to mainland Chinese residents. Most histories emphasize that Hong Kong was a "barren rock" at the time of its occupation by the British—its attraction to the British and its vast merchant empire was its location as a deep-water port. Nonetheless, precolonial Hong Kong was inhabited by a small number of Han Chinese and other ethnic groups who, like other residents of Southeast China, farmed the land and fished the sea (see, for example, Ko 1994). Today, Hong Kong's population is still 95 percent ethnic Chinese. Both Chinese immigrants and long-time Hong Kong residents enjoy similarities of language, foodways, and, as one of my informants said, "some traditional Chinese cultural values, such as respecting the elderly and filial piety." Many Hong Kong residents also originate from the same areas of Southeastern China as current immigrants. Furthermore, economic, consumer, and media links forged by participation in a global capitalist economic system (coupled with the social ties created through the interaction of individuals with family members abroad and in Hong Kong in particular) have resulted in the additional "blurring" of boundaries between residents of the mainland and Hong Kong, as families, businesses, recreational activities, and media straddle both sides of the mainland Chinese/Hong Kong border. From the points of view of many outsiders, China's lightning-speed economic development and the significant global links between the mainland and Hong Kong, combined with a powerful discourse that links Hong Kong, China, and Taiwan as part of one pan-Chinese cultural area, might well suggest that whatever cultural differences do exist between Hong Kong and the mainland are relatively minor (Shih 1998).

The government of the PRC has also been instrumental in trying to re-inforce the similarities between Hong Kong people and mainland residents. When Hong Kong was returned to the PRC on July 1, 1997, the political reunification of Hong Kong with the mainland was the source of much jubilation on the part of Chinese citizens on the mainland, who welcomed the "return" of their Chinese "brothers and sisters" in Hong Kong to the "motherland's" embrace. Through government-controlled media imagery, Hong Kong was described as returning to the "Chinese family," coming "home," and uniting family membership of the "same blood" (Pan et al. 2001). By making unambiguous connections between the "Chinese family" and the "Chinese nation," the PRC party-state attempted to focus world-wide attention on the symbolic "reunion" of Hong Kong and mainland Chinese citizens through their "supposed common ancestry" (ibid.). At the same time, this imagery served to deflect attention away from the question-able legitimacy of annexing Hong Kong—a former colony that had finally been "liberated" from foreign occupation—to its "motherland" in a semi-colonial relationship.

The rhetorical strategy of describing Hong Kong people and mainland Chinese residents as one reunited "family" not only minimized the ethnic, geographical, and other social and political differences between Hong Kong people and mainlanders (ibid.), it also tapped into deep-seated cultural ide-als focused on the importance of "reunion" held by both Hong Kong Chi-nese and their mainland counterparts (cf. Stafford 2000). Nonetheless, this view was rejected by many Hong Kong people as portraying a false sense of unity among mainlanders and Hong Kong people, who continue to see themselves as ideologically, socially, economically, and politically different from mainlanders (Shih 1998; Mathews 2001; M. Chan 2002).

These views of difference stem from the fact that the border between Hong Kong and the rest of mainland China is not only a location of move-ment. As demonstrated by the decade-long waits of mainland wives to join their Hong Kong husbands, it is also a location of impermeability. Hilary

Cunningham and Josiah Heyman write that borders, and the ports of entry situated along them, are "places where processes of both mobility and enclosure exist side by side" (2004:297). This is certainly the case of the Hong Kong/mainland Chinese border, where the complex social history of contemporary cultural, economic, and familial interaction continues to be strongly influenced by the shadow of the political separation that exists between Hong Kong and the rest of the PRC. For most of the second half of the twentieth century—from the establishment of the PRC in 1949 through the implementation of the PRC's economic liberalization policies in the late 1970s and early 1980s—the border served as both an actual and ideological marker of separation between Hong Kong and mainland Chinese residents. While Chinese citizens on the mainland were working in state-controlled work units, farming in village collectives, and making continuous revolution under the encouragement of Chairman Mao, Hong Kong people (as British subjects) were being schooled in English, learning about the rule of law, and making money by working in factories, engaging in international business, and speculating on property. Residents and visitors in Hong Kong who were curious about life in mainland China routinely parked at Lok Ma Chau, a high, wide-open vantage point, where, from the security of their own cars, they had unobstructed views across the Shenzhen River to the mainland (see, for example, Lui 2001). During this period of political and ideological separation, Hong Kong developed into a vibrant center of global trade and commerce, and the ethos of a Hong Kong identity, separate from that of mainland China, crystallized among the residents of Hong Kong. Cosmopolitan, engaged in a complex web of global social and economic relations, law-abiding, and self-enterprising, Hong Kong people see themselves as (and have proved to be) important actors on the global stage (Hamilton 1999). Surveys conducted both before and after 1997 indicate that Chinese residents of Hong Kong more often identify with Hong Kong rather than mainland China, whose residents have been portrayed since the late 1970s as "lazy," "dirty," and "uncivilized" in the Hong Kong media (Ma 1999; Mathews 2001).

Today, these two groups of PRC citizens are not equal. Hong Kong residents are governed by the rule of law and enjoy important civil and political rights, including free speech and limited suffrage. Hong Kong residents hold different passports from mainland resident PRC citizens, and these HKSAR passports allow Hong Kong residents visa-free access to over one hundred countries worldwide. Furthermore, Hong Kong residents are not subject to the one-child policy, and, most importantly, they do not need exit visas to cross the border to enter mainland China. In 2001 and 2002, Hong Kong husbands were free to cross this border at any time they desired. Mainland wives, on the other hand, along with all other mainland resident Chinese citizens, were still not allowed to cross the border without special exit permits issued by the PRC government. These exit permits were available once each year to individuals requesting permission to visit close relatives in Hong Kong for a period of three months or less, but many split-families had neither the financial resources nor access to suitable child care arrangements to enable such visits. Between 2000 and 2002, mainland residents could otherwise only visit Hong Kong with organized tour groups. Participation in such groups remained impractical for many mainland Chinese residents, however, because of the large monetary deposit required from each tour member, used to cover the cost of PRC government-imposed fines should an individual not return to the mainland with the group (Li 2001).

The political freedoms enjoyed by Hong Kong residents—despite (but also because of) their former subjugation by the British—not only underpin Hong Kong's worldwide success as an important financial center but also secure Hong Kong's place in the "first" rather than "second" or "third" world. With the creation of the HKSAR of the PRC on July 1, 1997, the differences in the political and economic systems of Hong Kong and the mainland were legally inscribed under the "one country, two systems" policy. As guaranteed by this policy, PRC Chinese citizens in Hong Kong will continue to have significantly different political, economic, and social rights than their PRC citizen counterparts on the mainland until the year 2047. Nonetheless, fueled by the uneasy memory of the harsh political suppression of student protesters by the Chinese party-state in Tiananmen Square on June 4, 1989, many Hong Kong people worry that their political and civil rights will be gradually eroded by the PRC government.

Hong Kong's return to mainland Chinese sovereignty sparked serious social consternation among many Hong Kong people (M. Chan 2003), not only because of Hong Kong people's desire to maintain their own identity separate from that of the mainland, but also because the future vitality of their political and economic ways of life was at stake.[2] Social tensions caused by concerns over Hong Kong's future political autonomy from the mainland were exacerbated by Hong Kong people's concern over their increased dependency on the mainland economy for trade, investment, and tourism to stabilize (and revitalize) the region's economic development (M. Chan 2002:13). As Chan explains:

> [Hong Kong people's] alarm at the prospect that such a China market dependency, which would soon be reinforced by increasingly extensive functional interfaces with the mainland, would result in the HKSAR's being more fully absorbed into the PRC mainland orbit, not just in the nominal political sense, but also into its powerful, much larger, but less liberal social and cultural loci. Then Hong Kong would gradually lose its unique cosmopolitan outlook and treasured global linkages, eventually becoming just another big city of the PRC. (ibid.)

Mainland immigrants, including those wives and children who had legally moved to Hong Kong for the purpose of family reunion, were at the receiving end of Hong Kong people's expressions of this uneasiness.

For mainland wives, whose moves across the border were profoundly circumscribed, the border had very real—and often devastating—effects on the well-being of their families and married life. Yet when women did finally immigrate and become Hong Kong residents, their legal status changed, and they, too, gained the mobility from which they had been restricted for so long. In this way, the migration experiences of Chinese women who moved from the mainland to Hong Kong remained substantially different from the migration experiences of the ever-growing numbers of female migrants who form an important part of China's internal "floating population" (see, for example, Davin 1999; Zhang 2001; Murphy 2002; and Gaetano and Jacka 2004).[3] For Hong Kong people, on the other hand, the border's symbolic importance is paramount. As economic and cultural interactions between Hong Kong and the mainland increase, the border serves as a concrete reminder of both the actual and perceived differences that exist between cosmopolitan Hong Kong people (Cantonese: *Heunggongyahn*) and their "backward" mainland Chinese "cousins."

Migration, Citizenship, and Imagined Community Membership

Throughout history, it has often been the norm, rather than the exception, that people have moved from one place to another (Glick-Schiller 2003). Yet there are a number of reasons why migration has attracted much important scholarly attention in recent years. The technological advances of the twentieth century—including air travel, cell phone technology, and Internet communications—have made travel and communication over long distances faster, cheaper, and less hazardous than in the past. And people do move: at mid-year 2005, total numbers of world migrants were listed at 190,633,564 (http://esa.un.org/migration/index.asp?panel=1).

Anthropologists and sociologists have responded to these massive movements of individuals in the contemporary world by developing growing bodies of research on both the increasing feminization of migration worldwide and on transnational family life.[4] The former body of literature documents the powerful role of accumulated capital and the high demand for physical and reproductive labor in industrialized cities in Europe, North America, and Asia in stimulating migration flows of women in addition to those of men (see, for example, Sassen-Koob 1996; Constable 1997; Mills 1999; Parreñas 2001, 2005; Massey et al. 2002; Choy 2003; Pessar and Mahler 2003). The latter body of literature focuses on the ways in which contemporary migration trends facilitate the abilities of individuals, including mothers and daughters, to leave family members to live and work in new locations—even if these separations are mitigated by the ability to maintain communication with those left behind (Mahler 2001; Parrenas 2001, 2005; Constable 2003). Increasingly, the literature on transnational family life has also drawn attention to the dense networks of family, friends, employers, and other individuals with whom migrants interact at each end of their migration experience—both in home communities and in their new host communities—resulting in complex webs of commitment and belonging that shape migrants' engagement with, adjustment to, and integration with the communities in which they live (see, for example, Glick-Schiller, Basch, and Szanton-Blanc 1992; Constable 1999; Levitt 2001; Pieke et al. 2004). Overall, these literatures paint a vibrant picture of the complex empirical realities of migrant experiences, which affect and are affected by economic, social, and political processes at both local and global levels.

The migration experiences of the mainland wives of Hong Kong men resonate with these theoretical frameworks. On the one hand, women's romantic motivations for marriage with their Hong Kong husbands mingled with their aspirations to gain access to first-world amenities and better social and economic futures for their children—futures that they thought they would experience once in Hong Kong. On the other hand, my migrant informants also experienced emotionally fraught family separations and reunions, through which they created and maintained dense networks of personal and social interaction on both sides of the Hong Kong/mainland Chinese border. These networks, comprised of family, friends, social workers, employers, and/or government officials, strongly shaped all phases of women's migration processes, including their adjustment once in Hong Kong.

Yet the particular situation of mainland Chinese wives, who wait for five years, ten years, or longer to enter Hong Kong as legal migrants, adds a new dimension of complexity to these frameworks. Why do these immigrants have to wait so long for entrance to Hong Kong *when they and the members of the society they seek to join are all citizens of the same nation-state* who also share similar racial, cultural, linguistic, and familial backgrounds? In other words, because these immigrant wives' spatial journeys take place across an internal—not an international—border, their journeys refocus analytical attention on a particularly salient aspect of migration experience. This analytical focus concerns the idea of membership, and how normative ideologies of membership and belonging are constructed and enacted, thereby influencing the empirical reality of individual migrants' journeys from one location to another.

Writing about the history of Mexican immigration to the United States, historian Mae Ngai has argued that immigration policy draws "lines of inclusion and exclusion that articulate a desired composition—imagined if not necessarily realized—of the nation" (2004:5). Ngai's argument is important, because it points to the fact that immigration policy never arises in a vacuum separate from localized or nationalist discourses that equate the possibility of membership with a set of imagined qualities desired of citizen residents. In this way, debates over immigration and citizenship are intertwined and rooted in shared beliefs and articulations over the concept of membership in particular communities. Since citizenship implies that members of a community share a sense of belonging, entitlement, and duties that define the possibilities of inclusion and exclusion, immigrants, who challenge—both literally and figuratively—the boundaries of the imagined communities that nations hope to establish and maintain, become the focal points for larger debates about national and community membership.

If, as Walzer contends (1983:31–63), we think of citizenship as determining the boundary between "strangers" and "members" of a given community, then immigration policy marks the first step in determining community inclusion and exclusion at a national level. The second step in this process, what Walzer calls the "second admissions" (ibid.), takes place *after* immigrants have already legally entered their new national communities. To what degree should immigrants have access to the same rights and resources held by other citizen residents of a particular nation-state? Should immigrants be subject to performing the same duties obligatory for citizens even if (or particularly if) they do not share the same rights? Should their rights as individuals be contingent on their modes of entry to a particular region? Or should they be contingent on the degree to which they have fulfilled their responsibilities as citizens? These questions of access to legal membership rights are all fundamental to the question of social and political membership, and the ways in which particular communities answer them have important repercussions on the everyday experiences of migrants and citizens. Nonetheless, the empirical "reality" of immigrants' everyday community engagement does not fit neatly into these abstract categories of legally defined belonging (Sassen 2005).

Discussions of immigrant incorporation extend well beyond the realm of legal rights and obligations. Just as an immigrant's first admission to a polity is governed by the interaction between the legal and discursive realms, so are immigrants' "second admissions," through their incorporation into everyday social, political, and economic life in new communities, also strongly shaped by this same discourse of the imagined qualities desired of citizen residents. In other words, citizenship cannot be understood as a legal construct separate from the imaginary of the ideal quality of citizen values promoted by the state (and, in varying degrees) accepted and internalized by the populace. As these values become part of the cultural/social landscape of communities, they define the possibilities for inclusion at local and national levels. This imaginary, which is rooted both in the possibilities of legal membership as well as more personal, social, and affective constructs of belonging (Chakrabarty 2002:101–14), interacts in complex ways with migrants' desires to reshape their personal and familial lives. Sara Friedman explains this imaginary "symbolic citizenship":

> Symbolic citizenship defines how a national community is imagined and sets the terms for identifying idealized citizens. It goes beyond characterizing "the nature of social membership within political collectives" (Turner, 1993:3) by establishing what kinds of people are eligible for that membership in the first place. Moreover, symbolic citizenship shows how civilizing processes define citizenship through intimate, often embodied, practices that mark individuals and groups as appropriately or insufficiently civilized, thereby establishing their eligibility for inclusion in or exclusion from an ideal body politic. (2006:243)

With this definition of citizenship, Friedman roots membership as a process that takes place not just between individuals and the state, but also as one that takes place among citizens themselves through the development of community-based bonds with each other—rather than directly to the state itself (Greenhouse 2002:196). This "social" quality of citizenship, which both reflects and contributes to the production of idealized conceptions of membership, is experienced in practice by immigrants through everyday interactions in and adjustments to new locations. In Hong Kong, the ideal citizen qualities that are framed through the "imaginary" discursive realm are consciously enacted by Hong Kong people to differentiate themselves from mainlanders; to outline the possibilities and impossibilities of Chinese immigrants' inclusion in Hong Kong social, political, and economic life; and to teach mainland wives the roles, rights, and duties of Hong Kong (rather than PRC) citizens.[5]

Migration from the Mainland to Hong Kong: Moving Across "Political Difference"

Immigrant incorporation (that is, how immigrants adjust to their host society) has long been a central focus of research interest for anthropologists and sociologists (see, for example, Alba and Nee 2003, Parreñas 2001,

Flores and Benmayor 1997, Portes and Rumbaut 1996). Most recently, through numerous studies of immigrant lives in urban locations throughout the United States, scholars have begun to challenge long-standing ideologies that put the burden of assimilation on immigrants rather than on the members of societies in which they live. These studies demonstrate that cultural definitions of "mainstream" American life are changing in ways that enable, and at times embrace, the integration of immigrants into social and community life (Alba and Nee 2003). They also document that immigrants—through exercising and demanding legal rights—can actively change the political and cultural landscapes around them (Flores 1997). In these studies, race and culture take center stage in discussions of immigrant incorporation, because in multiethnic societies such as the United States, many immigrants *do* tend to look, act, and talk differently from the so-called "mainstream" social and cultural actors.

Mainland Chinese wives who immigrate to Hong Kong to join their husbands and other family members there may also look, act, and talk differently from the majority of Hong Kong people. For example, some women may have outdated haircuts and wear unfashionable clothes, may not be used to waiting patiently for their turns in line, or may speak a strongly accented Cantonese that marks their rural mainland origins. On the other hand, many immigrant wives, particularly those who come from urban areas of the PRC or who have been in Hong Kong for a few years, may not be identifiable by these markers of difference and may look, act, and talk just like "Hong Kong people." Nonetheless, these women do not experience seamless transitions to Hong Kong life, nor are they necessarily deemed to "belong" to Hong Kong by other Hong Kong citizens. For Hong Kong people, the "difference" that separates them from their mainland "cousins" and other relatives is not cultural so much as political. As a result, in moving from the mainland to Hong Kong, Chinese wives immigrate over the "political difference" that separates Hong Kong—both actually and discursively—from the mainland. By political difference, I mean that mainland Chinese immigrants and Hong Kong people as individuals, but also as members of larger social groups, have been socialized with different expectations of privileges and goals for relating both to the state and also to society around them. These expectations are "deeply rooted in [their] personal and social imagin[aries]" (Aretxaga 1997:9) as citizens of the PRC or

Hong Kong, and influence not only their normative ideologies of belonging but also the ways in which they, as individuals, relate to time, space, and personal relationships in the communities in which they live.

Writing about the presumption of national unity that followed the reunification of East and West Germany after the collapse of the Berlin wall in 1989, John Borneman argues that the "creation of a single [German] market and a single national space" did not result in "an 'imagined community' in the sense explicated by Benedict Anderson, but [in] a territorial and fiscal community in a homogenous space with quickened time (Anderson 1983). No matter how much people imagined and experienced a national unity by reading a tabloid *Bild Zeitung* together in the morning, they were divided by their differential orientation and access to the new temporal and spatial world that afternoon" (1998:106–7). In other words, sharing a common ethnicity, language, and historical background was not sufficient to ensure that German citizens who had lived under significantly different political regimes for several decades would seamlessly integrate into a national whole. When the wall came down, the socialist East Germans traveled to capitalist, democratic West Germany to see, hear, taste, smell, and touch the consumer-driven experiences in which they had not been able to participate for the previous forty years (Berdahl 1999). In making their trips into the former West Germany, East Germans had the rather disorienting experience of crossing freely in and out of areas that had previously been restricted and which had served to mark the cultural, political, and economic differences between East and West Germans. These differences—experienced so completely and over such a long period of time—influenced the everyday values, thoughts, and actions of both groups and acted to create ethnicized distinctions among East and West Germans (ibid.). As a result, the incorporation of East Germans into West German life was not only difficult for both parties, but also unwelcome by many West Germans who vilified their newly reunited compatriots (ibid.) just as Hong Kong people distinguish themselves from (and also discriminate against) mainlanders.

The reunification of Hong Kong with the PRC has important differences from that of East and West German reunification, among the most notable being that—far from being integrated into one political and economic system—the actual economic and political differences between Hong Kong and the mainland have been legally reinforced through the creation of the "one country, two systems" policy. The differences that have been legally reinforced through the creation of this policy stem from the different political and economic histories that Hong Kong people and mainland residents have experienced since the mid-1800s, when Hong Kong became a British colony. As British colonial subjects, Hong Kong people were not actively encouraged to develop a conception of citizenship rooted in the rights-based vocabulary common to Western liberal democracies (Tse 2004). Nonetheless, Hong Kong people did have access to some of the civil rights accorded to members of liberal democracies—such as free speech, travel, and choosing how many children to have—that have not been consistently available to mainland resident PRC citizens over the past sixty years. Furthermore, in the thirteen-year period immediately preceding the return of Hong Kong to mainland Chinese sovereignty, Hong Kong people were granted more political rights than they had in the past, including partial suffrage, and were promised universal suffrage, including the ability to elect their own chief executive,[6] shortly after their reunification with the mainland. This actual and potential access to civil and political rights has not only distinguished Hong Kong people's daily life from that of mainlanders over the past sixty years, but it has also led to the desire for rights, along with the possibilities of action, thinking, and behavior that are enabled by access to increased rights. The articulation of this desire is one important aspect of the contemporary Hong Kong ethos of "belonging" and is also evident not only through the large-scale protests and demonstrations that have taken place in Hong Kong in recent years, but also through the actions of individuals who emigrated from Hong Kong to North America, Europe, Australia, and other countries in the years leading up to Hong Kong's return to mainland Chinese sovereignty, practicing what Aihwa Ong has termed "flexible citizenship" (1999).

In addition to this rights-based imaginary (and actuality) of difference, political difference between Hong Kong and the mainland is also framed around the construction of what Lam calls Hong Kong's "culture of depoliticization" (2004). This discourse, which has allowed Hong Kong people "to share a general self-perception that they took no interest in politics" (ibid. 221), has also allowed Hong Kong people to differentiate themselves from mainlanders, whose political activity as "communists," as perceived by Hong Kong people, casts them in a negative light and sets them apart from the essentially "law-abiding" and "orderly" Hong Kong populace. Under colonial rule, Hong Kong social, political, and economic life was generally prosperous, peaceful, and stable when compared to the political and social upheaval that has characterized much of twentieth-century life on the mainland. Nevertheless, the casting of Hong Kong as a "stable," secure," and "law-abiding" place was a deliberate policy on the part of the colonial government, which understood the colony's prosperity and stability to be precarious and easily undermined by political insurgency on the part of the colony's inhabitants or by influxes of mainlanders (Goodstadt 2005). Still, as Lam points out, Hong Kong people have consistently demonstrated over the past fifty years that they are political actors, and they have done this through repeated protests that challenged government policies seen as violating the principles of accountability, fairness, and justice championed by both Hong Kong people and the colonial government as part of the Hong Kong ethos of belonging (Lam 2004). This imaginary, which has its roots in the colonial systems of governance that continue to shape the post-1997 Hong Kong legal and bureaucratic system through such institutions as the legal courts of justice and the Independent Commission Against Corruption (ICAC), conveniently masks the fact that Hong Kong people *do* act in ways that contest and subvert laws while still enabling them to maintain that non-law-abiding individuals should be excluded from the Hong Kong polity.

At the time of my research, these politically based discourses combined with a firm emphasis on neoliberal principles of "self-help," individual responsibility, and "entrepreneurialism" (Ku and Pun 2004) to produce the imaginary qualities of civility that signified inclusion to the Hong Kong polity. Because they were seen as not conforming to this imaginary, recent immigrants to Hong Kong from mainland China[7] were portrayed by Hong Kong media in 2002 as presenting a significant threat to Hong Kong's current and future economic well-being. On the one hand, immigrants were criticized as causing a drain on government resources through their dependence on government-supported social services (see, for example, Chan and Moy 4/29/02; Moy 4/29/02; *Ming Pao* 4/11/02). On the other hand, immigrants were also portrayed as "stealing" jobs from more deserving "locals"—a claim that has often been made about immigrants in other parts of the world as well (Seller 1984). Finally, these concerns began to take on another form: fears about the "quality" and number of immigrants being allowed into Hong Kong on a daily basis. Drawing on their personal knowledge of immigration application procedures to Canada and the United States, economists and government officials began making calls to reduce the numbers of immigrants allowed into Hong Kong on a daily basis and suggested that immigrants should be graded on a "point" system in considering their applications for entry—to ensure that more highly skilled immigrants be given priority over those viewed as being less skilled (see, for example, Moy 4/29/02). Central to these arguments were two concerns. First, Hong Kong did not have control over who could enter its territory and stay there, since immigration permits for Chinese immigrants were granted by mainland PRC officials. Second, a better "quality" of immigrants was needed to ensure that Hong Kong could retain its competitive edge over other Chinese cities, such as Shanghai, which are rapidly developing into regional financial centers (see Lloyd-Smith 4/23/02 and Cheung 4/24/02, 7/4/02). Alternatively, suggestions were made that would-be immigrants and their families should be given a small monthly allowance and "resettled" on the Chinese side of the border ("Migrant Solutions" 4/29/02).

The shift in membership status that accompanied wives' legal moves to Hong Kong meant that they had gained civil and political rights already held by their husbands. In particular, they gained the right to cross the Hong Kong/mainland border at will. From the points of view of most Hong Kong people, however, the actual shift in membership status that accompanied mainland immigrants' legal moves from the mainland to Hong Kong was not enough in and of itself to allow these newest members of Hong Kong society to take full advantage of the political, economic, and social benefits that they should be able to realize as Hong Kong residents (Ku 2004). As a result, immigrants' everyday interactions with Hong Kong family members, government officials, and social workers were influenced by these individuals' efforts to encourage immigrants' conformity with normative ideologies of belonging. In this way, political difference, and its influence on immigrant incorporation, was not limited to the legal realm but extended into the domestic sphere and family life more generally.

After experiencing years of split-family life, mainland Chinese wives finally moved to Hong Kong, where they either lived in crowded tenements or in public housing flats with their husbands' extended families. These "reunions" with family members in Hong Kong were fraught with difficulties resulting from the disjunctures between women's expectations and the reality of the life they experienced in Hong Kong, and many immigrant wives took advantage of government-funded social welfare services in attempts to ease their transitions to Hong Kong life. Through their interactions at social service centers, immigrants were introduced to Hong Kong's legalistic and bureaucratic culture focused on rationality and fairness, along with the colonially inspired neoliberal discourses of "self-help" and "responsibility." Social workers and immigrants alike grappled with the implications of defining belonging to Hong Kong along these lines: How could individuals with no first-hand experience with the "orderly" and "law-abiding" norms of Hong Kong life be expected to understand the importance of waiting one's turn in a queue? Or in not engaging in corrupt practices like bribery that are still common on the mainland? How could individuals who had come of age in a postsocialist state that still provided many major social welfare benefits to its citizens be taught to become self-reliant individuals who would not make unreasonable demands on limited state resources? And how could immigrant mothers with little education act as empathetic, supportive parents so as to create the "healthy" family life that policy makers link to Hong Kong's social stability and successful economic development?

In short, political difference not only kept families separated while wives waited for the legal documentation that would enable their immigration to Hong Kong, but it also served to complicate wives' adaptation and integration to Hong Kong life once there. Because they facilitated the entry of mainlanders into Hong Kong, the marriages that I describe in this book tapped deeply into fears by Hong Kong people that their real and perceived differences with mainland residents—symbolized by the Hong Kong/mainland border but also reinforced by the ease of Hong Kong people in crossing that border—will gradually begin to fade. In this context, the incorporation of mainland immigrant women into Hong Kong life was a socially, politically, and emotionally charged issue that affected women's relationships with their Hong Kong family members in their homes just as it affected their interactions with social workers, employers, and government representatives outside their homes. When immigrant wives joined their husbands in Hong Kong, they joined households where the ordinary tensions associated with moving to a new environment or reuniting after long periods of separation were intensified by the fact that their husbands and other family members were Hong Kong people whose feelings toward them—as mainland Chinese immigrants—ranged from grudging accommodation to open hostility.

Methodological Issues: Locating Immigrant Wives in Hong Kong

Most brochure images of Hong Kong highlight Hong Kong's many gorgeous natural or human-made attractions: the glittering, tall skyscrapers that line Hong Kong's famous harbor, the lush green parkland that covers most of the region, the beautiful sandy coves, and the state-of-the art malls. Hong Kong is a bustling city—vibrant, colorful, and teeming with life. It is an exciting, consumer-driven city full of the manufactured trappings that people in industrialized countries have adopted as the necessary sidearms of everyday life. Tourists from places near (Asia) and far (Europe and North America) who travel to Hong Kong can marvel at these attractions and also enjoy the quaint remnants of Hong Kong's colonial past—the tram cars, the funicular railroad, and the small winding footpaths dotted with occasional gated mansions overlooking the harbor far below—or the carefully restored lineage halls and temples in the New Territories and outlying islands. The areas of Hong Kong in which I did my research, and in which most mainland immigrant wives and children live, are far removed from these idyllic parts of Hong Kong.

The West Kowloon area of Hong Kong, with its old tenement housing stock, street markets, and central urban location, has long been a low cost yet convenient living area for recent immigrants to Hong Kong. The Sham Shui Po district, in particular, registers a high number of immigrant residents, with 46.7 percent of its 365,927 residents reporting that they were born outside of Hong Kong, compared to 39.7 percent for the HKSAR as a whole (Census and Statistics Department 1996). Statistics recorded between 1996 and 2001 by the Hong Kong Home Affairs Department consistently listed Sham Shui Po as the area of Hong Kong in which the most "New Arrivals"—the Hong Kong government's official term for recent immigrants from the mainland—settled. Each year, 11 to 12 percent of all New Arrivals designated this area as their place of residence (newarrivals. socialnet.org.hk). Since 1996, the neighboring areas of Mongkok, Yaumatei, and Tsimshatsui in Kowloon, and Kwai Ching in the New Territories, have consistently accounted for an additional 15 percent of Hong Kong's mainland immigrant population (ibid.). Unlike many areas of the city, Sham Shui Po was not specifically targeted by the British colonial authorities for redevelopment, nor has it experienced substantial gentrification over the past few decades. As a result, many of the area's residents are older or poorer compared with many other Hong Kong districts.

The social service center where I did the bulk of my research was one of many social service centers—some government funded and others not—located in Sham Shui Po. This social service center, which drew its client base from these urban areas of high immigrant residency, was one of the oldest centers serving immigrant needs in Hong Kong, and it was conveniently located on the fifth floor of an old tenement building near a subway station and many bus routes. About 600 square feet in size, the center had at least sixteen staff members, eight of whom worked there full time. With the exception of an administrator, the fifteen other staff members sat at eight desks in a partitioned-off area of the office comprising less than 200 square feet. The service center had one small classroom, big enough to hold just fifteen students at five tables. There was also a bathroom and a small back storeroom, with a copy machine, refrigerator, and an additional desk that was used for client intake. On many days, with a full complement of workers, several immigrants and their families waiting to see social workers, and a class in session, the office was packed to capacity, and certainly no less crowded than the busy streets outside.

I spent a total of fourteen consecutive months conducting participant observation-based fieldwork at the social service center, from May 2001 through June 2002. Throughout that time, I spent on average forty to fifty hours each week at the center or with social workers or immigrants outside the center. I interacted with hundreds of immigrants (primarily women and children), along with several dozen service workers and government officials. Of these numbers, there were about forty or fifty immigrants and their family members with whom I interacted on a regular basis, and, from these, I had fifteen or so key informants who became close friends. Like other ethnographers, I do not claim to make generalizations about all mainland immigrants in Hong Kong based on my findings from my select number of informants. Nevertheless, when compared with Hong Kong government statistics on the 55,000 mainland immigrants who enter Hong Kong each year, my informants were representative—in terms of gender, ages, educational levels, incomes, and places of origin and residence—of immigrants overall. Furthermore, my in-depth and sustained involvements with these women and children over days, weeks, and months allowed me to gain a well-informed picture of their processes of adjustment to Hong Kong.

During my first few months at the center, I was put to use providing English conversation practice and game playing with classes of immigrant children and adults for several hours each week. While not teaching, I sat in the cramped office space, rotating from vacant seat to vacant seat, depending on which worker happened not to be in the office at any given time. This limitation of space, accepted with good humor by the center workers even as they never gave up hope of moving to a larger office, proved a significant advantage for my understanding of office work and practice as well as the social workers' interactions with their clients. Like all the other members of the center, I overheard all phone conversations, personal banter, and procedural debate that took place during the hours I was there. And the more I was there, the more social and welfare workers found creative ways to include me into the programs that they were planning for their clients.

Educational programs, mutual help groups, and recreational activities formed the core of services offered to immigrant clients. These often took place outside of the center, in various locations around Hong Kong, or on weekends, when the center's small classroom was not used for teaching. Over the course of my research, I attended over fifteen of these activities, which ranged in time from one two-hour meeting to five or more all-day meetings. Following the advice of James L. Watson, I went where my informants went and did what they did (1997: viii). For example, I went on orientations of the city with immigrants, where we ended our tours at Hong Kong government agencies like the Police Department, where immigrants and I saw empty jail cells, held handcuffs, and listened to presentations about the rule of law in Hong Kong. Another weekend, I participated on an overnight sex-education camping trip organized by the social workers at the center, and immigrant parents, children, and I practiced badminton and archery after completing the information sessions that formed the basis for the trip. On these programs and others, my roles varied widely. Sometimes I simply accompanied immigrant groups on tours as an additional chaperone.

More often, social workers integrated me into the thematic content of programs, in which I acted out various dramatic scenarios or was produced as a "novelty" to gain the audience's attention at a program's beginning or conclusion. Furthermore, the immigrant wives in my English classes were often recruited by social workers to join multiple-week adjustment-related programs, and in these cases I was always included as an additional participating member of the group. In the end, I enjoyed a unique status at the center, mingling with both social workers and clients, yet treated as an "insider" to both.[8]

The goal of ethnographic research is to establish in-depth connections with informants over time in order to be able to trace their movements and actions and, finally, to distinguish between *what people do* and *what people say they do*. As a result, the most significant data collected by ethnographers result more often from informal interactions than through formal interviews. Although my social worker informants were comfortable talking with me early on in my research, many of the immigrants, particularly those who had received little education, were quite concerned about how they presented themselves to me. These fears were even stronger when I asked to tape-record formal interviews with several informants. Nevertheless, my long-term involvement at the center with both social workers and immigrants allowed me to gain the trust of my informants and to compare interactions that I had observed over the course of many months. In the end, I was able to gather large amounts of material not just from social workers but also from my New Arrival informants, who continued to invite me to eat dimsum, to visit their home villages, or to participate in other activities to which they did not invite the social workers. All of my interactions with center employees and immigrants took place in Cantonese, with the exception of English classes, where Cantonese was still used as the language of instruction.[9]

While the majority of my research data is based on these in-depth interactions with both social center employees and their clients, I also conducted thirty open-ended taped interviews, ranging in length from one and a half to three hours, with most of the center's employees, with twelve of my own immigrant informants who were willing to talk to me in this more formal way, and with five immigrants and their family members who were identified as "model" clients for me by social workers at the social service center.

I also relied on the professional expertise of many individuals in Hong Kong in supplementing the data about immigrant life that I obtained through my participant observation-based research. These individuals included, but were not limited to, social workers at other Hong Kong nongovernmental organizations (NGOs); Hong Kong academics; and government representatives from the Hong Kong Home Affairs Department, Immigration Department, and the Police. Finally, I also conducted a substantial amount of archival research in order to map out the history of Chinese immigration to Hong Kong. This history provides important contextual information for understanding the ways in which the current immigration experiences of mainland wives who marry Hong Kong men continue to be influenced by past social, political, and economic processes in both the PRC and in colonial Hong Kong. The social effects of these processes, which are directly related to contemporary ideologies of membership and belonging in Hong Kong, were rendered significantly more complicated when Hong Kong was returned to mainland Chinese sovereignty on July 1, 1997. I present this historical information in the following chapter, where my ethnographic journey into the experience of reunited immigrant family life in post-1997 Hong Kong begins.

The Moral and Legal Landscape
of Reuniting Families in Hong Kong

In August 2000, two weeks before I would leave to begin my fieldwork, I opened a newspaper and read about a firebomb attack that had taken place the previous day at Hong Kong's main Immigration Tower. The violent protest, which resulted in the death of one immigration officer and one protester, had been initiated by upset illegal immigrants, angered at the seeming "indifference" (cf. Herzfeld 1992) of the Hong Kong bureaucratic apparatus to their claims to be recognized as legal residents of Hong Kong. Tired of waiting (over hours) for their paperwork to be processed on that day, and angered at waiting (over years) for the resolution of court cases that would ultimately decide whether their status in Hong Kong would be regularized, several men constructed a crude firebomb out of a soda bottle, lit it, and used it to threaten immigration officers in the area where they were waiting. Chaos erupted, and a fight broke out between the protesters and immigration officers, resulting in serious injuries and the two deaths. While the death of the illegal immigrant was largely ignored in the media, the state funeral of the martyred immigration officer, who was buried in one of Hong Kong's cemeteries reserved for government dignitaries, received major coverage.

This was one incident in a series of major protests that were carried out by illegal immigrants in Hong Kong, otherwise known as "abode-seekers" (that is, individuals seeking to gain the "right of abode" in Hong Kong),[1] in reaction to a specific series of political events in 1999 that had first granted, and then denied, legal residency rights to significant numbers of mainland immigrants who were illegally resident in Hong Kong. Like the majority of the 55,000 *legal* immigrants who enter Hong Kong from mainland China each year, most of the abode-seekers had immediate family members, including parents, children, and siblings, in Hong Kong. Furthermore, like legal immigrants, they shared the same nationality and similar racial and cultural backgrounds as most Hong Kong people; they also had homes, jobs (sometimes), and networks of friends and relatives in Hong Kong. In other words, these illegal immigrants had significant moral claims of belonging to the region (Sassen 2005), even if these moral claims were not recognized as legal claims by the Hong Kong or mainland authorities involved in determining which Chinese citizens could legally immigrate to Hong Kong (see also Ku 2001).

The mainland wives of Hong Kong men on which my study focuses were legal, not illegal, immigrants to Hong Kong. Yet the actions of illegal immigrants had significant repercussions for my informants, who, despite their legal status in the region, were often confused with illegal immigrants in public perception. Accounts of the firebomb attack and the trial that followed it (along with the other protests conducted by abode-seekers) continued to appear in Hong Kong newspapers throughout the period of my fieldwork. These accounts, which highlighted the potentially disruptive effects of mainlanders, reinforced local stereotypes that cast mainland immigrants as a dangerous threat to Hong Kong's economic and social stability (Ku 2001). In this public discourse, legal immigrants, as "mainlanders," were just as guilty of potentially imperiling Hong Kong's stable political environment as were illegal immigrants.

Immigrants from the mainland to Hong Kong have long been seen as a security threat to the region, not only because of Hong Kong's rather precarious physical status in relation to the substantially larger mainland, but also because Hong Kong has historically been the receiving point of large influxes of mainland immigrants. Several influxes of Chinese immigrants to Hong Kong over the past fifty years have resulted in Hong Kong government authorities becoming increasingly restrictive over which mainland immigrants would be (and which would not be) eligible for legal membership in the Hong Kong polity; yet the official distinction between recognizing some immigrants as "legal," and others as "illegal," only dates to the 1970s. Since that time, illegal immigrants have been seen as threatening to Hong Kong's "hegemonic" discourses of "law and order" and "political stability" (Ku 2001, 2004; see also Lam 2004). Legal immigrants, on the other hand, provided other causes of concern. In particular, the low educational status and rural origins believed to characterize many legal immigrants have fueled local fears that the inclusion of mainland wives and children into Hong Kong society will jeopardize Hong Kong's continued success as an elite center of global financial practice.

In the introduction to this book, I quoted historian Mae Ngai, who has argued that immigration policy draws "lines of inclusion and exclusion that articulate a desired composition—imagined if not necessarily realized—of the nation" (2004:5). Yet the eruption of violence, such as the firebomb attack described earlier, over the issue of whether certain individuals will be granted legal membership status in Hong Kong indicates not only that abstract ideals of belonging have concrete and powerful repercussions on the lives of individuals, but also that the very makeup of a nation's "desired composition" is necessarily contentious, with different groups of social and political actors voicing different opinions about what the nature of that "desired composition" should be. In this case, the firebomb attack at Hong Kong's main immigration offices sent a striking message that a particular group of people, Chinese immigrants who were officially "excluded" from Hong Kong membership status by virtue of their illegal mode of entry to the region, strongly disagreed with the official definitions of inclusion and exclusion in the Hong Kong context. How, then, are decisions about legal membership status determined in Hong Kong? Who has the power to set these definitions, and how are these definitions contested (and with what effects) by individuals who believe that their moral claims of belonging should supersede these legal definitions?

In this chapter, I answer these questions by charting the history of immigration policy to Hong Kong. In particular, I examine how the policies that control "family reunion" immigration from the mainland to Hong Kong have been constructed over time. Focusing on the central issue of how official decisions about "inclusion" and "exclusion" have been made in the context of Hong Kong, where almost all immigrants share the same national, ethnic, and cultural backgrounds as current Hong Kong residents, I explain why some Chinese citizens who wish to immigrate to Hong Kong for the purpose of family reunion are recognized as having legal claims of belonging to Hong Kong, while others are not. Tracing the history of immigration policy between the mainland and Hong Kong over the past sixty years, I argue that legal family reunion into the region has been made significantly more difficult because of the seeming arbitrariness of immigration policies, which not only frequently change but have also become increasingly restrictive over time. These official policies, which control how the "family" is defined in the Hong Kong context, have worked together with negative public perceptions of mainland immigrants to create significant difficulties for mainland wives who do in fact have the legal right to immigrate to Hong Kong.

Categorical Confusions: Defining Legal Membership in the Hong Kong Context

In the contemporary world, it is customary to equate issues of formal inclusion and exclusion of polity membership status (that is, citizenship) with nationality. In other words, "citizens" are included in national forms of membership status, while noncitizens (whether they be legal or illegal immigrants) are not (Bosniak 1998). Yet global economic and social processes that have facilitated the increased transnational movement of capital, infrastructure, and people throughout world areas have greatly complicated the problem of identifying which individuals qualify as citizens. By focusing on the many challenges that immigrants pose to policy decisions defining inclusion and exclusion, a number of scholars have recently argued that our understandings of citizenship should be dismantled from the immediate association of that concept with the nation-state (Soysal 1994, 2000; Bosniak 1998; Heyman 2002; Silverstein 2004; Sassen 2005). For example, Verdery (1998) and Ong (1999) have highlighted specific situations where transnational and national interests intersect and create state dilemmas in defining which individuals should be included or excluded from formal definitions of state membership. Verdery notes the case in Romania, where membership is defined by inclusion in certain blood lines or ethnic groups. This definition results in the inclusion of individuals of Romanian descent in the transnational arena but the exclusion of individuals of different ethnic backgrounds living within the "bounded" nation-state (1998). Ong, on the other hand, describes a very different situation among overseas Chinese, in which well-educated, professional Hong Kong residents actively seek citizenship status in different nation-states and then manipulate their different membership statuses to gain access to resources that will increase their financial or cultural capital (1999). Like Romania, Germany and China define citizenship along ethnic lines (jus sanguinis), while the United States, Canada, and France instead base citizenship on territorial claims (jus soli).

During most of Hong Kong's colonial period, official policies governing inclusion and exclusion were sometimes based on either of these principles but were more often based on *both* jus sanguinis and jus soli. In other words, individuals who were ethnically Chinese *and* born on the mainland were deemed to have the most important "claims" on Hong Kong (Ku 2004). Yet in the latter decades of the twentieth century, as Hong Kong people developed a social and cultural identity as distinct from the mainland as its political and economic policies already were, and as more and more mainlanders "flooded" into Hong Kong following the relaxation of PRC political and economic controls in the late 1970s, these claims were no longer sufficient to regulate the entry of mainland immigrants into Hong Kong. As a result, the jus soli requirement shifted from birth on the mainland to birth in Hong Kong. Also, more stringent policies, directly modeled on those policies controlling the entry (or refusal of entry) to British colonial subjects into the United Kingdom (Hampshire 2005), were adopted by the Hong Kong colonial government and remained in place even after Hong Kong's return to mainland Chinese sovereignty under the "one country, two systems" policy.

In Hong Kong, decisions about who can—and should—be "included" in the region's special membership status have been particularly fraught since 1997, when Hong Kong returned to mainland Chinese sovereignty as a Special Administrative Region (SAR) of the PRC. Hong Kong residents of Chinese descent are officially citizens of the PRC, not citizens of Hong Kong. "Citizenship" in the local sense in Hong Kong is obtained through permanent resident status, which is normally granted to individuals who have legally entered and resided in Hong Kong for seven years.[2] Since 1997, decisions governing which mainland resident PRC citizens can become Hong Kong resident PRC citizens have been made through legislation promulgated by both the Hong Kong government and the national PRC government. The historical permeability of the Hong Kong/mainland border, and the increasingly intertwined economic infrastructure shared by Hong Kong and Southeast China, makes the untangling of membership claims—from a practical as well as a legal point of view—even more difficult. In particular, the common practice of family reunion migration from the mainland to Hong Kong presents a particular challenge to these already complex problems of deciding which PRC citizens are eligible for Hong Kong membership by highlighting the conflict between moral and legal claims to belonging in the Hong Kong context.

As I explained in the introduction, 98 percent of Chinese immigration to Hong Kong is for the purpose of family reunion. The common practice of Hong Kong men looking to the mainland to find wives, combined with the strict entry quotas imposed on legal entrants to Hong Kong from the mainland, meant that many families were separated—often for decades—on either side of the border, with some members legally resident in Hong Kong and others legally resident only on the mainland. In these cases, the desire for excluded family members to be able to join family in Hong Kong could be extreme. Yet the large numbers of mainland residents who were legally eligible to immigrate to Hong Kong meant that those individuals who followed the bureaucratic practices in place and did finally enter Hong Kong as legal residents, like my immigrant wife informants, most commonly waited for periods of up to or exceeding ten years. In some cases, individuals did not want to, or were not able to (because of financial reasons or, more often, care-giving demands within the family), wait so long for paperwork to be processed. As a result, family members already resident in Hong Kong might help them to gain entrance to Hong Kong—either by crossing the border illegally, or by crossing legally on a visitor's permit and then overstaying that permit once in Hong Kong. In other cases, the arbitrary exercise of bureaucratic power, most often by members of the

PRC's Public Security Bureau (which controlled the allotment of exit visas to mainlanders), prevented mainlanders who should have had the legal right of residence in Hong Kong from exercising that right. I provide an example of the moral and actual difficulties encountered by one family because of this latter situation below. This case, which was regarded as particularly poignant since it involved the separation of identical twin girls, received extensive media coverage during my period of fieldwork in Hong Kong, yet the situation encountered by this family was by no means unique. Because legal entrance to Hong Kong was controlled primarily by the PRC rather than Hong Kong, many other families had also been separated through similar corrupt practices.[3]

Identical twins Lin Yeung-min and Lin Yuk-oi were separated at the age of twelve, following the family's application for Yeung-min, Yuk-oi, and their mother to immigrate to Hong Kong to join the twins' father, who had been living there for over fifteen years and who was already a Hong Kong permanent resident at the time of the twins' birth. The twins' parents had submitted their paperwork to emigrate at the same time, so there was no reason to suspect that their cases would have been treated differently. Nonetheless, mainland Chinese officials told the twins' mother and father that only one child would be allowed to emigrate with their mother. Faced with an impossible decision, the twins' father took them outside and had them play a game of "rock, paper, scissors" to determine which twin would go to Hong Kong and which one would stay on the mainland. Yuk-oi, the younger twin, won and went to Hong Kong. Yeung-min, the older twin, lost, and stayed on the mainland. For several years, their mother traveled back and forth trying to take care of both girls. (During her mother's stays in Hong Kong, Yeung-min lived with relatives.) When Yeung-min was sixteen years old, her family brought her to Hong Kong on a short-term visitor's permit. Like many other would-be immigrants, Yeung-min over-stayed her permit and did not return to the mainland upon its expiration, even though her illegal status in Hong Kong prevented her from attending school or even leaving her family's apartment—since her parents were worried that a neighbor might report Yeung-min's continued (but illegal) presence, for which she could be arrested and repatriated to the mainland.

Throughout the years that the family members were separated (and then living together illegally in Hong Kong), Yeung-min's parents continued to push for Yeung-min's legal claim to Hong Kong membership. During that time, however, the laws defining Chinese citizen eligibility for legal resident status in Hong Kong kept changing in ways that continued to deny Yeung-min the legal status that, based on the fact that her sister was a permanent resident of Hong Kong, should have been available to her, too. For a period of several years, while Yeung-min's case was being considered, she was temporarily granted legal residency rights in Hong Kong. Finally, a decision rendered by the Hong Kong Court of Final Appeal on January 10, 2002 (for more on this case, see below) denied Yeung-min the right of abode in Hong Kong, and she once again officially became an "illegal immigrant" subject to forcible repatriation to the mainland. Yeung-min's story did, however, have a happy ending. Unlike those many other "illegal immigrants," whose legal rights to reside in Hong Kong may have similarly been denied, Yeung-min was eventually granted legal membership status in Hong Kong. Following a major media campaign about her plight, the Hong Kong Director of Immigration exercised his particular discretion to issue her a permit that would allow her to reside in Hong Kong as a legal resident and, after seven years, apply for permanent residency. At the time of this governmental reprieve, Yeung-min and her sister were already nineteen years old.

Yeung-Min's story, like this next case, demonstrates some ways in which the disjunction between moral and legal claims to belonging in Hong Kong create possibilities of contestation to legal definitions of membership in Hong Kong. In August 2001, one Hong Kong Justice ruled that a Swiss national who had been convicted of fraud should have his sentence in a Hong Kong prison reduced by three months on the basis that, as a foreigner, he suffered particular hardships in prison because of "differences in culture, language and diet and isolation from family and friends" (Bradford 12/12/01). Following this ruling, a number of illegal Chinese immigrants jailed in Hong Kong argued that their sentences should likewise be reduced, on the grounds that they were "foreigners." One claimant from China's Hunan Province argued that he missed the spicy food characteristic to his native area—food, which was not, of course, on the menu at his Hong Kong prison. The cases of these mainlanders were dismissed with the ruling that "Hong Kong residents and mainlanders live under the same flag" (Bradford 9/27/01). Since these illegal immigrants, like most Hong Kong residents, were Chinese nationals, mainland Chinese individuals could not be defined as "foreigners" in Hong Kong. Nonetheless, the final judgments rendered in other cases from this same period indicate that many government officials in Hong Kong and the mainland would have preferred that these Chinese "nonforeigners" stop exercising their claims, real or imagined, on Hong Kong.

In sum, both legal and illegal immigrants in Hong Kong faced an uncomfortable situation that left them in positions that were neither fully "included" nor fully "excluded" from PRC and Hong Kong official definitions of membership status. Illegal immigrants in Hong Kong remained citizens of the PRC, whether they still had homes, families, or jobs on the mainland or felt that they belonged there. Legal immigrants in Hong Kong, on the other hand, despite being resident there with the possibility of obtaining Hong Kong permanent residency (that is, citizenship in the local sense) after seven years, were often denied many of the social welfare benefits (including, most importantly, public housing) eligible to Hong Kong residents and were conflated with illegal immigrants in the mind of the public. In these ways, their situations echoed many of the same kinds of exclusionary issues faced by immigrants in other world areas, such as the United States, where there have been increasing calls throughout the past decade to deprive both legal and illegal immigrants of the rights accorded to citizens. Just as "[s]capegoating and political rhetoric have created an atmosphere of open hostility toward Latino immigrants" in the United States (Flores 1997:260), mainland Chinese immigrants—whether legal or illegal—in Hong Kong were generally excluded from the social imaginary of the ideal qualities of civility that defined membership in the Hong Kong polity.

Unlike immigrants in other world areas, however, who generally retain their citizenship rights in their country of origin after their migration to other countries, Chinese citizen migrants to Hong Kong had their residency rights[4] on the mainland revoked when they immigrated legally to Hong Kong—even though in Hong Kong they were not eligible to be full "citizens" in the local sense. Borrowing from Victor Turner's terminology, one could say that these Chinese individuals were "liminal" citizens, whose moral claims to particular membership statuses often conflicted with Hong Kong and PRC government regulations stipulating where they should live or the public articulations of which Chinese citizens were seen as "belonging" to Hong Kong. These cases, like those documented by Ku (2001), ultimately demonstrate that no matter how powerful moral claims of belonging to Hong Kong are by immigrants, these claims are subordinated to local ideology that locates legitimate membership claims to Hong Kong in the discourses of "law and order" and "political stability" (ibid.). In the following section of this chapter, I describe the ways in which the historical processes surrounding the immigration of mainlanders to Hong Kong have led to the dominance of these discourses over decisions governing immigration policy to Hong Kong, along with increasingly restrictive definitions of legal membership in the SAR.

The Historical Trajectory of Immigration Policy in Hong Kong: From Inclusion to Exclusion

Before the establishment of the PRC on October 1, 1949, there were no restrictions placed on the movement of Chinese individuals over the Hong Kong/mainland border.[5] This "open" border between China and the British colony allowed merchants, fishermen, farmers, and other locals to continue their daily or weekly travel between the two areas, since many individuals routinely crossed the border to work, visit relatives, or take care of marketing needs. The complex economic and familial linkages that had developed between Hong Kong and the mainland over the first one hundred years of British colonial rule (roughly from 1842–1950) meant that the policy of keeping the border "open" to Chinese nationals was both necessary and practical. Guangdong Province has, for hundreds of years, been the starting point of journeys made by—primarily—Chinese males in search of better economic livelihoods to all areas of the world, including Southeast Asia, the Americas, and Europe (Kwok and Ames 1995:17; Watson 1975). Hong Kong was the "transit point" for this migration abroad, and many individuals waiting to leave for foreign places became caught up in the local economy, taking jobs in Hong Kong. These "waylaid" immigrants became "Hong Kong residents" (Kwok and Ames 1995:17). Strong kinship ties to their "native places" meant that many emigrants who left the mainland for Hong Kong or foreign ports abroad not only sent remittances—with the help of Hong Kong merchant intermediaries—to their family members left behind, but that many individuals also returned to China through the port of Hong Kong (see, for example, Watson 1975). Individuals returned to their home villages to get married, to retire, and to be buried with their ancestors. As the crossroads for this traffic in money, people, and goods, Hong Kong quickly grew. In the past, the majority of Hong Kong's residents—up to 98 percent—were ethnically Chinese.

By 1950, Hong Kong's population had grown to more than two million people, and controlling and limiting the growth of Hong Kong's population had become one of the most important policy issues concerning the colonial government (see, for example, *Problem* 1965; also Hambro 1955). Many of these residents (approximately one million) had lived in Hong Kong before World War II and returned to Hong Kong after having fled to China or been sent there while the Japanese occupied Hong Kong during World War II (ibid. 3). The sudden increase in population had been compounded by the inflow of political and economic refugees fleeing China's civil war and the subsequent establishment of the PRC on October 1, 1949. While the majority of prewar immigrants to Hong Kong had been individual males, the refugees who arrived in Hong Kong in the late 1940s and early 1950s included wealthy families, skilled workers, and Nationalist government officials who were fleeing the newly established Communist government (Hambro 1955). Although the majority of these postwar refugees were still Cantonese people from Guangdong Province (75 percent), 6 percent reported their "native" place to be elsewhere in Southern China and 10 percent reported their native places "elsewhere" in China (ibid. 151).[6] The Shanghainese industrialists who fled from the mainland's Communist government, along with their skilled workers, were highly instrumental in developing postwar Hong Kong as an international industrial center. Tens of thousands of less-skilled refugees provided a ready supply of cheap labor for the industrialists' enterprises (see, for example, Burns 1987 and Wong 1988). As Wong Siu-lun explains, perhaps the main reason why so many mainland Chinese refugees fled to Hong Kong was because, at the time, Hong Kong and Taiwan were the only places where "Chinese could freely enter" (1988:21).

Over the course of the next thirty years, a number of political events in the PRC would result in large numbers of mainland residents fleeing—or attempting to flee—to Hong Kong to seek refuge from war, famine, and political chaos. During most of this time, restrictions imposed by Beijing, reinforced through heavily guarded border areas, prevented large numbers of individuals from easily crossing from the mainland into Hong Kong. During periods when Beijing relaxed its control, however, Hong Kong officials had no real means of limiting the entrance of mainlanders to Hong Kong. In 1962, for example, when famine conditions following the disastrous Great Leap Forward campaign were at their worst, mainland authorities suspended their regular border control practices. Over 50,000 refugees fled to Hong Kong in May alone (Burns 1987:663; Lee 1979), and estimates indicate that at least 150,000 illegal immigrants entered Hong Kong undetected and were granted permission to stay there over the course of the year (Burns 1987:664). Another influx of mainlanders arrived during the Cultural Revolution in the form of "sent-down" youths[7] who escaped to Hong Kong (Siu 1988:1; Burns 1987:665). A third "wave" of immigrants to Hong Kong—in the mid-1970s—was comprised of overseas Chinese whose requests for mainland exit permits were processed after the liberalization of PRC government practices following the height of the Cultural Revolution. These previous influxes set the stage for the public panic and condemnation of mainland immigrants that began in Hong Kong in the late 1970s, when hundreds of thousands of mainlanders took advantage of political and economic liberalizations following Deng Xiaoping's rise to power to exit the PRC.

During this thirty-year period, from 1950–80, immigration policy in Hong Kong shifted from that of open entry for mainland refugees to a highly restrictive policy that forcibly repatriated illegal entrants to the region. In tracking this change, Agnes Ku has argued that colonial immigration policies shifted from "reactive measures to more deliberate control, planning, and hegemonic discourses" (2004:326) that developed in tandem with the rise of a Hong Kong identity separate from that of the mainland. In describing this process, Agnes Ku has shown how the British colonial government's policies related to immigration control and settlement during this formative period of Hong Kong's growth were actively involved in the development of local discourses that contrasted Hong Kong people with an inferior, "uncivilized" mainland other (ibid.).

Ku identifies the first stage in the discursive construction of difference by the colonial government as a "problem of people" (2004). This "problem," which resulted from the large numbers of war refugees who entered the colony in the early 1950s, created difficulties in governance for colonial authorities and also threatened the well-being of those Chinese nationals already resident in Hong Kong through the continued addition of individuals into a local infrastructure system that could not adequately meet the sanitary and housing needs of the local population. Furthermore, colonial government officials were concerned about ensuring the security of the colony in the face of Cold-War politics that placed Hong Kong in a perilous position on Communist China's doorstep. Seeking to change the "open-door" policy that had allowed unrestricted access to Hong Kong for Chinese nationals in the past, colonial policy makers began restricting entry to the colony. To justify the imposition of these new controls, members of the government stressed their past benevolence in having allowed entry to the colony to such large, unregulated numbers of people:

> In fact, what has happened has been, over the years, that in respect of Chinese who come from China an exception has been extended in practice, though not in law, from the ordinary applications of the Immigration Law, which, like the immigration laws of any other country in the world, makes a list of the types and categories of people to whom entry is refused . . . The consequence of such liberality in Hong Kong is that many persons come to Hong Kong and remain here who would never have been allowed at all had the normal operation of the immigration laws been applied. (*Hong Kong Hansard* 1949:240–41, cited in Wong 1988:21)

Practice and discussion over the means to limit the entry of Chinese nationals into Hong Kong took a variety of forms. For example, ration coupons and access to subsidized rice were denied entrants to Hong Kong in the early 1950s (Goodstadt 2005:6). By the mid-1950s, the Hong Kong Government had imposed a "quota" system on the entrance of mainland Chinese residents into Hong Kong, limiting their numbers to fifty per day. Beginning in 1952, individuals were also required to have valid exit permits that had been issued to them by the mainland Chinese government (Hambro 1955:16).

Because Hong Kong's population had grown so quickly in the years following World War II, the colonial administration was already faced with serious problems providing for the social welfare of the colony's residents. Housing, health care, and education were far from adequate for the majority of the colony's population, particularly for those individuals living in squatter areas. In a memoir about his experiences as a colonial officer in Hong Kong, James Hayes explains the enormity of the "problem":

> The huts were constructed of such material as they could lay their hands on at little or no cost—flattened sheets of tin, wooden boarding, cardboard, sacking slung on frames—every variety of two dimensional material that was light enough to carry and cheap enough to beg or steal or buy for a few dollars.
>
> There was, of course, no sanitation and there was seldom any organized system of refuse disposal. There was in most cases no mains water immediately available, and water for all purposes had to be carried long distances from communal standpipes or collected from such hillside streams as the season allowed . . .
>
> Chickens, ducks, and pigs shared the huts or the narrow congested areas around them. Sacking curtains over the doors gave privacy and they provided a measure of warmth in winter and or protection from torrential rains in the summer. (*Hong Kong Annual Report 1956:* 13, cited in Hayes 1996:8)

Colonial officials' need to improve the living condition of Hong Kong's Chinese residents was particularly pressing given that the PRC had indicated that it would not interfere in Hong Kong's governance, provided Chinese living there were well cared for by the British regime (Smart 2006). During the next few decades, the colonial administration employed significant resources in working to improve the standard of living of Hong Kong's residents. In the early postwar years, these efforts focused on meeting the immediate needs of Hong Kong's poorest Chinese residents—residents who were still believed to be living temporarily in Hong Kong until conditions on the mainland would enable their return there. While some accounts of policy-making decisions at this time emphasize the goodwill of colonial government officers who sought to aid the growth and development of Hong Kong's people (and, by extension, the colony itself; see, for example, Hayes 1996), others question such motives by pointing out both the economic and other gains ultimately realized through the colonial government's social welfare policies (Ip 2004; see also Goodstadt 2005). What seems most likely is that the Hong Kong colonial government worked in its own interest, in order to protect the security interests of the colony, and that these interests—because of Cold War politics—also coincided with providing sufficient resources to better the living conditions of Hong Kong's Chinese residents (Smart 2006).

Despite the prevalent discourse of the "problem of people" (Ku 2004), it was not until the late 1960s, when unrest over continued poor housing and social welfare conditions resulted in riots, that the Hong Kong colonial government began a planned campaign to build better quality public housing and increase educational and social welfare opportunities for Chinese residents of Hong Kong. Ku identifies the change in official discourse at this time to that of "settled residence," which, she notes, colonial officials implemented in response to several local conditions (ibid.). First, around this time, changing conditions on the mainland led international agencies to no longer classify Chinese nationals fleeing social and economic conditions in the PRC as "refugees." As a result, thousands of Chinese nationals who had been living in Hong Kong while awaiting to be resettled (primarily) in the United States were no longer eligible for resettlement and would be staying on in Hong Kong (IDAR 1971–72:13). Second, Hong Kong authorities by this time had become aware that many of the refugees who had "temporarily" moved to Hong Kong during the political and economic turmoil of the 1940s and 1950s were established in Hong Kong and were not likely to return. Third, the political chaos caused during China's Cultural Revolution in the late 1960s began to "spill over" into Hong Kong in the form of labor and other unrest. To keep governance of Hong Kong's "settled" population of Chinese nationals secure, British colonial officials embarked on the campaign of housing and social welfare provision mentioned previously. These provisions helped to encourage a sense of "belonging" to the colony by its Chinese residents, who had already begun to define themselves as culturally and politically distinct from their mainland "cousins" (ibid.; see also Ku and Pun 2004 and Lam 2004).[8] These distinctions became further reinforced through the decade of the 1970s, as immigrants began entering Hong Kong in successively greater numbers following the PRC's relaxation of political, economic, and social controls by Deng Xiaoping in 1978.

With the change in policy on the mainland, it became clear to Hong Kong authorities and people how vulnerable the colony was to being "overrun" by Chinese nationals who desired entry to the colony. From the point of view of the Hong Kong people and authorities, their fears were justified by the influx of mainlanders who arrived in the colony in the late 1970s and early 1980s. In the three years from 1978 through 1980, there were an estimated 193,300 legal and 161,000 illegal immigrants granted stays in Hong Kong, with an additional 180,800 illegal immigrants repatriated to the mainland (Burns 1987:664). In all, Hong Kong's population grew at a rate of 10 percent from immigration alone during these three years. The cover story of the May 25, 1979, issue of *the Far Eastern Economic Review* illustrates the powerlessness felt by Hong Kong people in the face of this onslaught:

> Hong Kong is under seige. So many refugees are now trying to cross over to the territory from China that surveillance teams have resorted to military terms to describe the situation. No longer do most of the refugees come across singly or in small groups. One alarmed intelligence officer recently reported "a large massing of people," the sort of phrase one would expect to be used only if troops were on the move. (Lee 1979)

Newspaper articles from that time further describe the many means employed by mainlanders to enter Hong Kong: swimming, with or without a "professional guide," through the shark-infested waters between the mainland Chinese and Hong Kong coastal areas; "skiing" on wooden planks through the muddy marshland areas adjacent to the official land border checkpoints; or paying vast sums to be smuggled into the territory in a local fisherman's boat. Armed with potentially inaccurate hand-copied tracing paper maps of the territory, Hong Kong "style" clothes, and a few Hong Kong dollars, immigrants hoped to evade detection from the Hong Kong authorities (ibid.). Potentially fatal risks taken to cross into Hong Kong were deemed worthwhile to would-be immigrants, who knew that they could achieve legal residency status in Hong Kong because of the "touch base" policy, which granted amnesty to illegal entrants to the colony who could reach urban areas. To stem the flood of entrants to the region, colonial officials quickly implemented new policies: first, to distinguish between "legal" and "illegal" entrants to Hong Kong, and second, to apprehend and repatriate those individuals who had entered Hong Kong illegally.

Ku outlines the way in which both the numbers and "quality" of immigrants in the late 1970s and early 1980s contributed to the overall negative perception of Chinese immigrants at that time (2004). She notes that, from the point of view of the colonial government policy makers, this wave of immigrants created problems of "lawbreaking, low productivity, and declining standards of living" rather than the problems of "poverty, poor hygiene, and overcrowding" that had characterized the 1950's version of the "Problem of People" (ibid. 351). The demographic characteristics of illegal immigrants during the late 1970s were at least partially responsible for these negative perceptions. While legal immigrants during this period included a roughly equal number of males and females, many families, and more educated individuals, the illegal immigrants were primarily uneducated males from Guangdong province, who had worked as farmers, fishermen, or laborers before coming to Hong Kong (Lee 1979). Also responsible for these negative perceptions were the Hong Kong media, whose portrayals of illegal immigrants during this time were so negative that they instilled in the Hong Kong public's imagination strong prejudices against *all* mainlanders (Ma 1999). These strong prejudices erased any sympathy once felt for "legitimate" mainland immigrants.

During the 1950s and 1960s, Hong Kong films had portrayed recent immigrants and mainlanders as "country bumpkins" (Cantonese: *tai heung lei*), individuals with less polish than current Hong Kong residents, but who could nevertheless learn local ways and assimilate to Hong Kong society. Ma explains that: "Tai Heung-lei became a social category in the popular media as well as in everyday life; however, this social label was far from discriminatory. The Tais were not deemed troublemakers but fellow countrymen who needed sympathy and help. These films inevitably concluded with a harmonious resolution of the differences with both locals and the Tais united in realisation that they were all Chinese" (1999:66).

Contrasting this sympathetic, "brotherly" account of mainlanders with a detailed analysis of the portrayal of mainlanders in the popular 1979 Hong Kong TV serial, *The Good, the Bad, and the Ugly*, Eric Ma demonstrates that Hong Kong people in the late 1970s already defined themselves in opposition to the negative stereotypes that they held about mainlanders (ibid.). One of the main characters of *The Good, the Bad, and the Ugly*, an illegal immigrant from the mainland who came to Hong Kong to join his family members there, was called "Ah Chian." Unlike the Tais, the character of "Ah Chian" represented the "dirty outsider" (ibid.). "Ah Chian" was "ill-disciplined and lawless," had an "insatiable appetite," and consistently violated "the sense of good taste among the established Hong Kongers" (ibid. 68). Most of all, he was foully dirty, personifying the threat of contamination that Hong Kong people were experiencing in the face of the seemingly uncontrollable masses of illegal immigrants arriving in the colony.

> In the serial, Ah Chian is dirty in the factual sense of the word. In the beginning, he is seen wearing dirty and ragged clothes (#1:4). When he eats, he uses his fingers instead of the chopsticks, and has bits of rice sticking all over his mouth (#1:16). He always laughs and talks while eating (#2.7). He tramples around in the rubbish bin and then smells out the Ching's house when [he] returns home (#24:6,7,8). Even down to the final confrontation . . . Ah Chian is depicted with a runny nose and greasy hair . . . The character of Ah Chian is heavily imbued with references, both verbal and visual, to garbage, dirt, faeces, urine, vomit, sweat, and nasal discharges. His dirtiness is excessive when seen in retrospect, but seemed to be very natural to the producers and local audiences at the time the serial was launched. To the locals, the dirty immigrants badly needed to be contained and controlled via a discriminatory name. (ibid. 67)

As a result of the serial, "Ah Chian" became "the public face of the newcomers" and "set in motion a stigmatising process that has persisted for years" (ibid. 63). Since the airing of this serial, Chinese newcomers to Hong Kong have been known locally as "Ah Chians," with all of the stereotypical baggage implied. Furthermore, they have been perceived as not just dirty but also lawless and generally destructive to Hong Kong social and economic norms.

From 1980 to 1983, the Hong Kong authorities took a number of steps to reduce the influx, which had swelled Hong Kong's population by almost half a million souls in just over five years. In 1980, the British colonial government abolished the "touch base" policy. As a result, all illegal immigrants, no matter where they were caught or in what circumstances, were repatriated to the mainland. New "forge-proof" identity cards were issued to Hong Kong residents, who were required to carry these ID cards with them at all times. Negotiations took place with the mainland authorities to ensure the imposition of firm (and reduced) limits on the number of PRC exit visas granted in any year. The practice of allowing mainland visitors to indefinitely overstay visitor's visas was ended, and removal from the colony was enforced. (Previously, policy toward these immigrants enabled the "regularization" of immigrant status [see Ku 2004] through the renewal of visas in six-month increments for periods up to seven years—the amount of time required to gain residency rights in Hong Kong.) Finally, Hong Kong authorities cracked down on "snakeheads," those individuals engaged in the illegal smuggling of persons from China to other areas (Burns 1987: 667–68). In short, these changes signaled an abrupt departure from previous practice and heralded the end of the liberal pre–World War II immigration policy that had allowed Chinese nationals visa-free access to Hong Kong. The enforcement of these new measures, designed above all to keep mainland residents out of Hong Kong, was reinforced by legislation, issued in the 1980s and 1990s, that targeted families as a further means of restricting official definitions of belonging to Hong Kong.

One of the concerns facing Hong Kong people in the early 1980s was that the large numbers of unmarried males who had entered the colony illegally during the late 1970s and early 1980s would marry mainland wives who would also immigrate to Hong Kong, thereby further increasing Hong Kong's population with "undesirable" mainlanders. During the past thirty years, this has indeed proved to be the case. Since 1995, Hong Kong immigration policy has allowed 55,000 mainland immigrants to settle in Hong Kong each year, and, as I pointed out in Chapter 1, the majority of the current immigrants (98 percent) are wives and children of Hong Kong permanent residents, some of whom were the "Ah Chians" mentioned earlier.

At the time of my fieldwork, the mainland-born wives and children of Hong Kong resident men waited for periods of up to ten years or longer before they could legally immigrate to join spouses, siblings, parents, children, or other immediate family members in Hong Kong.[9] These restrictions on entry to the region can be traced directly back to restrictive (and exclusionary) policies introduced in reaction to the massive entrance of mainlanders (both legal and illegal) to Hong Kong in the late 1970s. Prior to 1983, any Chinese national born in Hong Kong automatically had the right to live and work there. Beginning in 1983, however, birth to Chinese nationals in Hong Kong was no longer sufficient to ensure residency rights. One could only gain these rights—and all of the economic, political, and social privileges associated with Hong Kong (rather than mainland) residency—if both of one's parents were already permanently "settled"[10] in Hong Kong at the time of one's birth (Clarke 1986:344). Similarly, the British Nationality Act of 1981 had cut back the right of women to acquire Hong Kong membership status automatically through marriage, although it did allow for the "naturalization" of wives after three years of stay in Hong Kong from the date of marriage (ibid. 347). These changes continued the already well-established trends of making immigration policy as restrictive as possible and of focusing on "legal" entry as the primary criterion for admission to membership in the Hong Kong polity.

The Politics of Family Reunion Immigration Under the One Country/Two Systems Policy

Current policy defining which individuals are eligible for legal residency status in Hong Kong is defined in the Basic Law, Hong Kong's "mini-constitution" (Ku 2001) drafted by British and Chinese authorities in the period leading up to Hong Kong's return to mainland sovereignty in 1997. Although Article 24 of the Basic Law explains which categories of people should be eligible to be Hong Kong permanent residents, what has become evident in the period since the Basic Law came into effect is that the provisions defining exactly which Chinese citizens are eligible for permanent residency and the right of abode[11] were not spelled out clearly enough in the Basic Law. In particular, confusion has resulted from Article 24 (2) (1), which states that "Chinese citizens born in Hong Kong before or after the establishment of the Hong Kong Special Administrative Region" are eligible for permanent residency (Basic Law 1996). Notice that in this clause, no reference is made to the residency status of the parents of those "Chinese citizens born in Hong Kong." As a result, this clause seems to indicate a return to the pre-1983 more liberal policies of granting Hong Kong residency rights to Chinese nationals, and, as a result, it directly contravened the more restrictive policy in place at the time of the 1997 handover, which stipulated that only Chinese citizens who were born after at least one parent had already achieved Hong Kong permanent residency status would themselves be eligible for the right of abode in Hong Kong.

Whether this ambiguity was intentional is unclear; however, the controversy sparked by these disparities of definition has been significant and has captured Hong Kong people's imaginations through the media coverage of court cases focusing on Chinese citizens fighting for the right of abode in Hong Kong. Cases of Chinese children born in Hong Kong to nonpermanent resident parents, adoptive children, and illegal immigrants—like the protestors at the Immigration Tower and the twin Yeung-min discussed earlier—who believe they should be eligible for the right of abode in Hong Kong, have had major press coverage. The resultant (often much contested) rulings by the courts' officers on these cases have filled in some of the gaps left in the Basic Law's legal definitions of belonging. Furthermore, these rulings have served as touchstones that tap deeply into Hong Kong people's fears that their "political difference" with the mainland will be compromised because of the "one country, two systems" policy. As a result, local residents, officials, and government watchdogs focused on the outcomes of these cases as one means of judging whether Hong Kong's government and court system have maintained the autonomy from mainland interference that was guaranteed by the 1984 Sino-British agreement.

The final verdicts rendered in the three cases that I examine here were all received with criticism and a fair amount of local uproar. Either locals or government officials criticized rendered verdicts as not "correct," or Western-educated champions of democracy cited contested court decisions as indicators that Hong Kong's democratic process was failing. These cases, along with the public reactions to them, demonstrate that legal categories defining which Chinese citizens are seen as having valid moral and legal claims of belonging to Hong Kong remain contested at all levels of the population—not just by those government officials who are responsible for promulgating legislation and enacting policies on this subject. Although these cases did not directly involve the legal mainland immigrant wives who were my primary informants, these cases reinscribed the government's power to decide what legal forms of "family" and "family reunion" are officially recognized in Hong Kong. In so doing, the verdicts of these cases legitimated the previous policies that had kept families separated on either side of the border, just as they also allowed for the continuation of these policies in the future.

On the basis of the Basic Law's definition of which Chinese citizens were eligible for the right of abode in Hong Kong, thousands of previously "illegal" immigrants in Hong Kong sought to regularize their status there once the Basic Law came into effect on July 1, 1997. One case in 1998 was filed by over 5,000 claimants—all immediate family members of legal Hong Kong residents who, like the twin Yeung-min, felt they had significant moral claims of belonging to Hong Kong but had missed obtaining legal residency rights because of the arbitrary behavior of the mainland officials issuing exit visas or because of their illegal means of entry to the region. On January 29, 1999, Hong Kong's Court of Final Appeal awarded the right of abode in Hong Kong to children who had been born before their parents attained permanent residency status in Hong Kong. This ruling "regularized" the legal status of (1) illegal immigrants, such as Yeung-min, and (2) the children born to the mainland mistresses of Hong Kong men. Through its renegotiation of the categories defining legal membership status in Hong Kong, this court decision challenged prevailing assumptions associated with ideals of membership and belonging in Hong Kong. On the one hand, it tapped into the still strong fears of both Hong Kong people and government officials that this verdict would set the precedent for including previously excluded categories of mainlanders within the legal categories of Hong Kong membership status. On the other hand, the verdict also recognized the children born out of wedlock to mainland mistresses of Hong Kong men as having the right of abode. This decision was particularly problematic, since the substantial number of these children (according to Shih [1998], there were 300,000 such children in the mid-1990s) was perceived as a concrete threat to the well-being of Hong Kong families, who would be substantially less threatened should these same children and their mothers be required to remain on the mainland (Wu 2003). In the wake of that highly unpopular decision, the Hong Kong government, led by the Chief Executive, Tung Chee-Wah, decided that the judgment should be sent to the National People's Congress (NPC) Standing Committee for "reinterpretation."[12]

In late June 1999, the NPC's Standing Committee ruled that the Hong Kong Court of Final Appeal had misinterpreted the Basic Law, and it restricted the right of abode in Hong Kong once again to children with at least one parent who had been a Hong Kong permanent resident at the time of their birth. The claimants appealed their case, and by the time they once again made their way to the Court of Final Appeal in May 2001, they had attracted much international human rights attention. Their counsel argued that these particular abode seekers had been given "reasonable hope" by the SAR government to expect that they should be able to stay in the region, where they had families and had resided for years. Nevertheless, on January 10, 2002, the Court of Final Appeal ruled against the majority of the claimants, only granting the right of abode to (1) those illegal entrants who arrived in Hong Kong before July 1, 1997, and who had been born after one of their parents had attained permanent residency status, and (2) those claimants who were able to produce letters from the Legal Aid Department or other government agencies saying that, prior to 1999, their cases were already under review. Unfortunately, many claimants had never filed such paperwork, as they had been told that there was no need to do so by the government agencies involved (Chow 1/11/2002).

During the three-year period when the appellants in the 1999 case were waiting to find out whether they would be able to regularize their status in Hong Kong, other cases were initiated challenging the Basic Law's definition of which Chinese citizens could, or could not, become legal residents of Hong Kong. In July 2001, the Court of Final Appeal ruled on two cases involving the right of children in two different circumstances to qualify, or not, for the right of abode, as stated in the Basic Law. Although the final verdict rendered in one case acted to contradict the previous trend toward restricting entry in general, along with family reunion in particular, to Hong Kong, this verdict was publicly ridiculed by Hong Kong and PRC government officials, whose responses indicated that there had been no official change in position (from the point of view of either government) that would support the ease of family reunion in Hong Kong. In contrast, the final verdict in the second case was praised for upholding the restrictive definitions of family and belonging in Hong Kong—which it did by denying the right of children adopted on the mainland to legal residency rights in Hong Kong.

In the first case, a three-year-old boy, whose paternal grandfather was a Hong Kong permanent resident, had been born in Hong Kong while his mainland Chinese parents were both visiting Hong Kong on visitors' permits. On the basis that the Basic Law does not stipulate that Chinese citizens born in Hong Kong must have Hong Kong permanent resident parents in order to gain residency rights, the boy's grandfather filed an appeal for the boy's right to stay in Hong Kong after the family's first application for permanent residency on his behalf was denied by the Immigration Department. Throughout the three years of legal process that ensued, the boy stayed in Hong Kong with his grandfather, while his parents traveled back and forth from the mainland whenever they received visitors' permits that enabled their entry to the SAR. The final ruling made by the Hong Kong Court of Final Appeal unanimously decided that, given the wording of the Basic Law, this boy did have the right of abode in Hong Kong. Along with this boy, however, all children born to mainland parents in Hong Kong after July 1, 1997, became eligible for the right of abode. Hong Kong officials, such as the deputy secretary for security, were quick to point out their "disappointment" in the ruling, noting that at least 2,202 children born in similar circumstances would now be eligible for the right of abode in Hong Kong (Chow and Lau 7/21/01). Others expressed concerns that Hong Kong would be "flooded" with illegal immigrant mothers wishing to give birth to their children in Hong Kong. Prodemocracy legislative members of the Hong Kong government, on the other hand, lauded this court decision, saying that it "upheld Hong Kong's legal autonomy" (Leung and Chow 7/21/01).

On the same day, judgment was also given on a case involving the right of abode in Hong Kong for adopted Chinese children of Hong Kong residents. In this case, however, the Court of Final Appeal ruled in favor of the government, as the Basic Law makes no mention of the status of adopted children in its Article 24. Four out of five judges interpreted the phrase "born of" in Article 24 (2) (1) as referring to a biological parent-child relationship (Chow and Lau 7/21/01). Although this ruling affected a much smaller number of children overall, less than 200, the tear-streaked faces of parents and children—who, in most cases, had no actual "home" to return to on the mainland—were rich fodder for media stories focusing on the hardships faced by these devoted children and their parents. The story of one teenager, who ran from the courtroom in tears after the decision was announced, garnered extensive coverage.

Fourteen-year-old Agnes Tam Nga-yin had been adopted by her parents at the age of three months. While Agnes was still an infant, her Hong Kong permanent resident mother had moved to Shenzhen to care for her. Because Agnes' mother felt that the separation from her husband was too difficult, she and her husband decided to bring Agnes to Hong Kong on a visitor's permit in 1996. Agnes had been living in Hong Kong illegally since the expiration of that permit; however, Agnes had been raised as if she were her parents' biological daughter, and she had only learned of her adoption, and perilous legal status in Hong Kong, shortly before the final court ruling was to be announced. Upon the announcement of the court's decision, Agnes fled from the courtroom in tears—an act that was said to be the genuine result of her confusion in learning that she was to be separated from the only home she had ever known (ibid.). Over the following weeks, Agnes's plight continued to be covered extensively in both the Chinese and English media. Hong Kong people were soon well-versed about Agnes's dedication to her family, her musical accomplishments, and her support from friends and neighbors. Her classmates and teachers organized a massive signature campaign "urging the government to let her stay" (Chow 10/26/01). The ongoing sight of this beautiful, crying, devoted daughter proved too much for government officials, as increasing pressure was put on them to allow her to stay in Hong Kong. The Director of Immigration issued Agnes a temporary permit to stay in Hong Kong, and, several months later, he granted her the unconditional right to stay in Hong Kong on humanitarian grounds.

These two cases were important not just because of their "clarifications" of which children could be considered to be eligible for the right of abode in Hong Kong, but also because local and international audiences watched the outcomes of both cases in order to determine whether Hong Kong's legal system was continuing to operate autonomously from that of the PRC national government. The final arguments of both cases were closely related to the judgment rendered on the previous case, described earlier, filed by over 5,000 right of abode claimants and requiring "reinterpretation" by the PRC's National People's Congress Standing Committee. Although the ruling in the three-year-old boy's case was criticized by some Hong Kong and mainland government officials as being in violation of this previous NPC Standing Committee "reinterpretation," Agnes's case did not inspire official commentary of this kind, largely because the final ruling supported both the Hong Kong and PRC governments' positions of restricting entry to Hong Kong. On the other hand, her case fueled the imaginations of other young people struggling with the threat of having to leave their homes in Hong Kong. Shortly after the conclusion of Agnes's case, nineteen-year-old identical twin Yeung-min launched her successful media campaign along similar lines. When one of my teenage informant's legal claim to stay in Hong Kong was severely jeopardized in January 2002, she modeled the narrative of her own situation in Hong Kong along the lines of those highlighted in the media reports about Agnes's life, repeatedly telling me about her father's ill-health, her concern about her family's well-being should she have to leave, and her dedication to the ideals of democracy and freedom in Hong Kong. As my informant's legal options for staying in Hong Kong began to run out, her social worker suggested an appeal to the media as her final "chance." With her legal status still unresolved by July 2002, and her despair increasing, her initial reluctance to consider a media appeal was wavering the last time I spoke with her.[13]

The majority of claimants who had lost the cases described previously (and thus were illegally residing in Hong Kong) were granted an amnesty to stay in Hong Kong until March 31, 2002. As far as most members of the Hong Kong government were concerned, their responsibilities to these individuals had been satisfied. As the deadline to leave Hong Kong approached, however, rumors began to circulate that those individuals who were voluntarily returning to the mainland were being imprisoned and beaten. These rumors further fueled the resolve of abode-seekers to defy the court order requiring them to leave the region (Moy and Schwartz 1/30/2002). The Hong Kong Immigration Department worked to quell these fears by issuing special letters to those who would leave by the March deadline, exempting them from punishment on the mainland. But for individuals conditioned to Hong Kong's freer society, many of whom had been away from the mainland for years, and who would be "returning" to situations where they no longer had residency privileges, friends, or family, the faint promise offered by these letters was not sufficient incentive to leave Hong Kong. Nor did the warning addressed to the abode-seekers by the deputy director of the Guangdong Public Security Bureau's Exit-Entry Administration Department, in which he publicly called them "rats," inspire them with confidence

(Lee 3/23/2002). By mid-March, the threats of punishment to those who did not voluntarily leave Hong Kong by March 31 by government officials on both sides of the border were increasing: Hong Kong officials had made it clear that after March 31, forced home raids and repatriation would occur for their part, and mainland officials were saying that individuals who returned after that time would be likely to be "restricted from leaving the mainland to visit relatives" (ibid.).

With the exception of a few voices in the Hong Kong community, most Hong Kong people, including both long-time and newly arrived residents, agreed that these abode-seekers no longer had any place in Hong Kong, and that they should leave before more trouble was caused. Social workers at the social service center where I conducted my research told me that since these people had broken Hong Kong laws, jumped the "queue," or entered the region illegally, the court decision was "right." Legal immigrant informants—such as my mainland wife informants—were equally relieved at the decision, feeling that their years of waiting to come to Hong Kong legally were finally justified. One woman, who had waited for nine years in Guangzhou for the documentation to join her husband in Hong Kong, felt very strongly that a decision made in favor of the claimants would have encouraged even more illegal immigrants to come to Hong Kong without waiting their "turn." According to her, such a situation would cause "chaos" and make Hong Kong "just like" the mainland by undermining Hong Kong's important social and political focus on the rule of law. Only two of my immigrant informants, while condoning the court's decision, were able to sympathize with the claimants, noting that mainland officials are notoriously unreliable and subject to bribery. These women did not doubt that some of the claimants had indeed been cheated by mainland officials, or that they had suffered, as a result. Nonetheless, such behavior by mainland officials did not justify their right to continue to stay in Hong Kong illegally.

In this section, I have described the highly personal legal battles, fought in the public arena, which are some of the individual sites through which Hong Kong's and Beijing's government apparatuses have been "working out" the details of how to establish viable policies over which Chinese citizens can gain access to the legal privilege of residing permanently in Hong Kong. The outcomes of these cases are important, because they provide new possibilities for the lives of some Chinese citizens (and dash the hopes of others) by enabling (or not) moves across political difference—from the mainland's late socialist political economy to Hong Kong's legalistic, capitalist, and cosmopolitan culture. Yet their importance goes beyond these real-life repercussions for immigrant claimants, because these cases also focus attention on the rifts that exist in the political imaginary of belonging in post-1997 Hong Kong, where definitions about which Chinese citizens are thought to have legal claims to and "belong" in Hong Kong are highly contested. Through their reactions to these cases, Hong Kong officials and residents alike have demonstrated repeated signs of ambivalence, confusing groups and individuals of different legal statuses, agreeing with restrictive court decisions, but letting their emotions be swayed at other times by moving stories of youth, beauty, or exceptional hardship and filial piety in media accounts. The stories of Agnes and Yeung-min, in particular, demonstrate how prejudices formed against mainlanders in general dissipated when applied to the situations of individual immigrants who had been humanized through media portrayals that highlighted their resonance with the idealized qualities of belonging in Hong Kong.

Although the outcomes of these cases provide challenges to the hegemonic discourses of "law and order" and "political stability" that form the backbone of official definitions of membership in the Hong Kong polity (Lam 2004; Goodstadt 2005), they also highlight—as exceptions to the rule—the power that these concepts continue to exercise over public ideologies of belonging in Hong Kong, where they overshadow competing discourses that might privilege moral entitlement to polity membership (Ku 2001). Nevertheless, the rooting of membership rights in strict definitions of "legal" entrance to Hong Kong has paradoxically resulted in obscuring distinctions between legal and illegal immigrants in the Hong Kong social and political imaginary. The frequent historical changes in official policy outlining legal and illegal entry to the region—combined with Hong Kong judicial decisions that first grant and then deny membership status, mainland bureaucrats' corruption over granting official exit permits, and Hong Kong immigrants' (and sometimes citizens') shaky understanding of what "the rule of law" means—have robbed some would-be immigrants of legal entry rights and have also seemingly eroded the legitimacy of legal immigrants' claims to membership in the Hong Kong polity. Nonetheless, as I explain in the following sections, obtaining legal entrance to Hong Kong is critical for determining the possibilities of immigrant adjustment to Hong Kong overall. Legal entrance not only leads to increased opportunities to access social welfare resources, but it is also a crucially important variable in immigrants' attempts to legitimate their statuses as "Hong Kong people" in the eyes of locals.

Legal Membership: The Path to Accessing Social Welfare Resources

Traditionally, the problem of delineating membership privileges has been particularly important because it defines which individuals are deemed eligible for inclusion in the provision of political, social, and civil rights. With the increasing "multi-sitedness" (Soysal 2000) of citizenship, the quality of membership rights experienced by individuals is even more closely linked to the localities in which they live. Heyman notes, for example, that "labor markets and benefits are not formally part of nation-state citizenship, but in practice they have developed together historically and are important ways in which citizens distinguish themselves from non-citizens" (2002:480). In this analysis, citizens' access to the "web of rights and distributive claims across many legal and institutional terrains"—rights that are not usually available to noncitizen undocumented workers—fundamentally determine individuals' life courses as well as their views of noncitizens (ibid. 481). Over the past fifty years, this link between quality of membership status and residential location has been particularly important for Chinese citizens. The household residency system (Mandarin: *hukou*), created in the mid- and late-1950s by the government of the PRC, established a set of policies that permanently linked a person's place of residency to other social provisions, including access to food, housing, education, work, and welfare (Solinger 1999). This system not only served to facilitate state control over citizens, but it also "segregated the entire Chinese population into a two-tiered rural-urban ranking of privilege" (Clark 2001:106). Since 1958, PRC residents have been required:

> to register at birth with the local authorities as either an urban or a rural *hukou* holder of a particular fixed place . . . Rural *hukou* holders are prohibited

from migrating into the cities and are not entitled to receive state-subsidized housing, food, education, medical care, and employment; these are reserved for urban *hukou* holders only. Cut off from urban employment, guaranteed food supplies, subsidized housing, and other benefits of the city, peasants were anchored in the countryside for decades with virtually no spatial mobility. (Zhang 2001:25–26)

Furthermore, this inscription of unequal membership rights (and benefits) into the everyday lives of citizens was reinforced by the division of PRC "citizens" (Mandarin: *gongmin*) as either "people" (those who supported state-initiated processes of social, political, and economic change) or "enemies" (those who did not) (Yu 2002:293). As a result, "[t]o be a citizen would not necessarily be as good as being a member of the people—a citizen could be a criminal or a bad element, whereas it would always be safe to be one of the people" (ibid.).

This official inscription of differential structures of rights for citizens tied to particular residential (or class) locations, which has been a hallmark of political and social life throughout the history of the PRC, continues in practice through the differential access to rights and privileges accorded to PRC residents of Hong Kong. As previously mentioned, Chinese citizens who are Hong Kong residents carry passports that enable them visa-free access to over 100 countries worldwide. They also enjoy substantial freedom of speech, limited suffrage, exemption from the "one-child policy," and the right to cross the Hong Kong/mainland border at will. These privileges, which are not consistently available to Chinese citizen residents of the mainland, indicate both actual difference and also the potential for continued difference among residents of these two different political regions of the PRC. Furthermore, the access (or lack of access) to these rights—and the resources (including public housing, social welfare provision, etc.) that accompanied these rights—played an important role in immigrants' adjustment to Hong Kong life.

While illegal immigrants were denied access to these rights and resources, legal immigrants had some access to some of these rights and resources, even though a number of resources that were available to Hong Kong permanent residents (that is, citizens in the local sense) were not always available to newly arrived immigrants, such as the immigrant wives and children who entered Hong Kong as "residents" rather than as "permanent residents." For example, in 2001, to be eligible for state-subsidized public housing, at least 50 percent of one's immediate family had to have been living in Hong Kong for seven years. Even to apply to live in public housing (and it should be noted that in 2001–02, almost one-half of Hong Kong's population was living in some sort of state-subsidized housing), one was required to be a permanent resident. This provision excluded immigrant wives, who had to be legal residents in Hong Kong for at least seven years before they could be recognized as permanent residents. Likewise, one needed to be a permanent resident to vote, to stand for election, and also to be eligible for worker (re)training scheme classes. On the other hand, a shorter period of residency—only one year—was required to apply for welfare, locally known as Comprehensive Social Security Assistance (CSSA).[14] The residency requirements for disability and old age or retirement assistance (locally called "fruit money" as the HK$700 [US$90] per month stipend is enough to do little more than buy fruit) fell somewhere between the requirements for housing and CSSA, at three to five years.

Although legal immigrants who had been living in Hong Kong for only one year were ineligible to receive most kinds of government assistance available to Hong Kong residents, funding requirements of many Hong Kong government-subsidized programs for recently arrived immigrants, such as those at the social service center where I did my research, stipulated that legal immigrants who had been in Hong Kong longer than one year were no longer eligible for aid. Reflecting the strong ambivalence toward immigrants—whether legal or illegal—by the Hong Kong public and many legislators, these ambiguous policies reinforced already salient ideals of "difference" between newcomers and Hong Kong people (Cantonese: *heunggongyahn*) and reminded recent immigrants that their presence in Hong Kong remained sanctioned only tenuously at best.

Hong Kong ID Cards: Badges of Belonging or Nonbelonging?

One important marker of local membership status that was accessible to legal immigrants, but not illegal immigrants, was the Hong Kong Identity (ID) card. On the basis of needing to distinguish between legal and illegal residents of Hong Kong, ID cards are consulted before many daily life transactions in Hong Kong can take place, such as signing up for mobile phone service, connecting phone or Internet service, renting videos, opening bank accounts and conducting nonautomated transactions at the bank, paying bills, and registering to take classes. Residents over 15 are required by law to carry their ID cards with them at all times, and should they be stopped and submitted to a random search while not carrying their cards, they will be fined heavily. Frequent searches are common, as police officers station themselves—usually—in areas where illegal immigrants are more likely to reside. As people rush by on busy streets or in crowded subway stations, the police officers will target certain individuals, who look like "mainlanders," and require that they produce their ID cards. For someone to get by on an everyday basis in Hong Kong without an ID card—someone like an illegally resident abode-seeker—many aspects of everyday life would be not just difficult, but dangerous, as even routine errands would carry the potential threat of being found out and repatriated.

My legal immigrant informants were highly aware of the importance of their Hong Kong ID cards in "marking" them as legitimate members of Hong Kong's polity. According to one of my informants:

> Actually, there's nothing particularly special that you have to do to be a Hong Kong person, except that when you are a Hong Kong person, you have the right to do more things. You have to—when you just come on a visa you can't do anything. You're here, but you can't work, you can't take classes. The only thing that you can do is sit at home, waiting, because you don't know what to do.
>
> When I [got my ID card], I was so happy. I really felt that I had become a Hong Kong person . . . really happy. Because before when I came [on a visitor's permit], I couldn't do anything. Everywhere I went, people asked: do you have an ID card? I couldn't take classes. I couldn't participate in any activities. I couldn't do anything and was so bored. As soon as I got my ID card . . . , I really felt like a Hong Kong person.

Moreover, it was clear from my discussions with my legal immigrant friends that they often judged their own "progress" in fitting in with locals by not having recently been stopped as part of an ID card search by the police.

Almost every immigrant I knew well at the social service center where I conducted my fieldwork had, at some point, been stopped and searched by Hong Kong police. Most informants had been searched two or three times, most frequently on the rare occasions that they had visited Hong Kong on two-way visiting permits. Over time, as women had longer to adjust to Hong Kong ways of acting and dressing, they found that they became less frequent targets of police searches. Many mainland wives would brag about how long it had been since they had been stopped, or, if they had been recently stopped, they were quick to offer an excuse about why they had seemed particularly good targets at that time. That being stopped by the police was a terrifying and embarrassing aspect of their immigrant experiences was also clear from my interviews, as women routinely told me that as visitors to Hong Kong they had been afraid to leave their husbands' homes and risk being searched. Women also identified the brusque attitudes of the police who stopped them, along with the open curiosity of bystanders who watched while they were searched, as evidence of Hong Kong people's prejudice toward mainlanders in general. Nevertheless, as one informant made clear, having an ID card when being stopped and searched was much better than not having one:

> If you have an ID card, and other people see you [being checked by the police]—you know—because you are on the street and other people will be staring at you, and that makes you self-conscious. If you have an ID card, then that changes things. You can relax. You know that other people will see that you have an ID card, and they'll say, "Oh! That person has an ID card. There's nothing wrong. She came to Hong Kong legally." So the way that people think about you will be different.

On the other hand, these same informants made it clear that this "marker of belonging" also served as a double-edged sword, sometimes thwarting their attempts to integrate locally. I was frequently told that the ID cards, with their prominent record of personal details, made immigrants easier targets of discrimination by potential employers and other locals. My informants often told me that they had been "dismissed" from job interviews after showing their ID cards with recent dates of registration, making it clear to all locals that they were newly arrived mainlanders in the SAR.

Ultimately, through such encounters, recent immigrants to Hong Kong learned that having legal residency rights in Hong Kong—while demonstrating that their moral and legal claims to the region had been recognized—were not sufficient in and of themselves to ensure that they would be treated as if they "belonged" in Hong Kong.

The mass shaping of Hong Kong public perception against mainland immigrants in recent years echoes the processes described by Ma in the 1980s in which all mainlanders were stereotyped as "dirty" "Ah Chians" (1999). Not all Hong Kong locals were unaware of this blatant manipulation by both government and media representations. At least one of my Hong Kong permanent resident informants held the government responsible for negative perceptions of mainland immigrants, who were portrayed as a drain on Hong Kong's resources rather than as welcome, productive members of society. Furthermore, she noted, negative portrayals of "chaotic" abode-seekers, like those who were responsible for the fire-bomb attack that I mentioned at the beginning of this chapter, had directly negative effects on the public perception of legal immigrants. Comments made during my interviews with others verified these claims, as discussions with social workers about their families' and friends' perceptions of their work revealed that most Hong Kong people did not distinguish between these two groups of legal and illegal immigrants. In contrast to the vocal abode-seekers, who were often shown protesting, and otherwise disrupting "orderly" Hong Kong life, legal immigrants lived a quiet life away from TV and media reports and disapproved of the "chaos" caused by the abode-seekers as much as long-term Hong Kong residents did.

Far from attempting to clarify these distinctions for the public, most Hong Kong government officials, by mid-2002, were also questioning the number and quality of legal immigrants coming to the SAR. In particular, these officials noted that the resources provided to help these legal immigrants adjust to Hong Kong ways of life would deplete welfare and social security funds. Overall concerns were heightened by reports of a "brain drain" resulting from the emigration of skilled workers from Hong Kong during the mid 1980s and early 1990s (Skeldon 1994a, 1994b, 1994c). As a result, public perception in Hong Kong continues to be shaped by strong fears that the replacement of the local economic and political elite with mainland immigrant wives and children, with their low educational and skill levels, will make it difficult for Hong Kong to maintain its elite status as a global financial capital. Hong Kong people's fears of the social and economic burdens that they could face if immigration from the mainland were not controlled are legitimate. Certainly, the massive influx of mainlanders into Hong Kong had both positive—in the form of overall growth—and negative effects (in the form of the "problem of people") in particular periods of the twentieth century. On the other hand, the fears that remain as legacies from these past events continue to support policies that work against the smooth reunion of family members whose legal claims of belonging to Hong Kong allow them to immigrate there.

In an article entitled "Who Should Get in? The Ethics of Immigration Admissions," Joseph Carens points out that family reunification is a moral obligation, rather than a specific legal requirement, that nation-states are responsible for upholding. He notes that most liberal democratic states do willingly allow for family reunion between citizen residents as well as non-citizen residents (2003:96). The continued practice of PRC and Hong Kong government officials to test the limits of this international moral convention highlights the collusion that does exist between the mainland and local Hong Kong governments. During the period of my fieldwork, these governments began to look less autonomous, and more superficially alike, with the visible and well-publicized forced repatriation of the failed abode-seekers—Chinese citizens who speak the same language and with the same historical roots as current Hong Kong residents, with claims to Hong Kong in the forms of family members and community involvement there—to their "homes," which no longer existed on the mainland.

Although modern technology has been applied to facilitate the increasing number of people—200 million in 2006—who cross the Hong Kong/mainland Chinese border each year, the distinction between mainlanders and Hong Kong residents that was once unclear is now well established (see also Ku 2004). This distinction continues to be maintained through immigration practices and government policies that make entrance to the SAR both a long-term dream and a highly sought after status among most mainland Chinese citizens. For those mainlanders who do achieve the right of abode in Hong Kong, they still face significant obstacles in adapting to Hong Kong life. These concerns are particularly salient for the wives and children of Hong Kong men, who form the majority of legal immigrants to the region and who must integrate into local households where they face many of the same difficulties that they also encounter in Hong Kong society at large. In Chapter Three, I explain how mainland wives and Hong Kong husbands meet and marry, along with how their early lives together on the mainland and in Hong Kong are affected by the political difference between Hong Kong and the mainland. In particular, this "difference" keeps mainland wives and their Hong Kong husbands separated for years on either side of the border and, along with this separation, prevents their equal access to the right of movement during this time.

THREE

Mainland Wives, Hong Kong Husbands

Behind the anti-immigrant rhetoric that pervaded the Hong Kong media in 2001 and 2002 was the assumption that all mainland Chinese immigrants with the legal right to immigrate to Hong Kong would automatically do so. This assumption was certainly not completely unfounded: not only had hundreds of thousands of immigrants left the mainland for Hong Kong—often at their own peril—over the previous fifty years, but the immigrants in question at the turn of the millennium were also primarily women, whose traditionally cast gender roles made it a likely assumption that wives would necessarily join their husbands in Hong Kong. Although my interactions with informants made it clear that many women with the legal right to do so did indeed immigrate to Hong Kong, these same interactions also demonstrated that women (including both wives and mothers of Hong Kong people) faced difficult choices in deciding how and when to immigrate to Hong Kong. Their personal motivations for migrating were influenced by economic and familial concerns as well as by governmental control and bureaucratic requirements dictating the terms, time, and status of entry for mainlanders hoping to "reunify" with family members in Hong Kong.

In particular, the long bureaucratic waits that wives and children faced while waiting for their legal permission to emigrate had a significant effect on their feelings about moving to Hong Kong. During these long periods of separation from their husbands, wives often developed feelings of ambivalence about immigrating to Hong Kong. Such was the case of A-poh's daughter-in-law, a mainland wife waiting (in 2002) for the legal documentation that would enable her to move to Hong Kong to join her husband there. I met A-poh's daughter-in-law on a visit to Guangzhou in April 2002, when I was visiting A-poh, a cheerful seventy-year-old retired children's math teacher. Together, the three of us dined at a fancy hotel restaurant in Guangzhou, where we had an expensive meal that A-poh said her daughter-in-law could easily afford with the high salary that she made as a fashion designer. During our meal, A-poh's stylishly dressed daughter-in-law talked unreservedly about how much she enjoyed her work. Afterwards, A-poh told me privately that her daughter-in-law was worried about moving to Hong Kong, where her husband, A-poh's son, had lost his job and was working temporarily as a taxi driver. A-poh's daughter-in-law knew that she would not be able to find work as a fashion designer in Hong Kong because of her inability to speak English and because of her immigrant status. As a result, she was reluctant to leave her secure and interesting job in Guangzhou's cosmopolitan urban environment for uncertain prospects in Hong Kong. A-poh told me she believed that her daughter-in-law would choose not to emigrate.

The professional success of A-poh's daughter-in-law was not altogether typical of the situations of mainland wives I knew in Hong Kong, who tended not to have careers and to be much less well educated overall. In other ways, however—including her relative lack of physical mobility in comparison to that of her husband, the long period of separation from her husband while she waited for her immigration paperwork to be processed, and her ambivalence about actually immigrating to Hong Kong to live with her husband after such a long period of living separately—her situation was profoundly similar to that of the majority of mainland wives I encountered. In Chapter Two, I documented the history of the immigration policy between Hong Kong and the mainland that has resulted in the long wait periods (upwards of five and ten years) that mainland wives face before they can legally immigrate to Hong Kong to join their husbands and other family members there. During these long wait periods, mainland wives could not easily travel to Hong Kong and were therefore dependent on their husbands' goodwill in visiting them and in sending needed remittances to pay for housing, clothing, education, and other daily expenses necessary to living and raising a family. Wives also had little or no ability to monitor their husbands' sexual, social, or economic behaviors while they waited over periods of five, ten, or more years for the legal documentation that would allow them to immigrate to Hong Kong. Furthermore, because of the way in which immigration-related permits were processed and distributed, mothers and their individual children rarely had the opportunity to migrate to Hong Kong as a complete unit; more often, the family's migration took place, one by one, over a period of years. Under such conditions, balancing work and family caregiving needs on both sides of the border presented particular challenges that often reinforced the social and economic marginalization of mainland immigrants. Immigrant women already in Hong Kong were particularly vulnerable to being dismissed from their already low-paying jobs when a family crisis or sick child necessitated their immediate return to the mainland. In cases where children immigrated to Hong Kong before their mothers, wives were often further disenfranchised from their husbands and in-laws by being excluded from "familial" decisions made about their children's educational and social needs. All told, the disadvantages suffered by the mainland wives and children of Hong Kong men during these long periods of separation, further compounded by the downward mobility that they experienced once in Hong Kong, created real problems for their adjustment and integration into Hong Kong life.

Arguing that the lack of control over mobility can disempower individuals, Doreen Massey writes: "For it does seem that mobility, and control over mobility, both reflects and reinforces power. It is not simply a question of unequal distribution, that some people move more than others, and that some people have more control than others. It is that the mobility and control of some groups can actively weaken other people. Differential mobility can weaken the leverage of the already weak" (1994:150).

It is undoubtedly true that the long years of separation that women experienced from their husbands did "weaken" mainland wives' leverage over husbands and other family members and also contributed to many of the difficulties of adjustment that they experienced once in Hong Kong. Nevertheless, the effects of this period of waiting for immigrant women were considerably more complex than what one might assume taking Massey's quote into account. On the one hand, mainland wives' marginalized positions in Hong Kong society more generally, and in their reunited families in particular, meant that their acquisition of the legal right to control their own movement—which they acquired as soon as they immigrated to Hong Kong—was not sufficient in and of itself to empower wives. On the other hand, the legacy of wives' long separations from their husbands meant that they had developed both concrete networks of resources as well as personal imaginaries that *did* often render them more "powerful."

During their years of waiting to immigrate to Hong Kong, mainland wives acquired houses and also developed networks of friends in Shenzhen, Dongguan county, or other areas of Guangdong Province neighboring Hong Kong—to which they would actually (or sometimes just threaten to) return after they had become Hong Kong residents with the right to cross the Hong Kong/mainland border. In cases where wives did not have children, or where children migrated before their mothers, women often had the chance to study English, acquire job skills, and live on their own— developing a sense of independence that made adjustment to living with their Hong Kong families more difficult and also empowered women to make decisions to leave destructive family or employment situations once in Hong Kong. In other words, these same conditions of restricted movement that increased wives' anxiety and caused serious problems of adjustment once in Hong Kong also had transforming effects on women, which allowed them new potentialities of engagement with the world around them once they had legally migrated across the "political difference" that separates Hong Kong from the mainland.

In this chapter, I explore the complex interactions among gender, power, and movement that characterized mainland wives' migration across political difference to join their husbands in Hong Kong. These cases demonstrate that although women were not "powerful," they experienced both hardships *and* freedoms and were thus "empowered" in some ways, but not in others, through their immigration to Hong Kong. These complex effects on women's experiences were tied both to the lack of control they had over their movement while residing on the mainland as well as to the increased control they had over their movement once in Hong Kong. Overall, this situation, which demonstrates that the equation between mobility and empowerment is by no means straightforward, raises questions for conceptualizing "power" as a meaningful category of analysis in understanding the migration and living situations of these women (see also Freeman 2005:100). I also set the stage for the subsequent chapters by addressing the following questions: Who were the Hong Kong men who married mainland wives? How did mainland women meet their Hong Kong husbands, and why did they choose to marry them? What were women's expectations for living in Hong Kong? And how did women's mainland and Hong Kong living situations compare? After first providing some background information describing the general situation of Hong Kong husbands and their mainland wives, the rest of the chapter focuses on narrative accounts of four of my mainland immigrant wife informants, whose in-depth stories about their immigration experiences illustrate both the very real difficulties of adjustment that they faced as well as the new possibilities of movement that they experienced once in Hong Kong.

Hong Kong Husbands

The cultural, economic, and familial linkages between Hong Kong and Southeast China have long facilitated the practice of Hong Kong men taking mainland wives (Lang and Smart 2002). While political barriers provided a formidable deterrent to this form of marriage during the 1950s and 1960s, China's period of economic and political liberalization since the late 1970s, along with recent processes of globalization (which include the development of transnational economic linkages, transportation infrastructure, communication technologies, and increased media access) have once again facilitated cross-border marriages. Census data collected in the 1990s reported that 100,000 Hong Kong men were "regularly sojourning" in Guangdong Province on business or traveled regularly between Hong Kong and the mainland as container truck drivers (Tam 1996; Lang and Smart 2002). Many of these already-married men, encouraged by their workmates and fellow sojourners, opted to take mistresses or "second wives"

(Mandarin: *ernai;* Cantonese: *yinai* or *yilai*) on the mainland (ibid.). Taking mistresses on the mainland—demonstrating not only a man's "virility" but also his "economic status" (Lang and Smart 2002:554)—is a widespread phenomenon: a 1995 survey in Hong Kong showed that 20 percent of Hong Kong's male population did not disapprove of the practice (Lee and Lu 1997 cited in Lang and Smart 2002), and qualitative data gathered since that time indicates that "the approval of such relationships among men who travel regularly into Guangdong on business is much higher" (Lang and Smart 2002:554). Nonetheless, not all Hong Kong men visiting or working on the mainland were already married, and some took "first" wives on the mainland. One main distinction between the two situations was that while "first" wives could legally immigrate to Hong Kong, "second wives" could not. The children born to Hong Kong men and their mistresses were also not able to immigrate legally to Hong Kong. Nonetheless, the presence of these mistresses and illegitimate children of Hong Kong men just over the border was seen as a threat by the Hong Kong women whose husbands were involved in this practice (Wu 2003). In Hong Kong public perception, negative qualities that they assumed about mistresses were also attributed to the legitimate "first" wives of Hong Kong men as well.

In the 1970s, 1980s, and 1990s, most Hong Kong men marrying mainland wives were older, sometimes widowed, and often from lower class backgrounds without stable incomes. Many of these men had immigrated to Hong Kong from Guangdong to work in the 1960s, 1970s, and 1980s, initially arriving in Hong Kong as "illegal immigrants" but later regularizing their status there.[1] Before immigrating to Hong Kong, these men would have worked as fishermen or farmers in Guangdong Province; once in Hong Kong, these men regularly worked as construction workers, restaurant workers, or truck and taxi drivers. With their lower incomes and educational levels, these Hong Kong men were often unattractive to many Hong Kong women as potential husbands. Furthermore, when Hong Kong women did want to marry these men, these women were often older (mid-thirties to mid-forties) and not considered very beautiful (Li 2001). Searching for younger, prettier wives, these Hong Kong men would often return to their hometowns in Guangdong to look for brides. In many cases, men were introduced to their future wives by family or friends on return visits home. One of my informants, who had met her husband this way when she was in her late twenties, explained:

> A friend introduced us. At that time, my husband was living and working in Hong Kong, and he was getting older. So his mother—because he was so ugly and so old [this was said laughingly]—his mother wanted to help him find a wife. My mom said I was so old and still hadn't found a boyfriend— well, I didn't care, I thought I might as well go out with him. I was working in a factory then . . . He would come to visit once a month. When he came, I would have to work, so I didn't have much time to spend with him. Maybe it was fate—lo and behold, several years later, we got married.

In other cases, men married long-term girlfriends. Another informant told me: "We were students together. He went to Hong Kong because his parents were there. After he emigrated, he would often come back to visit. So, we knew each other, dated, and then got married after he had immigrated to Hong Kong. He [immigrated] to Hong Kong in '91. In '92 he came back and we registered our marriage."

As opportunities to work or to seek entertainment across the border opened up in the decades of the 1980s and 1990s, Hong Kong men had increased opportunities to meet mainland women. In these cases, Hong Kong men met their future wives through introductions from friends when they traveled for work or relaxation to Shenzhen. At times, men would have to be persuasive. One wife, whose husband had—six years earlier—walked into the Shenzhen shop where she worked to visit friends on his birthday, described her initial reluctance to go out with this unknown man. Laughing, she told me: "I thought it was really strange that he would invite me out with him to celebrate his birthday because I didn't know him!" Often, men met women whom they later married when not actively looking for wives at all (Li 2001).

Recent ethnographic research has demonstrated that by 2001 the profile of Hong Kong men marrying mainland wives had changed. Younger Hong Kong men, including those who were locally born and better educated with stable, white-collar jobs, might actively seek mainland wives through their participation in dating services or while working in China—despite the risk that their marriages to mainland women would be looked down upon by their family and friends. In these cases, younger men were willing to risk social censure through their desire to acquire young, pretty wives who men thought would be "more willing [than Hong Kong wives] to perform the 'traditional' roles [associated with] a Chinese wife—i.e., [being] faithful and submissive to the husband, serving the husband and his family without complaint, and [being] the child-bearer and child-rearer" (Li 2001: 162-63). According to Li, these men also preferred to marry Chinese women from Guangdong, since the similar cultural and language backgrounds should enable better communication between the couple (ibid.). Li found no correlation between a man's birth order and his tendency to marry a Chinese wife, nor were less expensive marriage costs cited as a motivating factor in these cross-border marriages (Li: e-mail communication 1/23/03).

My informants' husbands—all of whom had married their wives in the late 1980s or early 1990s—tallied with the descriptions above. Hong Kong husbands worked in a variety of service and professional capacities, including, but not limited to, factory management, construction, restaurant chef and service, business administration, and electrical repair. They met their future wives when working on the mainland, but more often through introductions from friends when visiting home or relaxing in Shenzhen. They included both men who had arrived in Hong Kong as immigrants from the mainland and men who were Hong Kong "natives." For wives, whether or not men were originally from Hong Kong or the mainland was important. Wives who married immigrants to Hong Kong (rather than Hong Kong-born and raised men) did not have to live together with men's families once in Hong Kong. Women who married into Hong Kong families, on the other hand, usually lived with their husband's Hong Kong family members—in contrast to most young Hong Kong married couples who preferred to live in households separate from those of their parents (that is, neolocally) (ibid.). Given the relatively low economic status of many Hong Kong husbands coupled with the very low earning potential of most mainland wives, living with in-laws may simply have been a financial necessity. Whether some Hong Kong men were interested in marrying mainland wives specifically for the purpose of remaining in residential situations where the wives would help take care of elderly parents or other relatives is unclear. My immigrant wife informants often did help care for elderly in-laws for at least a short period after their arrival in Hong Kong, but these same immigrants often left (or threatened to leave) their in-laws' homes once their in-laws acted in abusive or domineering ways.

Mainland Wives

A substantial number of the immigrant wives I met during my research were part of the ever-increasing internal migrant population in China. Throughout most of the Maoist period (from the early 1950s though the mid-1970s) mainland Chinese residents were not allowed to leave their place of "household residency" (Mandarin: *hukou;* Cantonese: *wuhhauh*) to live or work elsewhere without specific PRC government permission. As a result, there was little migration of any sort; that which did exist was tightly controlled by the party-state apparatus. Beginning in 1978, policies initiated by Deng Xiaoping ushered in a new period of political and economic reform, which, among other things, allowed mainland residents to explore increased possibilities for movement throughout the decades of the 1980s and 1990s. During this period, leaving one's legal place of residence to look for work was still technically illegal and certainly very difficult, but state methods of control, such as rationing, no longer prevented individuals from leaving their homes to move to other parts of the mainland. By the mid-1990s, such movement had become "routine." Individuals—both men and women—left their rural villages to work in urban areas throughout China, and families began to depend on migration as one strategy used to support rural families struggling to get by after the dismantling of China's collectivist system.

Recent estimates suggest that "more than 100 million rural Chinese have now migrated to cities," and half of that number have migrated to Guangdong (Rosenthal 7/2/02). This vast movement of people, officially labeled the "floating population,"[2] has gained much attention from scholars, who have documented both the characteristics of these migrants as well as the confrontations between these migrants and representatives of the Chinese Communist Party (CCP) state apparatus. The CCP has demonstrated its reluctance to recognize the social and civil rights of migrant citizens through such means as refusing to allow migrant children educational opportunities and by demolishing well-established migrant "villages" located in and around major cities such as Beijing (Davin 1999; Solinger 1999; Zhang 2001; Wang 2006). While recent estimates generally confirm that Chinese male migrants outnumbered female migrants in the last two decades of the twentieth century, women still accounted for a substantial number of the total—approximately 40–45 percent (Davin 1999:27). When further broken down between intra- and interprovincial migration, female migrants accounted for 45 percent of migration from rural to urban areas within the same province, and, in contrast to men, "were also strongly represented in all migration from rural areas to other rural areas" (ibid. 28). Of the total of female migration figures based on the 1990 census, 30 percent of female migration was for purposes of marriage, compared to 2 percent for men (ibid.).

The female migrants I met through my fieldwork in Hong Kong generally belonged to one of two categories. One group was comprised of older, poorly educated women from rural areas of Guangdong Province who had never left their home villages before immigrating to Hong Kong. Frequently, these women had married the Chinese men who had immigrated to Hong Kong in the 1960s, 1970s, or 1980s. These older (ages 40 to 65), poorly educated rural women from Guangdong had still been young—in their twenties and thirties—when they had initially met and married their Hong Kong husbands, who were commonly up to twenty years their senior. Because of the large numbers of immigrant brides from Guangdong Province, and because of the poor regulation and enforcement of the quota system for Chinese migrants prior to Hong Kong's reunification with the Chinese mainland in 1997, many of these women had waited the longest (fifteen to twenty years) to receive the documentation that would enable them to immigrate legally to Hong Kong. In many cases, by the time they finally immigrated to Hong Kong, their children were almost grown and often their elderly Hong Kong husbands were gravely sick or, perhaps, deceased. With few skills and little knowledge of urban areas, these women often required significant social worker involvement to adjust to their new lives; yet barriers of language[3] and shyness prevented many of these women from participating in social service-related programs or activities, making it difficult for me to get to know them well. As a result, very few of my core informants (although many of my acquaintances) were members of this group of migrants. This "older" model of the "cross-border marriage," which has become increasingly rare, remained the stereotype of Hong Kong-mainland marriages prevalent in the media and social discourse during the period of my fieldwork (Li 2001).

The second group of wives with whom I interacted over the period of my research was comprised of younger women who had left their homes in rural areas, usually during their mid-teenage years, and traveled to Chinese urban areas to work. The average level of educational attainment of my informants who fit into this category was junior high school level, although there were some women who had only studied for one or two years at elementary school. These younger immigrant wives (ages 25 to 39) were from Guangdong Province as well as from other provinces, most often Guangxi, Sichuan, Zhejiang, Hubei, and Fujian. When compared with the statistics on immigrants kept by the Hong Kong Home Affairs Department, the backgrounds of these women were representative of the general characteristics recorded for all immigrants during the last quarter of 2001, when most of my informants formally entered Hong Kong. During this period, 71 percent of all immigrants (over age 11) to Hong Kong were female, 52.5 percent of them between the ages of 20 and 39. The average level of education was through middle school, and 65 percent of immigrants cited Guangdong Province as their place of origin on the mainland (Home Affairs Department 2002). These numbers were statistically similar to those collected in the rest of 2001 and 2002, with the exception that in other periods, up to 80 percent of immigrants cited Guangdong Province as their place of origin (ibid.).

My informants had left their rural homes to earn money by working in factories in Guangdong Province or in the "Special Economic Zone" (SEZ) of Shenzhen, which borders Hong Kong. Since its designation as an area for experimenting with capitalist economic practices in 1980, Shenzhen has continued to attract large numbers of China's youth who flock to the SEZ with hopes of making their fortunes there. Likened to the American "Wild West" of the mid to late 1800s, Shenzhen "is often seen as an anonymous space with myriad possibilities for the re-creation of the self and for making a 'second start' in life" (Clark 2001:106). Not only did Shenzhen hold the "mystique of the urban" (cf. Brownell 2001) for these young women who moved there, but the narratives of my informants certainly attest to the independence and self-reliance experienced by young women (and men) who had "the freedom to explore their identities and their sexuality away from the watchful eyes of family and to take control over decisions regarding their future" (Clark 2001:106; see also Croll 1995). My informants told me that they had left their homes for a variety of reasons, including the need to make money to support their families, the desire to remove themselves from familial situations in which they were unhappy, and, in one case, because of rape. None of my informants cited "marriage" as a primary reason for originally leaving home, but that does not mean that these women were not aware that their moves to urban areas might carry with them the possibility of marriage to either urban-dwelling Chinese men or, possibly, to Hong Kong or foreign men.

Describing a visit she made to a Shenzhen beauty parlor set up by three female migrants, Aihwa Ong notes that the hairdressers "watched Hong Kong soaps on television and made a running commentary on what they imagined to be women's greater choices and strategies in overseas-Chinese communities" (1999:155). For these mainland migrant women, Ong writes: "Marriage to a traveling man enables one to expand one's accumulation of network capital [described as 'acquired personal networks based on friendship, school ties, and professional contacts'] and can also benefit the members of one's family, who eventually may also emigrate to the capitalist world, where their desires for wealth and personal freedom can be met" (ibid. 155–56). Ong's portrayal shares similarities with some of the motivations voiced by my informants, who often did indicate the pragmatic nature of their decisions to marry their Hong Kong husbands: one woman cited the need to help support her family as a primary motivating factor in her marriage, and another, who was clearly curious about the world outside of China, certainly felt that, in her mid-twenties, she was too old to be considered marriageable by most Chinese men. Yet this focus on the mere instrumentality of marriage ignores the importance placed on emotional motivations—specifically love—in cross-border marriages like those that took place between mainland wives and Hong Kong men.

The feelings of love and romance, and their potential compatibility with marriage, have a strong history in China that predates both "westernization" and communism (Jankowiak 1995:180). It is therefore not surprising that these sentiments also figured prominently in stories told by my informants, which often focused on the intense emotions felt, most often, by women during their initial periods of meeting and separation from their

husbands. One wife, for example, talked animatedly about how—before they were married—her husband would visit her in Shenzhen almost every night after work. When he could not come: "[W]e would talk on the phone for an hour or two at night . . . At that time, it was a lot more expensive to talk on the phone than it is now. We never wanted to hang up, and each phone call ended up costing more than the cost of transportation to come visit. So we thought he might as well just come—really!"
Another told me:

> It was really difficult [to live separately on the mainland and in Hong Kong]. Does everyone tell you it's really difficult (Cantonese: *sanfu*)? We— our situation was different [from lots of other couples]. No one introduced us, and we were in love (Cantonese: *yauh gamching*). Some people, their husbands would go back [to the mainland] to look for a wife . . . But for us, I got to know him, and I didn't know that he was going to go to Hong Kong. So, I felt so unfortunate (Cantonese: *chaam*).

These accounts highlight the romance that accompanied periods of meeting, courtship, and early years of marriage between mainland wives and their Hong Kong husbands. For many of my informants, however, much of the initial romance in their relationships often deteriorated during wives' and husbands' long periods of separation. One wife explained: "I didn't think about [my relationship] with my husband very much [while we were separated], because I spent all of my time looking after the kids . . . I thought we were still getting by pretty well. But I never imagined these past two years—I came to Hong Kong last year—there's been a change. Everything has changed."

The strong sentiments expressed by my informants also resonate strongly with the range of feelings described by Nicole Constable in writing about the premarital relationships between Filipina "mail order" brides and their American husbands (2003). Arguing that concepts of love are culturally constructed and "are intertwined with political economy through cultural logics of desire" (2003:119), Constable questions definitions of love that limit that emotion to a purely romantic notion, artificially severing the complex emotional feeling of "desire" from larger issues of stability, well-being, and economic security (ibid.). Similar to Constable, I found that the possibility of "love," either real or imagined, was an important motivation to my informants' decisions to marry their Hong Kong husbands. My informants told me that they had married their Hong Kong husbands because they loved them, because they valued their friendship, because they enjoyed their company, because they thought their husbands were "honest," or because they "got along." They also cited financial need, economic security, and (in the early years of relationships) the ease of access to consumer goods not available on the mainland as motivating their marriages. Nevertheless, the wives I knew remained highly sensitive to Hong Kong stereotypes conflating them with mistresses and portraying both wives and mistresses as "gold diggers." As one means of distancing themselves from this negative rhetoric that denied them emotional motivations for marrying their Hong Kong husbands, some of my informants refused to socialize with "second wives." From my informants' point of view, men's mistresses were the "gold diggers." In their eyes, not only were mistresses' relationships with their Hong Kong "husbands" not morally legitimate, but, financially supported by Hong Kong men, mistresses enjoyed comfortable living situations similar to those of my informants without the hardships involved in taking responsibility for the care of in-laws and other family concerns.

Waiting

My informants usually married their husbands in civil ceremonies. While those who had the financial means had opted to wear the now common Western-style white bridal dress and document their marriages with studio wedding portraits (see, for example, Adrian 2003), many of my informants told me that they wore much simpler dresses, sometimes complemented by one or two pieces of gold jewelry. Many informants had gone "home" to get married. In these rural locations, local marriage customs often varied from those practiced in wealthier Hong Kong, where gifts of gold and money play an important role in the marriage ceremony. One wife explained:

> For the wedding we went home to Guangxi—[the ceremony] was very simple. We followed the customs of my hometown. We bought some things, we made some offerings to the gods, and then we invited family members

to eat. My family doesn't do what people here [in Hong Kong] do—giving presents of gold or money. They will buy cloth, meat . . . That's the custom in my hometown. But my husband's family was far away, so we didn't completely follow that custom. Usually the groom's family will buy pork, chicken, cakes, lots of salt and sugar, and give it to the bride's family.

The physical separation between the bride's and groom's families also influenced ceremonies in other ways. In particular, many informants indicated that they had never had a wedding banquet—because of their inability to travel to Hong Kong or because their husbands' families had not wanted to travel to the mainland. One wife originally from Guangzhou told me, "We got married in Guangzhou. But we didn't have a wedding banquet. My husband's mother . . . wouldn't come to Guangzhou. And I couldn't come to Hong Kong. So we just went out to eat by ourselves; that was it. It was really simple." After marriage, wives were supported by their husbands, who either settled their wives in large (1,000 square foot), modern apartments in urban areas, or, if wives were originally from rural areas, built new three-story houses (or updated plumbing in older houses) for them in their home villages.

During their long (five to ten year) periods of waiting to immigrate to Hong Kong, my immigrant informants lived in the areas of Guangdong where they had grown up or, if they had migrated to Guangdong, they lived either in Shenzhen or one of the many new cities that had been built in Guangdong since the mid-1990s. These cities had sprung up in areas of Guangdong Province near Hong Kong and Macau where—less than ten years ago—there existed only tiny villages surrounded by vibrant green rice paddies. Still literally "under construction," these cities provide striking testament to the astounding speed with which industrialization is taking place in the PRC. Often only a few hours by train or bus from Hong Kong, these cities are not only filled with inhabitants (many of whom may be the wives and mistresses of Hong Kong men) but also with modern amenities, such as shopping malls, fancy consumer goods, and "international" style restaurants, serving Japanese, Korean, and "Western" foods. Offices, apartment buildings, shopping centers, and hotels—ranging from already "outdated" five-year-old cement tile-covered buildings to sleeker and more streamlined buildings that had been finished just months (or days) before—sit beside

Figure 3.1   Typical transitional area of Guangdong Province (May 2002)

temporary housing, makeshift food stalls, and wall-less public health centers opening directly onto the street. Many of my informants lived in "gated communities"—complete with restaurants, convenience stores, tree-lined "avenues," and recreational facilities such as gyms, tennis courts, and archery ranges—that existed as "civilized" islands in the midst of wide, as-yet "blank canvasses" of former countryside still being built into urban areas. This startling conjunction of the already built and the yet-to-be built was evident on bus trips throughout the region, as roads alternated between dirt "tracks," functional cement roads in the process of being widened, and virtually empty (in 2002) eight-lane highways.

For mainland wives waiting to join their husbands in Hong Kong, living in such areas meant that they had access to people, goods, services, and ideologies that would not have been nearly as accessible to individuals living in many other parts of the mainland. Supported by their Hong Kong husbands, most wives did not have to work, and many of my informants spent their days taking care of their children and, when time allowed, playing mahjong with friends (including other migrants, other wives waiting to immigrate to Hong Kong, and, from time to time, with the "second wives" of

Hong Kong men). Whereas certain kinds of "high-status" consumer goods had only been available through their husbands' provisions of such objects in the early years of their marriage, by the late 1990s, these wives had access to many of the same kinds of goods and services abundant in Hong Kong. Furthermore, wives and other residents of this region of Southeast China also had extensive access to media from Hong Kong and, by extension, abroad. Through radio and cable television, women could watch Hong Kong television programming and news reports, even if those news reports were still "clumsily censored" (Latham 2000:635). By watching Hong Kong programming, women who had yet to visit their husbands in Hong Kong could familiarize themselves with the English and Japanese-inflected Cantonese that is spoken in Hong Kong. Through watching soap operas and serials, they had access to media images of a Hong Kong middle-class lifestyle that few of them would share once in Hong Kong, but which served as a powerful motivating factor that influenced their desires to emigrate. More importantly, access to these forms of media, which were largely outside the control of the Chinese party-state and which presented a significantly different worldview from the state-sponsored line that was still promoted through official mainland sources of news and information (including radio and television) meant that these wives were living in a "semi-transnational frame of reference which was quite specific to [that] region [of] China" (ibid. 636). Access to these media not only familiarized wives with the world they would enter once they received the legal documentation that would enable them to immigrate to Hong Kong, but it also may have helped women to prepare for some aspects of Hong Kong life. One informant told me: "In Shenzhen, there are lots of opportunities to interact with Hong Kong people, and I watched the news a lot. So I had a good understanding of Hong Kong when I came. I adapted very quickly."

While China's fast-paced economic and infrastructure development allowed waiting wives to experience comfortable standards of living and facilitated visits from husbands, women's periods of waiting were also fraught with concern—over taking care of sick children, worrying about how children who had emigrated before them were faring in Hong Kong, or wondering why husbands did not visit more often.

> Before we got married, we would see each other three or four times a week ... At that time, I think [my husband] really wanted to come and see me.

As soon as he got off work, he would go back [to the mainland]. Most of his time was spent visiting me on the mainland. At that time, it was really good. But later, I didn't think it was so good . . . Right after we got married, then I got pregnant. I had to take care of everything myself. He would still come back to visit, but he was busier then at work—there was more to do. So, he would come twice a week, three times at the most. During that time, I was often sick or uncomfortable, and I was really worried . . . Sometimes I would think, "Why did I marry you? How come since we've been married you just abandon me here by myself?"

Wives' anxieties were exacerbated because of communication difficulties, which were more acute when wives did not yet speak Cantonese or husbands did not know Mandarin:

At that time, we often wrote things down. [My husband] didn't speak Mandarin, and I didn't speak much Cantonese. Lots of times when we were talking, there would be something I wouldn't understand. He wrote it down and showed me, or I wrote it down and showed him. [If we were talking on the phone], we would have to repeat the same sentence over and over. Repeat it, and repeat it again and again. In the end, we would have to use other words to understand—something that could describe the meaning of what we wanted to say.

Other communication problems stemmed from wives' and husbands' long separations and differential possibilities of movement. One wife remembered: "Sometimes, when there was a problem or when . . . I wanted to find him to help me with something, I couldn't always get in touch with him in Hong Kong. I would call, but there were lots of things I couldn't say over the phone. Calling was really expensive then." Another wife questioned her decision to marry her husband when she became dismayed at his poor command of written Chinese in the letters that he sent her. While some wives gradually became concerned about aspects of their husbands' personalities that had not been apparent in the early years of their relationships, others worried about the subtle shifts in character in their husbands' attitudes toward them as the years of separation increased.

In talking about their separation from husbands, wives generally emphasized the considerable difficulties—such as the physical and emotional distance from husbands and the challenge of raising children single-handedly

—rather than the many conveniences they enjoyed as wives waiting to immigrate to Hong Kong. Throughout the course of my research, I heard many poignant stories reinforcing the many everyday hardships experienced by mainland wives and children involved in a process of migration that entailed such long periods of state-enforced waiting. These stories were never about waiting per se, and in this way they differed significantly from the narratives of waiting described by Nicole Constable in her recent ethnography of "mail-order" marriages (2003). In Constable's ethnography, American men expressed their frustration with the bureaucratic process involved in sponsoring visas for their Asian fiancées, while Asian women remained concerned that their American fiancés would find "someone else" while waiting for their immigration paperwork to be processed (ibid.). In contrast, the mainland wives I knew talked about the concrete repercussions of "waiting" on their daily lives in both Hong Kong and on the mainland. Perhaps these differences stemmed from the substantially longer wait periods experienced by my informants—upwards from five years— compared to the six month to two year wait periods encountered by Constable's informants. That my informants were already married, as opposed to engaged, like Constable's informants, did not necessarily mean that they did not need to worry about their husbands' affections being otherwise occupied while they lived apart.

Taking for granted the complexity and length of mainland Chinese and Hong Kong bureaucratic processes involved in the acquisition of the legal documentation that would enable them to join husbands, parents, or children already in Hong Kong, most women settled into their own "ordinary" rhythms of daily life—working, raising children, socializing—that were finally disrupted upon the receipt of their one-way permits. One immigrant told me:

> When I first heard about [getting my one-way permit], I was really happy! I had waited for almost eleven years. But then I thought: how come they issued my permit first and not my son's permit first? If my son's permit had come first, I could have applied for a visitor's permit to take care of him [in Hong Kong]. But if I came first, and he was left [on the mainland], then I would have to hire someone to take care of him, and I was uneasy about that. That was a different feeling. But it was still better than not getting my permit at all, because I had really waited for a long time.

Another immigrant, whose son had already been granted his permit and had moved to Hong Kong to join her husband's family, explained:

> I was both happy and sad [when I got my one-way permit]. I was happy because I had waited so many years, and I finally got my permit. But I was sad, too, because I had lots of friends [in Shenzhen] . . . Going to a new place, I would have to start everything all over again. [In Shenzhen], I got along with my friends so well that they were like family, so I didn't want to have to leave them.

Thus, women's immigration to Hong Kong represented not just the fulfillment of long-awaited dreams; it also occasioned the dismantling of the everyday lives that their "waiting" had become. Sadly, the opportunity for the fulfillment of such dreams, after having waited for periods of at least five to ten years, came too late for many women, whose relationships with their spouses and family members both in Hong Kong and on the mainland were severely strained by years of living apart. These difficulties were exacerbated by the downward mobility that wives experienced in their moves to Hong Kong—where they had long dreamed of experiencing a modern lifestyle together with their husbands and children.

Women's Stories

In this section, I provide narrative accounts of four mainland wives' experiences first meeting and marrying their husbands, then going through the five- to ten-year process of waiting, and, finally, immigrating to Hong Kong. These stories highlight concrete examples of the familial and personal changes experienced throughout these life-altering events. Some hardships—in the form of loneliness, feelings of abandonment, anxiety over children's health and schooling needs, and separation from children already in Hong Kong—resulted from the lack of control that women had over their own ability to cross the Hong Kong/mainland border. A different set of difficulties—including exploitation in the labor market, separation from children still resident on the mainland, and conflict with husbands and in-laws—existed for women once they crossed that border. Yet women's experiences were not all bad. By living for extended periods of time in the "semi-transnational" (Latham 2000) spheres of influence in Guangdong Province, women had opportunities to learn Cantonese, develop networks of friends, acquire job skills, and live independently—all of which aided immigrant women's adjustment to Hong Kong by providing them with resources that they could draw on to try to counter the social and economic marginalization that they experienced once they, too, had control over their own mobility by becoming legally resident in Hong Kong. Although these women experienced both hardships and freedoms during their years of separation, at the time of my fieldwork—when women had just moved to Hong Kong after their long years of living separately from their husbands—they tended to articulate the hardships, rather than the freedoms, that they had experienced both before and after their migration to Hong Kong.

The four stories offered below are not meant to be "representative" of the experiences of all immigrant wives in Hong Kong; nor do they represent an unbiased sample of immigrant women. Nevertheless, these stories are relatively typical of the stories that I heard over the course of my sixteen months of participant observation research, and, as such, they serve to highlight the kinds of overall experiences described only as decontextualized passages in the other chapters of this book. These stories are not "life stories" in the traditional anthropological sense, meaning that they are not transcripts of interviews where informants related their stories themselves (Linde 1993); rather, I have pieced together these wives' experiences myself after spending dozens of hours over many months with each of these women at restaurants, on playgrounds, and in their homes—in addition to the time we spent together in class and in other activities sponsored by the service center. Nonetheless, in my "translations" (cf. Clifford and Marcus 1986) of our informal dialogues and taped interviews, I have tried to remain as faithful as possible to the ways in which the bits and pieces of their stories were told to me. In other words, what I emphasize in these narratives, which reflect women's feelings and reactions at the particular moments in which they were first experiencing their new living situations in Hong Kong, is what these women emphasized in our conversations about their experiences.

Finally, as members of my English class, these women had all requested that I choose English names for them, as they had all been eager to embrace the local Hong Kong practice of calling oneself by an English, rather than a Chinese, first name. Although some of these women adopted their English names for outside use with friends as well—just as local Hong Kong people do—others continued to interact only with me using this name. Since it was our practice to refer to each other by our English names in our various interactions, I have chosen English "pseudonyms" for them here.

ALLISON

At the time of my fieldwork, Allison was an engaging and enthusiastic woman in her late twenties, married to a Hong Kong plumber who was thirty-one in 2002. She was granted her one-way permit to immigrate to Hong Kong in July 2001, but she did not move to Hong Kong until January 2002.

Allison's father was a government official in a rural area of Sichuan. Allison still had very close ties to her family there despite having run away to Shenzhen at the age of sixteen. Once in Shenzhen, she quickly used up the money that she had taken with her and spent two months sleeping on people's roofs as she had nowhere else to go. Over time, she learned several trades and regained her family's support. She became a beautician, and she worked for several years in Shenzhen in this line of work. Allison also loved to cook the spicy cuisine of her native Sichuan Province. Supported with capital from her family, she opened her own Sichuan-style restaurant in Shenzhen for a short time.

Allison met her husband in 1995 while she was working in Shenzhen. The friend of a co-worker's husband, he invited Allison on a date the first time he saw her. At first Allison did not want to go out with him, but after he pleaded with her, saying that it was his birthday, she agreed. They dated for about six months. Every night after work, he would make the one-hour trip to Shenzhen to stay with her rather than return to the apartment he shared with his parents in Hong Kong. Finally, Allison's father found out that she had a Hong Kong boyfriend and interceded in their relationship. Alarmed by stories of Hong Kong men taking mistresses on the mainland, Allison's father was worried that Allison's boyfriend might have no intention of marrying her. As a result, he called Allison back to Sichuan where she stayed at her family's house for four months until her (now) husband traveled to Sichuan to meet her father and ask his permission to marry Allison. They got married in a civil ceremony there.

After their marriage, Allison returned to Shenzhen, and Allison's husband continued to visit her as often as his work allowed, at least several times each week. Allison traveled to Hong Kong on a special visitor's permit once—for a brief two-week visit—while she waited for the legal documentation that would enable her to immigrate to Hong Kong. In July 2001, after waiting five years, she finally received this documentation, but Allison's first reaction was not to immigrate. For one thing, her three-bedroom apartment in Shenzhen, rented for her by her husband, was more spacious and comfortable than the tiny public housing flat that she would share with her husband and his parents in Hong Kong. More importantly, she had a five-year-old adopted daughter whom she was raising in Shenzhen. Allison initially did not want to be separated from her daughter, who could not travel to Hong Kong or apply to immigrate there because she did not have at least one biological parent who was a Hong Kong permanent resident at the time that she was born. Nevertheless, by January 2002, Allison decided to send her daughter back to her home village to live with her parents, and she moved to Hong Kong to live with her husband and in-laws.

Although Allison had planned to help take care of her husband's parents and not work, she very soon started having problems getting along with them. While helping her mother-in-law prepare *laisee* (Mandarin: *hongbao*)—the money-filled red envelopes that are handed out during Lunar New Year—HK$30 (US$2.80) was misplaced, and Allison's mother-in-law accused her of stealing it. Her mother-in-law refused to drop the issue and would even call Allison names, such as *chaak poh* (female thief), around the family dinner table. Although Allison told her mother-in-law that she had no need to steal HK$30—that her family on the mainland was richer than her husband's family in Hong Kong—her mother-in-law would not believe her. Allison told me that she did not argue back with her mother-in-law, understanding that elderly people were easily confused and forgetful, but her husband could see her unhappiness and discomfort, and he suggested a short time later that, like his five brothers and sisters, they move out from his parents' house.

Just before they moved, Allison had found a job giving facials at a beauty salon right below their public housing unit. Although her income was low, about HK$3,500 (US$450)/month for full-time work, this added income was enough to enable Allison and her husband to move to a 100 square foot studio (with one room and a tiny bathroom but no kitchen) in a different part of Kowloon. Allison's work at the beauty salon went well, and, just before I left Hong Kong, her salary was increased to HK$5,500 (US$705)/month. She still gave her parents-in-law some money to help support them each month, but she never dared to visit them alone, as she was afraid of their anger at her. She noted that although they knew that she worked just below where they lived, her parents-in-law had never once come by to visit her during the two months since she and her husband had moved out. Allison was hoping to save enough money to bring her aging parents to Hong Kong for a visit before they got too much older. She regretted, however, that working in Hong Kong meant that she would most likely not be able to get enough time off to go back and visit her parents and adopted daughter in Sichuan that year.

CYBIL

In 2002, Cybil was thirty-two years old and married to a local-born Hong Kong man about forty-two years old. They had one daughter, who was four. They lived in a modern, 400 square foot public housing flat in an urban part of Kowloon, not far from Sham Shui Po, with Cybil's husband's parents. This new flat was a big improvement over the old flat where Cybil's husband's family had lived until 1999, in a building slated for demolition just across the street from their new residence.

Cybil had arrived in Hong Kong on her one-way permit at the end of August 2001. She was originally from a rural, tea-growing area in Zhejiang Province, where her parents and brothers still lived and harvested tea. Cybil had left home at the age of sixteen and had lived and worked in Xiamen for ten years from the late 1980s to the mid-1990s. When Cybil first moved to Xiamen, she found work in a factory. For three months, she spent eight hours each day painting the eyes on wooden Easter rabbits that were being manufactured for export. She then received a promotion that landed her in the company's central office, where she worked her way up the hierarchical ladder from the position of "coffee girl." Her husband's aunt had also worked in this office, and when her husband (then single) was in Xiamen on business in 1995, his aunt introduced Cybil and her husband to each other. The couple went out once. By their second meeting, several months later, they had become formally engaged, and Cybil's husband's parents came with him from Hong Kong to meet her. Cybil told me that her friends laughed at her when they learned that she had met and married her husband in such a "traditional" way, but Cybil argued in her own favor that she knew of many women who had dated for years without getting married, and as she and her husband had found each other to be agreeable, why should they have waited? Cybil often told me that she had married her husband because he was honest: when she first met him he told her that although he had a good job, he supported his family and had "no money."

Immediately after their marriage in 1996, the couple went together to Cybil's hometown in Zhejiang to apply for her one-way permit to immigrate to Hong Kong. Soon afterwards, Cybil's husband bought an apartment in Dongguan—an area of Guangdong about two hours away from Hong Kong by train. By buying an apartment there, Cybil could transfer her residency to that location, which was close enough to Hong Kong for her husband to visit her on weekends. Cybil was not very happy with her residence and its location when she first moved there. Her apartment was situated in a community that had just begun development in the mid-1990s in response to Hong Kong's people's needs for vacation homes and housing for mainland wives and mistresses, and, as a result, it lacked the community infrastructure to which Cybil had become accustomed during the years she lived in Xiamen. Cybil had also disliked the apartment because she did not have sufficient money to decorate it in a way that she considered to be "modern" and "tasteful." Nevertheless, she settled into her new home, and, over the next few years, she learned to speak Cantonese as well.

Cybil became pregnant soon after moving to Dongguan, and it was the period after her daughter was born that she described as the most difficult. Although her husband and father-in-law came from Hong Kong for the birth, they did not visit her much in the hospital. Cybil noted that staying in the hospital in China is different than in Hong Kong in that no food is provided, and the irregular meals that she received from her husband for the week she was in the hospital after her daughter's birth left her long hours of feeling hungry. Although Cybil's mother-in-law and, later, her own mother came to stay with her to help her take care of the baby, these visits apparently caused Cybil additional stress. When we talked, four years after these events had taken place, Cybil told me that she continued to have health problems that stemmed from this time. In her mind, the neglect that she had experienced during these past events were still of relevance when talking about her current adjustment to Hong Kong and her relationships with her husband and his family members.

Cybil's daughter received her permission to enter Hong Kong when she was two and a half years old. For one year, her daughter lived with Cybil's husband and his parents, and each Sunday her husband would make the two-hour (each way) trip to Dongguan, bringing their daughter to visit her. Cybil described herself as being very "satisfied" with her husband during this time, as she knew of many women who were visited by their husbands only one or two times a year. During that year, Cybil was free to live as she liked, and she contrasted her freedom in going out with friends, eating casual meals (such as an apple for dinner, for example), and watching TV while in her pajamas with her current life in Hong Kong. Finally, in August 2001 she received her one-way permit, and she was able to go to Hong Kong as well.

In the months after she first arrived, Cybil had much trouble adjusting to living with her husband's family. Before she began working at a nearby restaurant, Cybil was criticized by her parents-in-law as being lazy, but when she began working at a twelve hour day, seven day a week job from which she got home at two o'clock each morning, she was also criticized as being a "lazy pig" when she would go back to bed after taking her daughter to school six hours later. Cybil had other disagreements with her parents-in-law, particularly in terms of the way that they disciplined her daughter. In part because of these disagreements, Cybil had trouble adjusting to the smaller living space and longed to return the 1,200 square foot apartment in Dongguan, which her husband still owned. After immigrating to Hong Kong, Cybil craved the apartment's spaciousness, "modern" or not, as well its solitude.

Despite this difficult relationship with her in-laws, for many months after Cybil arrived in Hong Kong, she remained confident that she would be able to work out her problems with her in-laws. Before she began working, Cybil's husband would take her and her daughter out to various spots around Hong Kong each Sunday. Such trips served not only to introduce Cybil to the wealthier communities in Hong Kong to which she was able to compare her own working-class living situation, but they also provided an important means of allowing her and her husband to escape from the watchfulness of her in-laws. Her husband's income was stable, since he was employed in a managerial position in a local company, so that, unlike many of my other informants, Cybil did not need to work. She liked the feeling of independence that she got from working, however, and she wanted to learn more about local life by working in Hong Kong. Although she complained about it, Cybil's mother-in-law was willing to help her look after Cybil's daughter when she came home from school at four o'clock each afternoon, and this help allowed Cybil to work outside the house. Her first job, which she quit after about six weeks (since she never had days off and the late hours meant that she saw her husband and daughter very little), was at a Thai restaurant near her house. The pay there was HK$20 (US$2.50) per hour. A short time later, Cybil was able to get a second job with more regular hours, from 9 A.M. to 7 P.M., at a Chinese medicine shop. The pay was equally low—less than HK$4,000 (US$500)/month—but she felt that her boss treated her well and she once again had Sundays free to spend time with her husband and daughter.

By the time I left Hong Kong, in July 2002, Cybil was still feeling unhappy and stressed because of the ongoing tension between herself and her in-laws. She told me that she would wait one more year—in all, two years from her arrival in Hong Kong—and then if things were still not working she planned to leave her daughter with her husband and in-laws and return to the mainland to support herself there.

MAY

At the end of 2001 when we first met, May was twenty-eight years old. Like Cybil, she was also married to a local Hong Kong man who was ten years older than she was, and they had two children, ages four and seven. May had moved to Hong Kong on her one-way permit in May 2001.

May was from a rural area near Foshan, a city less than one hour from the Guangdong Provincial capital of Guangzhou and about three hours from Hong Kong. She was the oldest of four brothers and sisters, who were all college educated except for May, since she had had to drop out of school at a young age to help earn money to take care of her siblings. In her late teens, May had moved to Shenzhen and worked as a clerk in a factory there, and she met her husband when he was sent to that factory by the Hong

Kong company that employed him. She did not know her husband very well when they got married, but she told me that she felt that she "had no choice" but to get married when she did, as the family was in desperate need of money, and her husband and his family were willing to pay for a house and other needs as part of their marriage contract. May never told me the details of her engagement, but she told me that her marriage had been a simple ceremony, without finery, in a bureaucratic office. I often wondered, however, if May did not cling to her special status as a "Hong Kong wife" as a means to help boost her image in the eyes of her siblings, who had all become professionals on the mainland. Interested in the world at large and a capable English-language student, May clearly regretted the fact that she had not been better educated.

During the nine years in which she waited for her one-way permit, May visited her husband in Hong Kong once each year, and he visited her and the children every few months, as his work schedule allowed. Although the mainland Chinese authorities do not usually grant two-way visiting permits for Hong Kong to pregnant women, May had been able to travel to Hong Kong when she was seven months pregnant with her older child and gave birth to her daughter in Hong Kong. (May told me that she had been able to circumvent bureaucratic regulations because her pregnancy did not "show" much and she wore a big coat when picking up her travel permit and going through immigration.) When she visited that time, she stayed with her husband in the old, temporary housing flat of 300 square feet that he shared with six of his other immediate family members in the New Territories. She absolutely hated staying there, at least in part because she could not sleep well at night with her husband's younger sister sleeping on the top bunk of the bed she shared with her husband. She managed to have the baby and stay the full three months of the visit, but May did not enjoy her subsequent visits because of the cramped space and because of her difficulties in getting along with her in-laws.

May kept her daughter with her in Foshan until she was two and a half years old, at which time May's husband took her back to Hong Kong to begin kindergarten. May had another child, a son, who was four in 2002 and who had always stayed with her until May immigrated to Hong Kong. Because her son's one-way permit to Hong Kong was only granted one full year after her own, May's son stayed in their home village with May's parents while May went ahead to Hong Kong. May spent her first year in Hong Kong torn between her daughter, who was failing at her schoolwork there, and her son, who missed May terribly—and had begun wetting his bed at night and crying each time she called to talk with him on the phone or if his grandmother was late to pick him up from school, thinking that he had been "forgotten." While May had thought that it was difficult to be separated from her daughter who was in Hong Kong while May waited on the mainland for her immigration paperwork to be processed, May felt that it was even harder to be separated from her son. May frequently noted that her daughter, who had never liked living in Hong Kong, suggested that everyone would be happier if she (the daughter) could return to the mainland to live with her grandparents while her brother came to Hong Kong to take advantage of the school system there.

To add to her troubles, May's husband had lost his job about the same time that May had arrived in Hong Kong, and it took him over one year to find a new one—at considerably less pay than he had been making previously. Because of the seriousness of their financial situation, May finally took a job working "part-time" (eight hours a day, six days a week with a monthly income of HK$3,000 [US$385] once transportation was subtracted) at a dry goods store in Sham Shui Po in March 2002. Although she had completed a local training course that prepared her to work as a housekeeper, at a significantly better salary level, she was never able to find this type of employment, in part because Hong Kong locals preferred to hire a Filipina maid who would work longer hours for less pay. Furthermore, the economic downturn had negatively affected sales at the dry goods store, and all the store's employees—all mainland new arrivals—had still not been paid for their previous months' work when I left Hong Kong in July 2002. Although May's social worker had counseled her to cut her losses and take another job instead (she had turned down at least two other jobs as the hours conflicted with those of the job she already had), May had decided to keep working at the store, afraid that she would never get paid the money originally owed unless she stayed on. During that time she continued to look for a second job that she could work in the late afternoon or evening.

In June 2002, May's son's paperwork was finally processed, enabling him to join the rest of his family in Hong Kong. Even though May had missed her son and had worried about him while they were separated during the time that I knew her in Hong Kong, by the time that I left she felt that his coming was a mixed blessing. With her family's economic difficulties, she was worried about having enough money to pay for his kindergarten fees, clothing, and other needs, since all of his expenses had been paid by her parents while he lived with them on the mainland. Furthermore, she was worried about being able to keep working while needing to look after him.

In 2002, Amber was twenty-six years old, and she lived with her husband, who was thirty-three, their son, six, and her husband's mother in an old public housing flat in an urban area of Kowloon. She had moved to Hong Kong on her one-way permit in December 2001.

Originally from a poor rural area in Guangxi, Amber left home at the age of fifteen to work in Shenzhen. She had worked odd jobs there, including that of chef, to support herself until the time that she met her husband. She and her husband were introduced by mutual friends one night when she was about nineteen years old. They dated for one year before returning to her hometown to get married, and during this premarriage period, Amber was happy with her husband and their relationship, as he would travel to Shenzhen three to four times a week to visit her.

After they got married, however, Amber became increasingly disillusioned about her husband and their relationship, so that by the time she arrived in Hong Kong, things were already quite tense between them. To begin with, her husband's work became more demanding after their marriage, so that his visits to Shenzhen became less frequent, at most twice a week. Then, when they applied for her one-way permit to Hong Kong, Amber was shocked to find out that it would take at least five years for her application to be processed and accepted. Amber was extremely unhappy about the long period of enforced separation while she single-handedly experienced the difficulties of pregnancy and caring for their small child. She felt terribly lonely during this period, despite the close relationships that she had with several friends in Shenzhen, including one woman, described as an "older sister," also married to a Hong Kong man. Over time, visits from Amber's husband enabled her to form a negative impression of him as having been too coddled by his mother, who still "took care" of him in Hong Kong. This impression was not helped by the tensions that she experienced with him and his mother when she visited Hong Kong three times, each for three months, on visitor permits.

When Amber's son was three years old, his one-way permit was granted, and, like Cybil's and May's daughters, he moved to Hong Kong to live with his father and grandmother and begin kindergarten. Although Amber missed him very much, she began to occupy herself by preparing for her future life in Hong Kong. In particular, she watched Hong Kong television news reports, and, using tapes and books, she began to teach herself English. In her free time, she surrounded herself with friends who were university educated, and she also read a lot. (Later, she would complain to me about the difficulties that she had communicating with her husband in Hong Kong, and she attributed his inability to discuss issues with her, in part, to the fact that he, like other Hong Kong people, read newspapers and comics but not books.) By the time she received notification that her one-way permit had finally become available, Amber's initial reluctance to stay in Shenzhen separated from her husband had completely disappeared. Instead, this reluctance had become replaced by the fear of leaving an environment now familiar to her and moving to one with fewer friends and many unknowns. Since her son had preceded her to Hong Kong by almost three years, Amber's husband and in-laws had already established well-formed routines revolving around his school and care—routines about which she disagreed, and in which she was not allowed to interfere. Amber's husband and mother-in-law would consistently make decisions affecting her son's well-being without consulting her.

Amber channeled the discontent stemming from her interactions in her living environment into positive interactions in an increasing number of activities outside the home. She had taught herself basic English vocabulary and grammar while still in Shenzhen, and, once in Hong Kong, she was quick to take advantage of the government-subsidized language classes offered by the social service center where I volunteered. There she completed five different English classes—all that were offered at the center—in less than three months. She was also an enthusiastic member of several volunteer activities and mutual help groups, using her interactions with other immigrant wives in these groups to form a network of friends who may have been experiencing similar difficulties with their husbands and Hong Kong families.

Eager to learn about all aspects of Hong Kong life, Amber was also quite successful in her initial job search, landing a cashier's job at a busy 7-Eleven outlet, which provided her the training in Hong Kong work ethics and conditions that she needed to get the higher paying job that she found soon after—as a night-time cashier at a twenty-four-hour diner in Mongkok. At that location, her monthly salary of HK$10,000 (US$ 1,282) was not only considerably higher than the average wage earned by other new immigrant employees, it was also higher than the income earned by many immigrants' Hong Kong husbands. Amber told good-natured stories of the personal difficulties inherent in such work, and her humorous accounts detailed the unwanted attentions she received from lonely male customers and other colorful Mongkok characters (including prostitutes, pimps, and triad members) who frequented the diner each night. These anecdotes conveniently masked the true reason she had taken the position: by working at night she had sought to minimize her interactions with her husband and mother-in-law at home.

Although the outcome of her situation was not yet determined when I left Hong Kong, Amber was actively considering using her income to support herself and move out from her husband's house. Even though she had already decided not to get divorced for her son's sake, she had also given up her previous hope of having another child, which she felt would be irresponsible given the general unhappiness of their family's living situation. Her husband refused to talk about either separation or divorce with her; nonetheless, he was certainly not above making rude put-downs and jokes about her in public—as I experienced when I met him.

From Guangdong to Hong Kong: Hypergamy or Downward Mobility?

Many of my informants had experienced what they considered to be "downward" mobility in their moves to Hong Kong. In part, this phenomenon can be explained by China's tremendous economic growth, by the relaxation of political control in China during the last years of the twentieth century, and by the extensive periods of politically enforced waiting that these wives experienced before their immigration to Hong Kong, during which time the Hong Kong economy entered a recession. When many of my informants first met and married their husbands, in the late 1980s and early 1990s, Hong Kong men still had privileged access to consumer goods that were scarce in China. One informant from Guangzhou recalled: "At that time on the mainland, the market economy hadn't opened up yet. It was difficult to buy infant formula or medicines. Back then ... you could buy better quality formula or medicines in Hong Kong and Shenzhen. My son was drinking formula, so my husband would buy four large canisters of powdered formula each week and bring them to me."

During the intervening years, however, the mainland economy continued to grow rapidly, and consumer goods became increasingly more available. In contrast, economic downturns in Hong Kong following the Asian financial crisis of 1997 resulted in significantly reduced employment opportunities, particularly in those sectors of the population most vulnerable to layoffs, such as the service industries, where many Hong Kong husbands were likely to have been employed. Several of my informants reported that when they married their Hong Kong husbands, their husbands were working in white-collar jobs making as much as HK$20,000 (about US$2,500) per month. I knew at least four women whose husbands had lost their higher-paying jobs during the period that these women were waiting to come to Hong Kong. In two cases, the husbands remained unemployed even after their wives' arrival; in two others, the husbands had begun working blue-collar jobs in the restaurant industry, with an average monthly salary of HK$8,000 (US$1,000), rather than remain unemployed.

Women's initial adjustments to living with their "reunited" families in Hong Kong, and the loss of independence that often accompanied these transitions, were made more difficult by their families' financial difficulties —related both to Hong Kong's ailing economy and the significantly greater cost of living in Hong Kong than on the mainland. Yet mainland wives also faced significant difficulties in finding employment in Hong Kong, where employers did not want to hire them because of their accented use of the Cantonese language as well as their lack of English language skills, "proper" educational training, or previous work experience in Hong Kong. The immigrant women I knew who did find jobs—like Allison, Cybil, May, and

Amber—worked, on average, for twelve or more hours a day, six to seven days a week, with monthly salaries ranging from about HK$3,500–$5,500 (US$450–$700). In her 1997 ethnography documenting the hardships faced by Filipina domestic workers in Hong Kong, Nicole Constable described Filipina women at the bottom of social and economic hierarchies in Hong Kong. When compared with the situation of local Filipina domestic workers whose contracts included lodging, health insurance, a food allowance, and a monthly minimum wage of HK$3,500 (US$450) (Constable 1997), Chinese immigrant women in Hong Kong were actually making less. Furthermore, because of government-enforced restrictions that limited application for social welfare to individuals who had been legally resident in Hong Kong for at least one year, immigrants could not apply for these benefits which, at HK$10,000 (US$1,282) a month for a family of four, were significantly higher than the average monthly combined income of immigrant women and their Hong Kong husbands.[4] Housing conditions for these immigrant women and their Hong Kong families were also very poor: families of four or five frequently lived in 80 square foot rooms sharing one kitchen and bath with as many as twenty other individuals; in other cases, three generations lived together in small apartments, with not more than 300 or 400 square feet of total living space.

In her ethnography of Filipina "mail order" brides, Nicole Constable problematizes the anthropological concept of hypergamy (that is, to marry "up" in status), questioning both what it means to marry "up" as well as the "gender-biased assumption" inherent in the concept that "women are the ones who marry up or are 'exchanged'" (2003:167). Documenting the historical trend of marriage in China, she notes that while "status-matching" was the norm during the Maoist period, during other periods of Chinese history and even today in China, problems are thought to result from marriages in which a woman marries beneath her family's social position (ibid. 165–67). Extending the concept across borders, Constable refers to "global hypergamy" as "the notion that Asian women who marry western men marry 'up'" (ibid. 167). In such marriages, which she documents between Asian women and American men, women and their families are thought to benefit from the social and geographical positioning of husbands who are "citizens or residents of 'the world's greatest super power,' as the United States is widely viewed from both the inside and outside" (ibid. 167).

Certainly, the Hong Kong-Chinese cross-border marriages that I discuss could also be characterized within this model of "global hypergamy," as the Chinese women who marry Hong Kong men marry "into" a capitalist economy with access to first world communication, technology, and information, as well as increased possibilities for political rights and social movement. Furthermore, while still residing on the mainland, most wives appeared to have improved their social status through the comfortable living situations and increased access to local commodities made available to them by their Hong Kong husbands' financial support. Nevertheless, the value of arguing that these women had made marriages defined as "hypergamous" remains highly questionable.

Like the young Thai migrant laborers that Mills describes in Bangkok, my young women immigrant informants desired access to "modernity" through their ability to participate in a capitalist, consumer-oriented lifestyle (1999). In preimmigration imaginings, Hong Kong's international orientation, capitalist economy, and widespread use of English made the city a hallmark of "modernity" that these women had hoped to experience. Ironically, however, "modernity" remained more readily accessible to Chinese women who remained on the mainland, where—subsidized by their husband's Hong Kong incomes—their independent living styles and greater spending power allowed them to achieve a higher standard of living than they could experience in Hong Kong. Once in Hong Kong, their "advantages" (in comparison to many mainland residents) seemed to disappear, as immigrant wives' and husbands' incomes were almost always low by local Hong Kong standards. Hong Kong's "first-world" lifestyle "perks," such as the increased access to travel and consumer goods mentioned earlier, were not necessarily available to immigrant residents of Hong Kong, particularly those wives whose husbands were older, sick, or blue-collar workers. For example, while many of my immigrant informants expressed an interest in traveling to the United States or Europe, the reality of their everyday economic situations meant that not only did they not have enough money to pay for travel expenses, but, because of their husbands' overall low incomes, they were likely to be denied visas to travel to the first-world destinations of their desire. Furthermore, many women did not have the knowledge base or disposable income to allow them to visit Hong Kong's more upscale locations or partake of Hong Kong's "first-world" commodities. Instead, most immigrant women remained located within the densely populated, older areas of urban Kowloon that remain stigmatized by many local residents. In these cases, their only access to a "modern," glittering Hong Kong was through tour bus windows while participating in the orientation tours of Hong Kong offered by social service centers to recent immigrants. Nonetheless, these women had benefited from "global hypergamy" in a not insignificant way: they had achieved a level of mobility that was unavailable to them before their marriages by acquiring the legal right to pass back and forth over the Hong Kong-Chinese border.

It was clear from the discussions that I had with my informants that the proximity of their pre–Hong Kong homes to Hong Kong, along with their networks of friends and relatives who remained in nearby places on the mainland after the wives' immigration to Hong Kong, gave these women a measure of "choice" in their decisions to come to or stay in Hong Kong. Some of my informants, like Cybil, longed for a house in Shenzhen, rather than Dongguan, so that she and her husband could live there together (separately from her in-laws) while he commuted to Hong Kong. In Cybil's case, and many others, husbands clearly dominated the family's decision-making regarding location of residence. Nonetheless, like Constable's Asian bride informants (2003) and Mills's Thai migrant informants (1999), the immigrants I knew had clearly exercised their agency not only in terms of their individual choices to marry a Hong Kong husband but also in deciding whether to move to and/or remain in Hong Kong. When women were able to exercise power in influencing such decisions, this power was the combined result both of their new membership status as Hong Kong residents (which allowed women the freedom to cross the border) and of the transformations women experienced—through the acquisition of houses, skills, feelings of independence, and networks of friends—as a direct result of their long periods of limited mobility while waiting to emigrate. As a result, although women's migration across political difference resulted in increased anxieties and concrete difficulties of adjustment with their family members, these same moves had also engaged migrants in new possibilities of action and behavior. In this way, their situations draw attention to the problematics associated with trying to map out set equations of power and mobility. As Freeman writes, "it [is] difficult to distinguish those 'in charge' of migratory

Figure 3.2   Visions of Hong Kong's modern lifestyle (January 2007)

processes from those who are not, those who benefit from those who are deprived" (2005:100).

Most immigrant Chinese women I knew in Hong Kong not only had fantasies about returning to the mainland, but they often had the actual opportunity to do so. Women unhappy in their marital relationships could use the threat or actual return to the mainland as a means of leverage in dealing with their difficult husbands, and even happily married women visited the mainland as often as they could, frequently once a week, just to spend time with friends and see family members. Women who were mothers of young children had less flexibility in crossing the border, since their children's Hong Kong school schedules often prevented them from the ease of coming and going so readily enjoyed by their immigrant friends who were childless. Yet in cases where in-laws were available to help look after young children or where children were deemed old enough to look after themselves, many women still found opportunities to return to the mainland once every four to eight weeks.

While their moves across the border had increased the freedom of movement for most immigrant wives—after having been trapped into a politically regulated separation with their husbands over a period of years—this move also made their lives and familial relationships more complex. As newly arrived residents of Hong Kong, immigrant wives juggled the demands made on them by their husbands, family members, and friends on both sides of the mainland Chinese/Hong Kong border while often harboring lingering desires to maintain the higher standards of living and independent lifestyles they had experienced on the mainland before immigrating to Hong Kong. In Chapter Four, I focus my ethnographic lens on immigrant wives' adjustment to living in Hong Kong with their "reunited" families and the expectations, tensions, and struggles over adjustment and control that took place in immigrants' new homes. Once in Hong Kong, the personal changes that women had experienced while waiting to emigrate had important repercussions for wives' relationships with their Hong Kong husbands and in-laws. These transformations were also influential in leading women to seek alternative sources of adjustment outside their Hong Kong homes when relationships inside the home became too strained.

FOUR

Immigrant Homespace

Both in casual conversations and more formal interviews with mainland Chinese immigrant wives in Hong Kong, the lack of "space" (Cantonese: *deihfong;* Mandarin: *difang*) was highlighted as a constant problem and point of tension and anxiety. Indeed, immigrants quickly picked up the saying used by local people, that Hong Kong is a place of little space, but many people (Cantonese: *deisiu, yahndo*). Population densities in urban districts of Hong Kong are among the highest in the world, primarily because of the government's practice of controlling land sales and restricting development to a small portion of the region's total land area. Most of the land that has not been developed is steeply mountainous, and not at all suitable for the skyscraper apartment towers that comprise the majority of housing stock in the region. Although 1999 figures indicate a total population density for the HKSAR at only 16,102 people per square mile, urbanized areas of Kowloon, where most of my immigrant informants resided, averaged 117,778 people per square mile—an astounding figure almost twice as high as the population density of Manhattan, listed as having an average of 65,500 people per square mile (www.demographia.com; www.csun.edu/~hbgego69/ NY/ Population. html).

In contrast, immigrants from mainland China, particularly those from rural areas, were used to living in less dense residential situations than the tiny apartments that they found waiting for them upon their arrival in Hong Kong. One informant succinctly described her dismay, saying "my bathroom in Dongguan is larger than my house in Hong Kong," which, in her case, was a 100 square foot windowless room that she shared with her mother and father. As one social worker told me, the immigrants "may not have many electrical appliances in their mainland homes, but they have lots of space, and people need space. This is the biggest difference for them." Even immigrants from urban areas had usually lived in apartments at least three times as large as their new residences in Hong Kong—residences that were often shared with their Hong Kong in-laws as well as their husbands and children.

The immigrant wives I knew in Hong Kong had been easily supported in a very comfortable way by their husbands' relatively low (by Hong Kong standards) incomes while they continued to live on the mainland. Families with wives living in more spacious rural areas had usually built their own three-story houses, or had at least updated older houses with modern plumbing facilities. A wife coming from Guangzhou, Shenzhen, or other urban areas in Guangdong Province would most probably have been provided with a modern, large (at least 1,000 square foot) apartment with multiple bedrooms and baths, either bought or rented by her Hong Kong husband.[1] Although rented apartments were not kept after the wife's immigration to Hong Kong, family-owned homes were, and in most cases these homes would be locked up and empty, available for use on weekends or vacations, if the families' Hong Kong schedules enabled their return. The very high cost of housing in Hong Kong, however, meant that immigrant families, once in Hong Kong, lived in housing vastly inferior to that to which they had become accustomed on the mainland. Although urban housing conditions on the mainland had been very cramped for most of the Maoist era due to rapid population growth that "outstripped housing construction" (Fraser 2000:30), most of my immigrant informants were not old enough to remember housing conditions as crowded as what they experienced in Hong Kong. At its most dense, during the mid-1960s, per capita floor space in Shanghai was about 24 square feet—roughly equal to the spatial allotments provided until the mid-1980s to rehoused families in Hong Kong's public housing blocks (ibid.). By the 1990s, Chinese housing reform had resulted in average per capita floor space of 81 square feet for urban residents of Shanghai (ibid.) and of 91 square feet for urban residents of Guangzhou (where the aim was to increase this space to approximately 150 square feet by the year 2000) (Ikels 1996:79).

Thus, immigrant wives' family reunions in Hong Kong took place in particularly crowded living conditions that further exacerbated the difficulties that families experienced in learning how to live together (often) for the first time. At the same time, however, these crowded spaces—whether government-provided housing units or older tenement stock where immigrant families lived together in small apartments with twenty or more people sharing one toilet and one kitchen—figured strongly into Hong Kong people's discourses of local life, where it is taken for granted that "there is little space but many people" and that hyperdensity, crowding, and clutter are the norm. These spatial constraints, along with the flexible uses of spaces that have resulted from these constraints, are both the product and legacy of British colonial housing policy from the early 1950s on and, as such, are strongly linked to the colonial government's "strategy for building a sense of citizenship and commitment by Hong Kong residents" (Smart 2006:2). For many Hong Kong people, who have grown up in these crowded conditions, there is also a strong sense of collective memory around family life in both older tenement and public housing units (see Rooney 2003:51; Luk 1995).

Since immigrants' Hong Kong homes were the locations in which newly arrived mainland wives had the most sustained daily contact with Hong Kong people—including their husbands, their in-laws, and any siblings or children who had migrated before them—they were important sites of social intimacy. Yet the social intimacy that immigrants experienced through their daily interactions with Hong Kong locals in these spaces was fraught with frequent misunderstandings and, often, quite serious discord, resulting both from the Hong Kong locals' negative perceptions of mainlanders in general as well as from the mother-in-law and daughter-in-law conflict that has long been featured at the heart of writings about Chinese family life. As a result, Hong Kong's tiny domestic spaces served not only as the settings for interactions among "reunited" family members but also became sites of struggle where immigrant wives and daughters-in-law challenged the local norms and memories of Hong Kong middle- and lower-class modes of belonging to which they were introduced by Hong Kong family members in (and through) these settings. Immigrant women, rather than "accepting" the lessons about adjusting to Hong Kong life that they received in these environments, often found ways to remove themselves from contentious family problems by returning more often to the mainland, by searching for employment outside of the home, by becoming involved in activities and programs organized by social service centers, and by socializing with other friends outside the home.

In this chapter, I discuss immigrant wives within the context of their Hong Kong homes in order to explore the ways in which these spaces, and the individuals inhabiting these spaces, shaped immigrants' experiences of adjustment during their first months in Hong Kong. After first situating the complex dynamics of family "reunion" within the context of traditional Chinese mother-in-law/daughter-in-law conflict (a recurring theme in my dialogues with immigrant women in Hong Kong), I focus the rest of this chapter around the theme of domestic space in Hong Kong. In particular, I concentrate on describing Hong Kong's densely inhabited spaces where the flexible use of space has become the norm, and I show how these spaces (and the objects within them) became the sites of contested meaning and control between mainland wives and their Hong Kong family members, including their mothers-in-law.

Mother-in-law/Daughter-in-law Conflict

Since my immigrant informants had lived both in larger spaces and independently of their Hong Kong families for long periods of time, it was not surprising that conflict with Hong Kong family members, particularly within their domestic spaces, was a common problem faced by all immigrant wives. One social worker told me that the first thing immigrants had to learn in Hong Kong was how to get along with their family members. She noted that, after having lived so far apart for so many years:

. . . all of a sudden, you have to cook dinner and wait for everyone to be together. What are your family members' daily habits like? Or what help do they need? Do you know how to help them? To reunite as a family with them? How will you start over to establish a relationship with them? And spend more time observing how you can help these people close to you? No matter whether they are old or young, how will you help them? If you don't do this, then problems will appear.

Implicit in this quote is the effort that immigrants must make to understand the needs of their Hong Kong relatives. Indeed, there was a clear difference between the adjustment experiences of immigrant women who married into local families—where the husband had been raised in Hong Kong and still lived with his parents or other family members—and women who married husbands whose families were still on the mainland. I knew many women who were experiencing significant marital difficulties with their husbands even when these husbands had no other relatives in Hong Kong; however, many women in this situation were more likely to have a "supportive" husband and thus have more positive feelings about living in Hong Kong. In contrast, women who had moved into their husbands' family homes in Hong Kong talked constantly about their conflicts with their in-laws and their lack of personal space. Conflicts covered all sorts of issues related to domestic life, such as appropriate roles and behavior in the home, but also carried over into the outside world as well, influencing activities and employment. Not confined to words, these conflicts were often defined and expressed through the use of space and the manipulation of domestic items in the space of homes. The situation of one wife, whose family's household space was confined to one bunkbed within her in-law's 300 square foot flat, was not uncommon. Although some of my other informants had their own rooms that they shared with their husbands, their in-laws nevertheless consistently circumscribed their activities within the household's common areas by forbidding them to straighten up the cluttered environment or cook what they wanted.

As these immigrants' most sustained point of contact with daily life, habits, and thought in Hong Kong, immigrants' Hong Kong family members and their homes had the potential to serve as important sources of information about their adjustment to life in Hong Kong. Instead, frustration and confusion resulted in many cases, where lessons about "life in Hong Kong" were rejected by these wives and daughters-in-laws who struggled to understand how their dreams of integration with their Hong Kong in-laws were falling apart before their disbelieving, and increasingly disillusioned, eyes. Furthermore, the attempted control imposed by family members over their new immigrant relatives created unbearable tension between wives and their spouses, providing the proverbial "final straw" to relationships already strained by years of being separated on the mainland and in Hong Kong. Amber, a twenty-six-year-old woman who had been married for five years before she came to Hong Kong in December 2001, told me:

> I feel like many people's husbands would ask them: since you've come here, are you used to living here? We've been together so many years, and I've just come to this new place, and he should ask if I am having trouble adapting . . . [My family] won't ever ask me: 'Do you like your work?' or 'How do you get along with your coworkers?' I am really disappointed when I think about this. It's not to say they won't help, but they should listen to what I am thinking, or should explain more about Hong Kong people to me, tell me more. But they don't.

Amber saw her situation in a strikingly different light from that indicated by the social worker quoted previously. From Amber's point of view, she tried her best to help and "fit in" with her family, but it was they who had done nothing to help her. She saw her own initiative as the only source of her newfound knowledge about Hong Kong people and society. Yet the similarity of her complaints to those of other new immigrant wives indicated that such family interaction had already "taught" Amber much about Hong Kong people's way of life. Because these realities contrasted so strongly with what Amber had imagined about life in cosmopolitan Hong Kong while waiting to immigrate, she may not have accepted these "lessons" on adaptation for what they were.

Although it is a newer trend that anthropologists have begun to focus more attention on the rifts—rather than the cohesion—that animate Chinese family life (Yan 2003:3–7), relationships between daughters-in-law and mothers-in-law have traditionally been characterized as tense rather than harmonious (see, for example, Ikels 1996, Wang 2004, Watson 2004, Yan

2003). This actual conflict sits uneasily beside the strongly idealized (and important) roles that daughters-in-law play in the practice of filial piety, both through their production of sons who will carry on the family line and also through their care and support of aged parents.[2] In her groundbreaking ethnography, *Women and the Family in Rural Taiwan*, Margery Wolf first linked mother-in-law and daughter-in-law conflict in Chinese families to the "ambiguous" positions of men whose strong affective ties to their mothers took precedence over the interests of their wives within their patriarchal families (1972). This past predominance of the mother-in-law's interests over those of the daughter-in-law has been challenged in many areas of contemporary China, where anthropologists have documented the increasing importance of the conjugal unit (see, for example, Yan 2003 and Fong 2004a). This reversal in "traditional" Chinese family norms has resulted primarily from the greater economic power enjoyed by younger generations, who have the financial means to live separately from parents and in-laws and choose when and how to help their parents with their financial needs (Yan 2003). In Hong Kong, by contrast, immigrant women's power within their husbands' families is still relatively weak. Many wives are dependent on their in-laws' subsidized public housing flats as their only means to achieve affordable housing. Although some wives work, their incomes are usually well below the wages of locals, and their incomes are rarely sufficient to allow them and their husbands to rent a private apartment elsewhere in the city. As a result, it is easy for mothers-in-law to continue to exercise significant control over their immigrant daughters-in-law. That my immigrant women informants were aware of the potential for having difficult relationships with their husband's mother was made clear in many comments they made to me. For example, one informant listed her knowledge that her husband's parents were both dead as a consideration that had positively influenced her decision to marry him.

Daily conflicts between immigrant wives and their Hong Kong mothers-in-law were common, and wives, upset by these conflicts, frequently told me that while still resident on the mainland they had imagined that they would avoid such conflict by being "better than Hong Kong daughters-in-law." But what exactly did they mean by that statement? The wives I knew were predominately from rural, rather than urban, Chinese backgrounds, which meant that they may indeed have grown up and been socialized to anticipate the more idealized views of daughter-in-law/mother-in-law roles that Wolf and others have documented as including the performance of daily household tasks such as cooking, cleaning, and child care, along with subservience to the desires and commands of mothers-in-law.[3] But unlike their mainland rural-dwelling contemporaries, the immigrant women I knew in Hong Kong had also predominantly left their natal homes by age fifteen or sixteen in order to work in factories or service industries in the SEZs of Southeast China. In these areas, women lived in factory dormitories or in apartments with other migrant women friends, rather than in "traditional" family settings. In this way, their expectations associated with gender roles may have also been influenced by the more active and economically independent roles of women and daughters-in-law that have recently been documented in contemporary Chinese urban locations. In these locations, wives enjoy the benefits of strong conjugal relationships and perform idealized wifely and daughter-in-law roles while still maintaining personal distance from the traditional subservience associated with these roles (Ikels 1996; Evans 2002; Adrian 2003; Fong 2004a; Whyte 2004). Furthermore, women's residences away from their natal families, coupled (in some cases) with strict factory discipline modeled on hierarchical family relationships (see Zhang 2001:115–36), may have also made them more receptive to the influence of PRC-sponsored media promoting "socialist family virtues," which has drawn on traditional ideals of filial virtue to encourage "individual civil (and family) obligation to take care of elderly parents" (Wang 2004:24). Thus, through the physical separation from both their own parents and their husbands' families, immigrant wives invested strong personal desires in the symbolic importance of their "reunified" family lives in Hong Kong, where they dreamed of enacting the idealized wifely and filial roles that they could not practice on the mainland.

Hong Kong mothers-in-law, on the other hand, had different expectations of their new daughters-in-law.[4] Hong Kong is, of course, a cosmopolitan urban city where many women, both married and unmarried, work. Furthermore, local ideologies of belonging—at least among younger and well-educated residents—champion women's roles as independent actors who resist the patriarchal subservience that dominated discourses of women's wifely roles in the "traditional" past (Law et al. 1995; see also Chapter Six).

Nevertheless, many Hong Kong elders (and even some new immigrants) frequently explained to me how Hong Kong—because it had not experienced the PRC's socialist revolution—was a more "authentic" source of traditional Chinese cultural practices, including family relationships, than the mainland.[5] Thus, it is reasonable to assume that many Hong Kong mothers-in-law—as members of an older generation—were suspicious of their new daughters-in-law, whom they did not trust to act in "traditionally" subservient (that is, "filial") ways. Thus, no matter the intentions of daughters-in-law, the interactions that took place between them and their Hong Kong mothers-in-law were rife with possibilities for misunderstanding: Were working daughters-in-law ignoring their household duties or in fact performing expected roles through their contributions to the family income? Could mothers-in-law depend on their daughters-in-law to provide for them, should something happen to their sons? Would daughters-in-law be willing to have more children, thus ensuring the continuation of the family line? This potential for mistrust, and the resulting conflicts that ensued from it, were exacerbated by the crowded housing conditions that are one hallmark of Hong Kong daily life. Forced to interact and live together in tiny spaces, immigrants often had no place to escape from the watchful eyes of their parents-in-law, whose surveillance of their daily actions they found hard to tolerate.

Through their interactions with Hong Kong in-laws, their contestation of the meanings associated with objects in their domestic spaces, and their struggles to control—at least to some degree—the use of their inhabited spaces, immigrant wives fought to understand why their parents-in-law treated them as if they were children rather than competent adults. On the one hand, such treatment can be understood within the context of local Hong Kong attitudes of superiority over mainlanders as a strategy to contain the "dirty" influence of mainlanders (see Chapter Two), who, as daughters-in-law, represented a double threat to the stability and harmony of their in-laws' homes. On the other hand, this infantilizing of daughters-in-law would also allow parents-in-law the necessary authority to focus significant attention on shaping the bodily actions of their daughters-in-law (see, for example, Kondo 1990 and Herzfeld 2004) to conform to familial and community norms of Hong Kong belonging. As I discuss in the following pages, however, immigrants' access to alternative value systems and residences, as well as to opportunities for employment, provided them with important means of countering the everyday attempts at control over them exercised by their Hong Kong family members.

Crowding

Beginning with World War II, Hong Kong's constant inflow of Chinese refugees and immigrants created a population growth significantly higher than that from natural increase alone.[6] As a result, the Hong Kong British colonial government was constantly faced with an awareness of the shortage of "adequate" housing for Hong Kong residents.[7] Hong Kong census data from the early 1960s provides a graphic picture of the "crisis in housing" at that time. Out of a total population of approximately 3.5 million people, over 500,000 individuals were catalogued as living in regular domestic situations consisting of bed spaces, cubicles, rooms, or apartments shared by two or more families (Hong Kong Government 1966:8). Nondomestic living arrangements also recorded significant numbers of people living on verandahs or rooftops and in basements, storerooms, shops, cocklofts, or in squatter areas (ibid. 9). From the 1950s onward, both local people and recent arrivals often occupied squatter homes, concentrated in different communities around the region. As late as the mid-1980s, recently arrived immigrants from the mainland were still routinely living in squatter areas, and even in 2001 the clearing of one of the last remaining such areas—whose inhabitants had long-since become permanent residents—was being strongly contested by its inhabitants.[8]

Despite the often poor conditions living in such improvised, outdoor spaces, residents have always had mixed feelings about leaving such homes for living spaces in government constructed housing blocks (Smart 2002: 342). One of my local friends, who had legally immigrated to Hong Kong with her family in the early 1980s when she was a young girl, remembered her family's transition from a Kowloon squatter area to Hong Kong public housing. She and her family had lived in the squatter area for their first three years in Hong Kong. One night while her father was out working, there was a huge fire that destroyed much of the area, including her family's home and all of their belongings. Her mother successfully led her and her infant sister to safety, and the family was relocated to a temporary shelter in the New Territories—a location far removed from the urban areas and convenient infrastructure to which they had become accustomed. There, they lived as a family on one bunkbed in a large room with many other families also waiting to be rehoused. When they were finally removed eight months later to a Temporary Housing Area—where they lived for the next seven years while waiting for a public housing unit to become available for them—the family was relieved to have, at least, a room of their own, rather than a bed hidden behind a bamboo mat barrier, on which all eating, sleeping, and homework took place. Such spatial constraints were an important reason why squatters might resist leaving their more spacious squatter homes; maintaining control over one's living space was an important factor as well (ibid.). One woman's mother, who escaped a squatter fire—although she broke her toe in her jump from her top bunkbed to the ground—was not happy about the prospect of being rehoused by the British in a new H-block flat. She was worried about the control of her space by agents associated with the colonial government and remained convinced that the British poisoned the water with kerosene, which she could smell. Smart cites other reasons why residents of squatter areas might resist leaving their homes, including the fact that they would be required to pay rent in public housing, that their squatter dwellings had fewer constraints than other forms of housing in Hong Kong (allowing them, for example, to keep pets or take in lodgers), and that their community attachments and social organization would be disrupted (ibid.).

Devastating fires were a common occurrence in Hong Kong squatter areas (Smart 2006). One particular fire—in the Shek Kip Mei area of Kowloon on Christmas night in 1953, in which 50,000 people were left homeless— has for the past forty years generally been cited as the impetus for the creation of the first public housing flats in Hong Kong.[9] One reason for the continued dominance of this "myth" (ibid.) in the social imaginary of Hong Kong people is that the history of public housing in Hong Kong is strongly intertwined with the history of all aspects of colonial Hong Kong's social, political, and economic life, and numerous scholars have focused particular

Figure 4.1 Newly constructed public housing blocks, Hong Kong (January 2007)

attention in trying to explain why Hong Kong's famously nonintervention-ist colonial government would have subsidized the housing of half of Hong Kong's population (see, for example, Yeung and Drakakis-Smith 1982 and Smart 1992, 2006). The underlying commonality in all hypotheses, how-ever, is the program's strong links to the collective visions of identity and memory of Hong Kong's past (see also Rooney 2003).

One result of the colonial government's huge housing program, which has been continued by the post-1997 SAR government, is that Hong Kong's residential areas can easily be identified as either publicly subsidized or not by residents and visitors familiar with the distinctive building designs that differentiate government-built towers from privately funded ones. Never-theless, the purely functional (at its inception) design of public housing has so improved that new public housing units are at least as nicely outfitted as new private housing units and are significantly better than older private housing stock. These new units are unrecognizable in comparison with the original H-Block housing models dating from the 1950s and 1960s, in which individual families shared one room along an outside corridor of similar rooms, with cooking done along the corridors, no electricity or elevators, and up to 300 people on each floor sharing two communal bathrooms (Yeung and Drakakis-Smith 1982:221). At that time, the standard spatial allotment per adult was 24 square feet, and children counted as half (despite the fact that they would grow up, and thus require more space later on). In 1970, the spatial allotment was increased to 35 square feet per person, and currently the allotment system is even more generous, since units built beginning in the 1980s now include private kitchens and baths (Rooney 2001:56–57). Although many older family members continue to inhabit older style flats while their children have bought private units in more desirable areas of the city, the public housing program is still crucial to the overall Hong Kong economy and housing situation. In 2002, over 50 percent of Hong Kong's population of almost 6.8 million individuals were living in some form of public housing (www.housingauthority.gov.hk). Over 30 percent of these public housing tenants were living in public rental housing, with another 18 percent living in subsidized sale flats (ibid.).[10]

Residents of both older and newer public housing stock are responsible for all of the "fitting-out" finishes of their individual units, including the partitioning of rooms and the installation of flooring, cabinetry, lighting fixtures, and all appliances (including air conditioners and refrigerators). While the current units are sufficiently large to accommodate the partitioning of one or more bedrooms while still retaining some common living space for the family, residents of older units often kept their one room unpartitioned, to allow for the maximum use of space in the unit. The restrictive size of such units makes the "flexible" use of space and furnishings the norm: bunkbeds may serve as work and storage areas as well as a place to sit or sleep; dining tables, as well as tables used for children's homework or mahjohng, can be folded out at meal times and put away when not being used; fold-out sofas or extra beds are common as well (see, for example, Rooney 2001:67). Residents of private units have, for most of Hong Kong's history, also lived in very small apartments, often shared with other families, and have likewise made creative uses of available spaces to enlarge their actual living spaces. Balconies, in particular, have often served as "separate

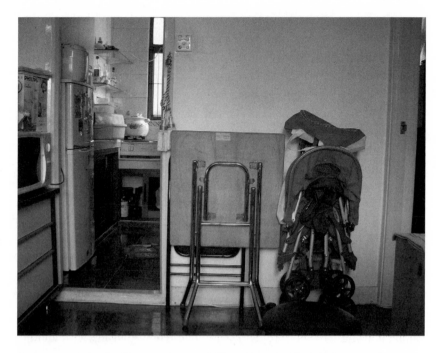

Figure 4.2   The flexible use of space: fold-up dining table and chairs in the main living area of a Hong Kong flat (January 2007)

rooms" for sleeping, playing, and doing homework. One local friend remembers, for example, often having to run down several flights of stairs to the street to retrieve the pencil that fell through her balcony's metal slats while she was doing her homework there.

The "improvisation" of outside spaces likewise parallels the kinds of multiple uses embodied in indoor spaces. Particularly in older areas of the city, vendors co-opt empty sidewalk spaces for selling any manner of new or used household goods, and alleyways between buildings become barbershops or places to get a quick snack. Along these lines, Ackbar Abbas describes the effects of what he calls the "hyperdensity" of Hong Kong:

> The tendency then is not toward specialization and separation, but toward the multiplication and concentration of different functions in the same space. But perhaps the most characteristic way of all of dealing with hyper-

density is to transform the facades of anonymous apartment blocks by the construction of illegal and semilegal structures: balconies, indoor gardens, additional storage space, and so on. It is as if the flat surfaces of these anonymous buildings were now covered in pleats or folds, multiplying in volume and interest and providing a zone of mediation between inside and outside. (1997:89)

Although the colonial and SAR governments have worked hard to "clean up" both the streets and the outsides of buildings by discouraging vendors and clearing away illegal structures (see, for example, Smart 2002), in older areas with primarily private housing stock, such uses of space are still common. The illegally constructed balcony space of one of my immigrant informants, a man of twenty-eight living with his mother, father, and two sisters in a 200 square foot apartment in an old area of urban Kowloon, was used as a storage area for household goods and a bicycle, provided a home to two cats and their food dishes and litter box, and held some stools for sitting outside. Furthermore, my informant had just "enclosed" the far end of the balcony with plywood, constructing a room about 3 feet by 3 feet, complete with a door and small "window." He planned to use this space as his home "office," and, in addition to a desk, chair, and table lamp that he had placed inside, he was also storing his squash racket there. The experiences of domestic spaces encountered by the majority of my immigrant informants, however, stood in stark contrast to the "flexible" use of space indicated by these other stories. For immigrant wives, the "malleability" of their own domestic spaces was a mere illusion: restricted from cleaning or otherwise transforming their domestic spaces by their Hong Kong relatives, wives remained frustrated with these spaces and their family relationships, interpreting the actions in and about these spaces as personal attacks on them by family members.

Dreamspace Lost

Many of the immigrant wives I met had visited Hong Kong with special "visitor" permits at least once before immigrating there to live with their husbands. Often, women's memories of their first visit to Hong Kong demonstrated the wide gap that existed between what they expected to find in Hong Kong and the reality of their experiences there. One woman, whose parents as well as her husband lived in Hong Kong, remembered her first visit, when she was a teenager in the late 1980s. At that time, she had visited for the purpose of helping out in her father's store—although working while in Hong Kong on a visitor's permit was (and still is) illegal. She thought that Hong Kong would be "as pretty as heaven," and instead was both dismayed at the state of the old, walk-up building that her father inhabited and disgusted by all of the trash left lying in the stairwells by other tenants. Furthermore, a strong impression was made on her by the homeless people she saw sleeping under highway overpasses, as well as by the large numbers of older people she saw working. Overall, she felt that the lifestyle in Hong Kong was not nearly as good as what she had imagined.

In the late 1980s, the access to information about Hong Kong by residents of Guangdong Province would not have been quite as easily available as it is today, with Hong Kong TV broadcasts, both local and satellite, available to most Guangdong (and other Chinese coastal) residents (Latham 2000). However, even with this increased information about Hong Kong, the images of Hong Kong and Hong Kong living spaces—often formed through the more comfortable, middle-class images seen on Hong Kong sitcoms and soap operas—did not do much to prepare these women for the realities of Hong Kong living conditions that they encountered on their first visits. Amber, one of the immigrant wives whose life story I presented in Chapter Three, described the surprise and upset that she experienced on her first visit to Hong Kong and to her husband's public housing unit:

> Before I came to Hong Kong, I thought that the places where Hong
> Kong people lived would probably be better than where we [lived]. I never
> thought they would be so small . . . It was terrible. I didn't know how to live
> there—a place for five was smaller than a place for one on the mainland.
> So I said to my husband: "Oh! So your house is so small! I thought it would
> be big and beautiful!" He never told me that it would be so small. He just
> told me that there were two bedrooms and how many people lived there,
> and so on. In my mind, I thought that so many rooms would be much
> bigger—that the rooms would be as big as we had on the mainland. I didn't
> know a room would only be big enough for a bed, no more—without even

Figure 4.3 The reality of public housing for many newly immigrated mainland wives, Mark V (1967) public housing block in Kowloon, Hong Kong (January 2005)

enough room for a dresser. So he didn't say anything then. He didn't say a word. He didn't know how to explain. I was so disappointed.

Although she had obtained the relevant information from her husband about number of rooms and people living in the house, without actual knowledge about the social and housing context of Hong Kong, the imaginary details that Amber supplied in terms of space size and décor of her prospective home were far different from the reality that she found. The apparent breakdown of communication between spouses on this subject was not uncommon. May, whose story I also told in Chapter Three, told me that she was shocked by her husband's family living situation, and that her husband had never described it for her, despite the questions she had asked before visiting.

More surprising to me, however, was that in talking to many women, it was clear that the experiences of their previous visits had not at all prepared them for the realities of living in Hong Kong on a long-term basis. May, for example, knew that her family would soon be eligible for their own public housing unit. In her case, she must not have expected to have to live with her husband's family at all, imagining only a life in Hong Kong with her nuclear family in a more comfortable public housing unit. Gaining access to a modern, low rent, public housing unit was, in fact, a dream shared by many wives living in housing situations that they found difficult to endure. Although some families—like May's—were lucky enough to have been able to apply for a unit when one of the children had been born in Hong Kong in the early 1990s, families who had not applied before their arrival in Hong Kong had other choices to make. In 2001 and 2002, new families could no longer apply for public units in the central urban areas, but instead had to choose between the relatively isolated New Territories areas, for which they would most probably be allotted a unit in three years, or a suburban area—more convenient to transportation, the main urban areas, and jobs—for which they would need to wait at least five years.[11] One immigrant wife, living with her husband and young son in a small room in the same run-down, low security building where her husband had lived in a boarding house before her arrival, did not know how to choose between the wait-list options: although she much preferred the idea of living close to the city in the long-term, she did not feel that she could possibly survive five years in their current environment. In some situations, this extreme lack of space may have been largely responsible for wives' difficulties in adjusting, since they had never actually shared these domestic spaces with their husbands before arriving in Hong Kong. Several women had stayed with their husbands' friends when they visited. One woman, who was particularly unhappy with this arrangement, was even a bit relieved when her daughter, being cared for by a friend on the mainland, got sick two weeks after her arrival in Hong Kong and thus provided her with an excuse to leave.

In other cases, women may simply have experienced their Hong Kong living spaces differently while visiting. Several women told me that they were treated completely differently on their earlier visits than after they had moved to Hong Kong permanently. On previous visits everyone treated them nicely, helped take good care of them, and took them sightseeing to Hong Kong's famous tourist destinations. On these visits, some wives were welcomed into families and treated as the visitors to Hong Kong that they were. Nevertheless, once in Hong Kong on their one-way permits, their roles changed from "honored visitor" to "wife," ensuring that they were expected to work, cook, clean, or otherwise keep themselves busy with the everyday tasks of running the household in the ways dictated by their Hong Kong in-laws. This example was brought home to me by a woman I met on one of the service center's orientation tours—a full-day trip around Hong Kong Island available only to immigrants who had been in Hong Kong for less than one year. This woman had taken a day off from her restaurant job in order to visit places that she remembered having visited with her Hong Kong husband's family on the trip to Hong Kong that she had made before immigrating. She told me that she thought it would be fun to see "the Peak" (one of the tallest points on Hong Kong Island and a popular tourist destination) again. But when I asked her if she thought that Hong Kong had changed much since her first visit almost a decade earlier, she noted that she did not know: since immigrating, she had not had the time, money, or encouragement to spend looking around the city, and so she could not say if it had "changed."

The relatively pleasant family encounters during first visits must certainly have altered when the dynamics associated with living together on an everyday basis became clearer. It took some time, often a period of months, for family relationships to begin unraveling in the upsetting, destructive ways described next. As these family relationships grew more difficult, women became increasingly more aware of qualities about their living spaces on the mainland that were not available to them in Hong Kong. Their longings were easily exacerbated by the media images of ideal homes available both on the mainland and in Hong Kong, where advertisements and "infomercials" routinely emphasized qualities of comfort, peacefulness, and serenity along with their idealized images of happy nuclear families inhabiting newly constructed homes.[12] Yet many immigrants' desires were much simpler than the idealized family lifestyles portrayed in these advertisements. One wife complained to me that "there was no place where [she] could cry" in Hong Kong. All she was looking for was a space where she could walk, or sit, alone, where no one would stare at her while crying, but she could not find any such space, either indoors or out.[13] Not knowing whom else to ask, she asked me if I could suggest some place that she did not know about.

"Clutter"

In describing their domiciles in Hong Kong, the amount of "clutter" and "useless things" collected by mothers-in-law and other relatives was the number one complaint that my immigrant informants would make. In some cases, the "clutter" was the cumulative result of a number of family members living together in tiny places over many years. The living arrangement in May's husband's family's home, where she lived during her first nine months in Hong Kong, was a case in point. Her husband's family had been living for the previous thirty years in one 300 square foot room in an old housing estate that had, at top occupancy, fifteen people living there. By the time May moved to Hong Kong, there were still eight people living in this room. A narrow entry corridor, just barely big enough to allow one person at a time to stand in the area, led in and out of the apartment. While a large television cabinet took up the entire wall space of one side of the room, the rest of the room held only four bunkbeds, which served as sleeping, living, and storage spaces for the family members. May's husband's two sisters slept on one bunkbed. May's mother-in-law used another bunkbed, both for sleeping and storage. A third bunkbed was used to sleep May's family of three or four—depending on whether her youngest son was visiting from the mainland. The last bunkbed was used by May's brother-in-law (and had previously been occupied by her late father-in-law as well). At mealtimes, a fold-out table was set up in between May's bunkbed and that of her brother-in-law, and the family members would sit on the edges of the beds and watch TV while eating.

May described the items stored by her Hong Kong family members, particularly her mother-in-law, as "trash." Likewise, she blamed this "trash," and the restriction of her family's life to one bed, for her inability to bring anything of her own from the mainland when she came to Hong Kong. This lack of personal things was not a concern for herself so much as for her children, particularly her four-year-old son, who could not bring any toys with him on visits to Hong Kong, since there was literally no "place" to keep them. Her concern about the unhealthiness of the living space provided for her children in Hong Kong contributed to her personal anxiety about her unhappy relationship with her husband, and it also made more concrete her concern about the best route for her children's future. Although May's living situation improved dramatically with her family's acquisition of a public housing unit big enough for her husband and children, her relationship with her husband and his family had so severely deteriorated by the time they moved in that she was certain she wanted a divorce.

My informants' complaints about the "clutter" in their living spaces usually, but not always, identified this tendency for collection as a habit of "old people." Nuala Rooney likewise describes a generation gap in the attitude toward keeping one's old things by her public housing resident informants. She writes that:

"Reducing things by half" was not an option this family was prepared to consider as a solution to density. As one mother in her fifties observed: My children always say that I keep all these things in the house, and maybe it's true. For example, I put these useless things underneath the beds. You know, old people are like this. These things may be of no use now, but they may be useful in the future. Right? There's no point in wasting money. (2001:69)

But what is perceived as "useful," and what is not? When I asked the staff at the social service center how they dealt with decisions about what to keep and what not to keep, the younger people all agreed that, no matter what, things just have to be thrown out. But the administrator, the mother of two grown sons, had a different view, about the difficulty of parting with such important objects as her sons' childhood projects or letters from close friends and relatives. She mimed her actions, clutching at an invisible piece of paper with both hands, and with such intensity, staring at it and finally throwing it out, that I felt as if I had actually watched her in the process of throwing out some dear object.

In the case of the immigrant wives, all young women who had already moved at least several times in their lives, and who had all made a conscious break with their mainland families and childhood homes, their mother-in-law's old clothes, musical tapes, and other objects were not understood, for the most part, as repositories of memory. Instead, these objects were appraised with a calculating air of monetary value, and, under this inspection, such junk was seen only as wasting space that could be better used. Most informants, while unhappy about this situation, resigned themselves to accepting that they could not control the fate of these items, as most mothers-in-law would not tolerate their daughters-in-law disposing of their clutter. But, despite an otherwise difficult relationship, Amber's mother-in-law and husband were somewhat more compliant in this regard. She said:

> I think there's too much stuff [in the house], and it's really bothersome. I've already helped [my mother-in-law] throw out a lot. She is willing. I told her these things are useless, and they are wasting space and are ugly . . . Like an old-fashioned dehumidifier, made from wood. You can still use it, but no one would. It was sitting there for 30 years, and no one was using it. It was useless, so I threw it out. Sometimes there are other old things . . . My husband used to go fishing, but now he doesn't like to go anymore. There was so much fishing stuff! So I threw it out, we didn't need it. And there were these shoes, these old shoes of his he couldn't bring himself to throw out. Now shoes are so inexpensive, but these styles are so old, no one would dare to wear them—it would be better to throw them out! [My husband] said, "Whatever, if you want to, throw them out. Do what you want." He won't say, "No! My things are too expensive—don't throw them out." Lots of people talk about throwing things out, and I think that it's better to do this. But there are lots of things that [I] can't throw out, like lots of old clothes, 30 year old clothes, that they can't stand to throw away. I think this is really bothersome, because [they] are never going to wear these clothes outside—so why keep them? But [they] must keep them. I can't do anything about it.

The substantial clutter in their homes, belonging to their Hong Kong family members and also mirroring the density of the constant crowds outside, contrasted sharply with the amount and kinds of personal belongings that most of these immigrant wives were able to bring with them to Hong Kong. Like May, every one of my informants told me that she had brought only a small, hand-carried bag when moving to Hong Kong. Each indicated that she had brought just a few clothes, and that she had either sold or left everything else behind. Some women had items that they had intended to bring, useful things like household appliances bought by their husbands for their mainland residences, which their in-laws rejected on the grounds that there would not be enough space or that these items would use too much electricity. One woman hoped to be able to bring some of her photographs of friends and family, although she had no place to put them. Another woman was proud that her eight-year old son gave all his toys away to friends, since he knew that there would be no space, or time, for them in Hong Kong. Although some women felt that their being able to come to Hong Kong with so few personal belongings indicated a ready adaptation to their Hong Kong families' living spaces, others may well have resented the fact that so little attempt at accommodation was made for them by their Hong Kong in-laws.

These Hong Kong interiors bring to mind Kathleen Stewart's descriptions of the accumulation of knick-knacks in the inhabited spaces of families living in Appalachia, where homes were also "piled high" with objects, inside and out (1996). Stewart focuses on describing these objects in terms of the meanings that they held for the people who amassed them, and she argues that the accumulation of these objects has allowed her informants to "occupy" the places where they live and inscribe their memory on the landscape around them. For Stewart's informants, possessions provided a concrete means of remembering past actions, people, and events. In Hong Kong's intensely "inhabited" domestic spaces, "clutter" seems to serve a similar purpose.

Hong Kong's history as a British colony provides an important context for understanding the relationship between clutter and identity in my informants' houses. This relationship is significantly different for older Hong Kong residents who immigrated to Hong Kong during periods of political and economic hardship than it is for those younger residents of Hong Kong, who have grown up in a relatively prosperous and politically stable environment, or for recent immigrants, whose lives on the mainland were much more comfortable than in times past. The interaction between identity and memory is made even more complex by the ever-changing—almost ephemeral—nature of Hong Kong's built environment (Abbas 1997). Colonial government planning decisions and private developer interests have both been responsible for the constant destruction of older housing stock, buildings, and neighborhoods. Replaced by new construction, entire parts of the city are unrecognizable from earlier decades (ibid.). In conjunction with the "temporariness" of the older public housing units, little room has been left for the inscription of memory in most of Hong Kong's outside built environment. As a result, the fiercely guarded "clutter" of older Hong Kong locals provides both a tangible memory of times past as well as concrete links to a precolonial identity.

"Collecting" has often been cited as one characteristic of "Hong Kong culture" (Bosco 2001). Tied to discussions about local people's love of speculation—a practice in which a commodity is bought for the sole purpose of immediately selling it at a higher price to someone else—and the "refugee mentality" held by older Hong Kong residents, in particular, "collecting" in Hong Kong has been described as "the activity of a 'paranoid population desperate for anything of value'" (Cook 1998 cited in Bosco 2001:269). For Hong Kong locals, homes as well as many of the objects in them may often be seen as sites of transactional value, in which the potential for realizable assets largely determines a thing's perceived worth. Nevertheless, that there is more meaning to such collections of objects than their potential monetary worth was evident from the intense debates that arose over these objects between immigrants and their family members. For example, when May's husband was out of work and the family desperately needed money, May complained about her husband's habit of collecting stamps, asking: "Why did he not sell them, since he said they were valuable?" Interestingly, such focus on collecting objects has not been described within the contexts of Chinese homes in other locations, such as the mainland or Taiwan. Writing about the interior spaces inhabited by families living in Shanghai, Deborah Davis describes interiors that reflected private tastes and concerns in contrast to the heavily political environment outside of her informants' houses (1989). The marked absence of state-influenced decorations in her informants' homes was notable given that they had lived for many years under a socialist regime in which individuals' private lives were subjected to the same intense political scrutiny as their public ones. In the 1980s, the period of time about which Davis writes, mainland urban residents were still not living in a political or economic system that would have valued overt displays of conspicuous consumption, demonstrated perhaps through such means as the collection of objects. Now, however, life on the mainland has changed, and the active consumption of consumer products is a part of everyday life, just as it has been for a younger generation of local Hong Kong people (Davis 2000).

For young immigrant wives, their Hong Kong in-laws' habits of collecting "clutter" prevented them from being able to consume local goods that they perceived as being more desirable than the objects hoarded by their elderly family members. Not only had they had access to more desirable consumer goods while still residing on the mainland while being supported by their Hong Kong husbands, but increased access to such goods must also have factored into immigrant wives' dreams of achieving a more modern lifestyle once in Hong Kong. As such, the objects in their Hong Kong homes were at the heart of immigrant and Hong Kong locals' conflicts over control within their domestic spaces.

Control

Nowhere was the open ideological conflict over the arrangement of domestic space more evident than in the public housing flat shared by Cybil with her husband, their four-year-old daughter, and her husbands' parents. Their 400 square foot flat was a new unit, with a bright exposure and on a desirable floor—within the top ten floors of the over-thirty-story building. The family had moved out of the tiny room they had previously occupied for thirty years in an old public housing block across the street just a year before Cybil came to Hong Kong on her one-way permit. Cybil was relieved they had moved out of the old unit, in which her husband had no bed, and where, on a previous visit to Hong Kong, she could not stay because there was no place for her to sleep. Nevertheless, she was very frustrated by the fact that her parents-in-law had not used the occasion of the move to dispose of some of their old, ugly belongings. She showed me the tattered, fake wood and vinyl pull-out sofa in the main living area, and complained that her mother-in-law had paid someone HK$400 (US$50) to move it for them. This was wasted money as far as Cybil was concerned, since her mother-in-law could have bought a brand new sofa for twice that price. Her mother-in-law, in contrast, saw nothing wrong with the old sofa and felt no need to replace it with a new one. Indicative of the general appearance of the central living area of the flat, this sofa, on which Cybil's father-in-law slept, was centered along the longest wall, and a fold-out table would be set up in front of this sofa for meals, doing homework, or playing mahjong. All other wall space was completely covered by large pieces of furniture—dressers holding old clothes, a large TV cabinet, and an old bunkbed. Every possible surface on these furniture items was covered with what Cybil called "junk," mostly collectible figures from McDonalds or other popular promotion campaigns carefully arranged according to type.[14] The bunkbed was also completely covered, with the exception of a small space of about two feet by three, reserved for sleeping by Cybil's mother-in-law. The rest of the area on both beds and underneath was packed with cardboard boxes filled with what appeared to be old newspapers, covering up whatever else was inside.

In stark contrast to this "shared" family area was the arrangement and décor of the 60 to 70 square foot room that had been partitioned off for Cybil and her husband. In fitting with the small size of the room, Cybil had chosen only two pieces of furniture: a darkly stained, wood double bed and matching dresser. Accented by curtains of bright yellow, the sleek cleanliness of this room, in which everything had a fixed place out of sight, provided an effect of light airiness far removed from the crowded, old clutter of the main room. In the bathroom as well were traces of this conflict over newness and simplicity versus oldness and clutter: tiny, threadbare towels hung neatly arranged on hooks, carefully placed rather than heaped up, piled, or even folded on the counter.

Cybil constantly complained about "dirt" and clutter in the apartment, and she was further frustrated that her parents-in-law did not like her to touch or move anything in the apartment, which prevented her from being able to clean anything. As a result, Cybil would wait around the apartment until both in-laws were out, and then she would clean the floor. (Cleaning the floor was a particular concern of hers, since her daughter often spent time playing on the floor.) But in other matters interacting with her in-laws, she was not able to reach such an adequate "compromise." When she attempted to move one dresser to create a more spacious arrangement in the common living area, her mother-in-law became angry and almost abusive toward her. After a distraught argument with her parents-in-law about how unwelcome she felt in their house, Cybil's father-in-law bought a washing machine for Cybil to use. Cybil greatly appreciated the gesture behind this purchase and was very happy not to have to wash her clothes by hand any longer. Less than two months later, however, she was no longer allowed to use the appliance, as she was told it was a waste of electricity and water, and Cybil once again began doing the family's laundry by hand. Finally, Cybil was conscious of what she felt was an overt show of disrespect toward her by her husband' sisters, who would routinely join the family for evening and weekend meals. Although both women had jobs with good salaries, they made no contribution to the meals—either by helping monetarily or by shopping, cooking, or cleaning up afterwards. Cybil was further angered when, just before leaving, both women would put their shoes back on and walk around the house, muddying the floor that they knew Cybil had cleaned just before their arrival.

Most upsetting to Cybil was her husband's increasing "disengagement" from these family issues and his increasing reluctance to offer an open show of support for her in the face of these family disagreements. Issues such as his large consumption of alcohol and his chain smoking had worried her before her arrival, but as their relationship was otherwise good, she had accepted these habits. Once in Hong Kong, however, her concern about his habits grew: What, she asked him, would she do if he died? How could she support his parents and sisters, and would they help her and her daughter? Instead of addressing her concerns seriously, he would note that he was in no danger of dying, as his parents were old, strong, and healthy, and chain smoking did not seem to have taken any years off Deng Xiaoping's long life. Other future concerns about their living space worried her as well: at four, her daughter was still sleeping in bed with her and her husband as there was no place for her to have her own bed. This was interrupting Cybil's sleep, and causing other problems, such as when her parents-in-law would give her daughter a large glass of water to drink before bed. In these cases, her daughter would invariably wet the bed, and Cybil would have to clean up the mess and wash the sheets out by hand. The stress involved in living in this environment took a marked toll on Cybil and exhibited itself through a number of different physical symptoms, such as difficulty sleeping (initially because of Hong Kong's background noise), which later became an almost chronic insomnia; a chronic sore throat, which she attributed to the air

pollution; and colds and flus, which she invariably came down with immediately upon her return to Hong Kong from her house in Dongguan, where
the atmosphere was completely different.

At the house in Dongguan, where my husband, three-year-old son, and
I spent a three-day holiday with her, her husband, and daughter in April
2002, she was able to relax with her husband, enjoy time eating at their
favorite restaurants, and watch TV. There, it was clear that Cybil's husband
was not only supportive of her—praising her efforts and progress in learning some basic English and her quick mastery of Hong Kong geography and
transportation—but that they seemed very close. Unlike many Hong Kong
people, he was fond of spicy foods, like Korean and Indian, and loved to
partake of Western "staples" like steak and coffee. Also interested in travel
and the outdoors, he had taught Cybil about these unfamiliar foods and had
taken her on trips to many different, beautiful sites in China. They both
talked animatedly about a trip they would like to take together to Japan, at
some as yet undetermined future time, and, most striking to me, he kept
his hand placed lightly on the small of her back when sitting or walking
together—perhaps the only public display of affection between a married
couple that I witnessed during my research. In contrast to the Hong Kong
flat, the apartment in Dongguan, three times larger than the Hong Kong
unit, was spotlessly clean, nicely provisioned with a washing machine and
large, plump towels and a separate bed for Cybil's daughter. Cybil also kept
the large screen TV tuned to her favorite mainland soap operas, complaining that Hong Kong programs were too silly and shallow for her taste.

Not suprisingly, Cybil viewed her Dongguan house as a possible shelter,
where she could turn should things in Hong Kong become too stressful
for her to stay any longer. By late June 2002, three months after our visit
with her and her family in Dongguan, and ten months after her arrival in
Hong Kong, she told me that she and her husband were talking less and
less frequently, that she was fighting more and more often with her in-laws,
and that she was considering possibly leaving her husband to return to the
mainland. She felt that although she had become familiar with life in Hong
Kong, she could not adjust to her living situation there, and that she would
give herself one more year to adjust, but no more. Because Cybil had been
working, she felt that she had maintained a measure of her own independence, proving that she could take care of herself while also removing her-

self from her Hong Kong family members. She was also putting a small amount of money away for herself—money that she had offered but had been rejected by her in-laws—in case the need arose. Since Cybil used her employment as a means to absent herself from her home, and her in-laws seemed to resent that absence, her husband was likely on the receiving end of both his parents' and Cybil's complaints.

While Cybil's frustration about her relationship with her in-laws was expressed often through complaints about their refusal to let her clean, decorate, or use their house as she would have liked, another immigrant wife, Allison, who lived with her husband and his parents in an old public housing estate unit, was more concerned about the attempted control exercised over her behavior by her in-laws in their living space. Although Allison frequently noted that their living space was only "small" because of all the clutter that her parents-in-law kept there, it was not clutter about which she complained; instead, it was their constant watchfulness and questioning of her activities that bothered her. If she wanted to go out, they would ask her where she was going and what time she would be back; if she was out longer than planned, she would face more questions on her return to the flat. Although she had been happy to help take care of her husband's elderly parents at first, and made sure that any activities that she did outside the home did not interfere with their care schedule, she soon became annoyed at their constant questions. Both social workers and friends at the social service center, on hearing of her concerns, were quick to assure Allison that it was quite natural that her elderly parents-in-law would worry about her, and that her parents-in-law's questions were merely their way of showing their care and concern about her—a concern that would seem justified in this new environment, as she had only visited Hong Kong briefly before immigrating there.

Allison, however, could not get over the feeling that she was being treated like a small child, and that this seeming "concern" was more an attempt to control her activities than anything else. The refusal of her parents-in-law to let her cook was particularly upsetting to her, as Allison's adjustment to Hong Kong was made substantially more difficult by her dislike of standard Cantonese fare. Chinese cuisine varies substantially by region, and although the Cantonese are known throughout China for their willingness to consume everything (meaning all parts of an animal as well as all manner of exotic species—from water cockroach to bear), they are equally famous for their dislike of spicy foods. In comparison to almost all other regional Chinese tastes, Cantonese food is exceptionally bland.

Allison's primary memory of her first weeks in Hong Kong was that she was constantly hungry. She missed the spicy cuisine of her native Sichuan, and found both Hong Kong "luxury foods" (shark fin soup, abalone, and swallow's nest soup) and the everyday emphasis on meat unpalatable. She told me:

> When I first came to Hong Kong, at every meal, when I saw the things on the table, the food on the table, I don't know why, but tears would start rolling down my face. I would pick up a bowl and chopsticks, but I wouldn't know what to eat, in part because there were so many things to eat, but nothing was right for me to eat. [My parents-in-law] wouldn't let me cook, and I thought that it was so hard.

At first, she thought that her parents-in-law just didn't know how to cook well. Later, she gradually became more accustomed to Cantonese style food. However, the tears that she had shed, without meaning to and seemingly without the ability to stop them, had already done damage to her relationship with her in-laws, who had been angered that she would cry over food.

In Shenzhen, where Allison had lived in a three bedroom apartment with her young, adopted daughter, her husband had visited her almost every night, commuting from his work in Hong Kong rather than returning to his parents' Hong Kong apartment. As the cost of food in Shenzhen was so much less expensive than in Hong Kong, she had regularly cooked them three main dishes every evening. It seemed that it had never occurred to her that she might not be able to continue to cook in Hong Kong. Once she had immigrated, however, her parents-in-law made it clear that they would not eat spicy foods and that vegetables (a staple of Allison's previous diet) were largely unsuitable for an elderly person's digestive system. They did "give-in" and let her cook once, warning her not to use too much hot pepper. Her mother-in-law stood behind her the whole time, looking over her shoulder and sneezing constantly—presumably from the excess of pepper being used—so that Allison was not able to enjoy even that experience. Her mother-in-law also went so far as to tell her that if she was not happy with the cooking arrangements, then she could just move out. Little did her mother-in-law think that she would actually do so!

After her mother-in-law's allegations that Allison had stolen HK$30 (US$2.80) from her rocketed out of control—so that her mother-in-law had taken to calling her "thief" and shouting at her at the dinner table— Allison's husband made the decision to follow the example of his five other siblings and move out. Concerned about his wife's welfare, he understood her extreme unhappiness when faced with his mother's temper and strictures. Nevertheless, her mother-in-law blamed Allison for the fact that her son had moved out. Although her parents-in-law continued to accept the monthly allowance that Allison had begun giving to them after she started working, they refused to talk to her, blaming her, among other things, for jeopardizing their son's health through his "improper nutrition" in their new living situation. In particular, since their new apartment was a studio with no kitchen facilities, Allison's mother-in-law was worried about Allison's inability to cook her husband "soup." Cantonese style brothy soups are the cornerstone of all Cantonese meals and are believed to have rich nutritious and healing properties. To be cooked properly, these soups are generally simmered over low heats for several hours, and although ingredients can be varied to help prevent against different kinds of illnesses or health problems, the cooking process—the length of time cooked over what level of gas fire—is crucial to both the soup's taste and nutritional outcome. The care put into cooking such soups is popularly perceived as indicative of caring between family members—usually demonstrating a mother's concern for her child, but also frequently referenced (even through jokes) as demonstrating a wife's ideal treatment of her husband.

Although such soups are not a part of Sichuan cuisine, and Allison did not find them particularly tasty, she respected the value placed on soup by her husband, and she also felt that it was important for his health to continue to have soup on a regular basis. When she and her husband had first married, and her husband was with her almost every night in Shenzhen, her mother-in-law, worried that her son was not getting any of the soup that she would cook for him at home in Hong Kong, would call her and tell her how to make the different kinds of soup that Allison's husband liked. Even after Allison and her husband moved out, although she could not get off work in time to join her husband for dinner, she would encourage him to return to eat at his parent's house when he could—since she felt that the soup for him there would be more nutritious than that which they regularly ate at the inexpensive cafeterias near their studio apartment. Thus, on the one hand, Allison's mother-in-law's refusal to let her cook may have been quite simply a power play, demonstrating her own position within the domestic hierarchy. On the other hand, what kinds of food were cooked, and how they were prepared was, in this case, indicative of other meanings, particularly that of caregiving, within the family context. As Allison had not been "schooled" in the correct forms of "local" eating, her mother-in-law could not accept Allison's food preparation within the domestic space she controlled. Instead, Allison's cooking represented a threat not only to her mother-in-law's family control but also to her son—potentially jeopardizing his health through Allison's insistence of eating her traditionally spicy and otherwise "different" Sichuan dishes.

Despite not having her own kitchen, Allison was nonetheless delighted with the tiny studio space that she shared with her husband after they moved out of his parents' housing unit. Not only had they been able to fit everything they needed into the 100 square foot space (including a tiny TV and stereo), Allison was also considering returning to Shenzhen to pick up photographs of family and friends that she had left with a cousin there and which she wanted to have with her in Hong Kong. Most importantly, however, was the feeling of independence and freedom she had gained from moving out: although she and her husband had had their own room in her in-laws' house, should they talk or laugh, they would always be overheard by others. In their own space, she said, they would stay up late at night—until after midnight—just talking and laughing and enjoying each other's companionship in a way that had not been possible before. Of course, she was also free from the constant scrutiny she had previously faced, and decisions about meals and eating were now her own again.

The solution that Allison and her husband achieved to ameliorate the friction related to her entry into the family—their joint removal from his family's apartment—was one that Cybil had expressed a desire for as well. In her case, however, her husband did not seem either interested or willing to explore this option. Instead, Cybil, like many other women in similar positions, found that working enabled her to have the freedom to be removed from the household tension for long periods of time, while also providing her with a sense of her own independence. Unlike long-term resident Hong Kong people, these women immigrants were denied the opportunity to find improvised ways to use domestic space more flexibly, even as they refused to submit easily to their Hong Kong in-laws' lessons about local belonging that sought to socialize them as compliant daughters-in-law within tightly controlled domestic spaces. Instead, these women had to remove themselves from those spaces in order to find ways to create some "space for themselves" in an environment that did not readily appear to allow for any significant personal space.

These women's experiences of old and crowded living environments in Hong Kong were made even harder to accept by their treatment as marginal members of society by both Hong Kong family members and strangers. Allison, laughing, told me that her father-in-law would preface any complaint about her with the words, "You people from the countryside are all . . ." Of course, she pointed out, he was originally from the countryside as well, but having lived most of his life in Hong Kong, he no longer identified himself with that background and instead used it to imply that Allison did things differently, and not as well, as a "Hong Kong person" (Cantonese: *heunggong yahn*; Mandarin: *xianggang ren*). Subject to the negative stereotypes of mainland immigrants prevalent in the media, some wives were also keenly aware that, in the eyes of many Hong Kong residents, they were viewed as "profiteers" and "gold diggers," and they felt resentment at being judged in this way. Cybil, in particular, was extremely critical of the hypocrisy she sensed between typical Hong Kong living conditions and local attitudes of superiority toward mainlanders.

> [Hong Kong people] think that the economy here is prosperous. But, by my way of thinking, most [Hong Kong people] are not very well off. At least, they don't live well. Only those few that have money do. And that's not to say that everyone [here] has money. Those who have money are fine everywhere: they don't have to be in Hong Kong to live well. But those who are poor, they will be poor anywhere, and they are even poorer than us mainlanders. Because, for example, where I work, there I've seen a woman who lives in the gutter. She's put up a house—about two-thirds as long as this bench [that we were sitting on]—divided into a top and a bottom. A dog sleeps at the bottom, and she sleeps on top. The old woman collects

garbage. How is she better than I am? I hope that in the future I never have to live like that. It's really pitiful. Really . . . I think, at least my whole life I've always had a bed to sleep in and a place to live. But my husband's situation has been different. Before we got married, he didn't have a bed to sleep in. He had to sleep on the sofa. He didn't have any private space . . . I really think that the poorest people in Hong Kong are worse off than we are on the mainland. In my village, even the poorest people have a place to live and food to eat.

Faced with discomfort in their own living spaces, upsetting relationships with their in-laws, and disillusionment at the impoverished living conditions in urban Hong Kong, these women struggled to understand why they were consistently targeted as "inferior" and "outsiders." Without the ability to create either spaces for themselves or the potential comforts that they had imagined prior to their immigration, many women took refuge by returning for frequent visits to their mainland homes or by visiting friends on the mainland. Once there, however, they were hard-pressed to explain the true nature of their difficulties to others. Cybil, for example, had heard such stories of hardship with in-laws before coming to Hong Kong, but she had dismissed her friends' complaints as exaggerated, deciding that she would not make the same "mistakes" that they had. Allison, on the other hand, simply did not tell her family members about the details of her living situation for fear they would worry about her too much. Such omissions contributed, along with media images, to misconceptions that many women still waiting to immigrate to Hong Kong would form about their future lives there.

For wives who had lived as single mothers on the mainland, immigrating to Hong Kong to live with their husbands had held the expectation of relief: of shared responsibility in making decisions about the children's futures, of companionship to help them through the worrying and exhausting periods of childhood illness, and of support in disciplining the children. These expectations of being relieved of some of the difficulties associated with child rearing may have also colored these women's expectations as to what they would find in Hong Kong. Instead of relief, however, many women found only new concerns and frustrations, which were intimately linked to the lower-class social and economic positions that characterized the majority of living situations faced by my immigrant informants and their local husbands. Would women's husbands help them locate a good school for their children, perhaps outside of the lower-class urban areas where many immigrant women and their families lived? Would their husbands be available to spend time with the children, when not working long hours in restaurants or driving taxis? What dangers, in the forms of triads, drugs, or crimes, lurked in the hallways of local schools and run-down apartment buildings and threatened their children? And where would children find space to play—as they had in rural areas—or concentrate on doing their homework well?

Only one of my informants, A-Chun, in her late thirties with three children under nine years old, viewed her move to Hong Kong in a completely positive light, both for herself and for her children. On more than one occasion, A-Chun characterized this time for her as a time to relax and enjoy herself, to make new discoveries and new friends, and to educate herself about things that she had not had the opportunity to experience before, when she had the sole responsibility of raising her three children on the mainland. In her case, her husband, an immigrant himself twenty years earlier, worked construction, and he often had periods between jobs where he helped with the children, their schoolwork, and cooking. Although his support was obviously an important aspect of his wife's positive attitude, she coped as well with difficult living conditions—as her family of five occupied one room in an apartment with twenty-two other people for the first year after her move to Hong Kong—without the upset or turmoil that I often witnessed in other wives. Intrigued, I asked how she had been so successful in adjusting so well to her new life. She responded that she had understood that she should not have high expectations in immigrating to Hong Kong. Knowing that she would be at the bottom of the social hierarchy, she had accepted this fact before coming, and was therefore not plagued by any disillusionment after her arrival. A-Chun's relative freedom in Hong Kong was also directly related to the fact that she did not have to live with her mother-in-law, who remained on the mainland. As a result, her Hong Kong family life was considerably less regulated than that of my informants who married "into" Hong Kong families.

In all cases, the restrictions that these immigrant women encountered in their Hong Kong living spaces were experienced in stark contrast to the

living situations they had enjoyed on the mainland during years of waiting for the legal documentation that would allow them to emigrate. The
hardships suffered in terms of constraints of space, behavior, and activities
while undergoing the adjustment of learning to live with their Hong Kong
family members were hard to reconcile with the "advantages" they had experienced on the mainland as individuals with a "Hong Kong connection."
These women had access to a "way out" from the mainland—as access to
Hong Kong ensured the possibility of increased information, travel, and
untold dreams. Furthermore, the money sent by their Hong Kong husbands to support these wives and their children, while insufficient to live
well in Hong Kong, enabled these families to build or buy nice houses and
generally live at a level far above the local norm—a fact that contributed to
frequent misconceptions that their lives once in Hong Kong would be even
more glamorous. In Hong Kong, however, these women were seen as inferior to and less "civilized" than local Hong Kong people, including their
Hong Kong family members, who sought to minimize their power within
their homes.

Arguments over domestic spatial constraints and the exercise of control
within these spaces caused significant problems between immigrant wives
and their Hong Kong family members—problems which were, in turn,
interpreted differently by mainland immigrants, their Hong Kong family
members, and local social workers. The attempts to integrate these wives
into their local living spaces should have served as one way to encourage
knowledge about local ideologies of belonging, educating these women in
the roles they would be expected to play in Hong Kong family, social, and
economic life. But most wives I encountered were so unhappy about their
interactions with their family members that this exercise in socializing
mainland wives through interaction in the domestic context seems to have
largely backfired. Although these women had certainly gained a more thor-
ough understanding of typical lower class housing and living conditions
in Hong Kong, as well as a clearer picture of the expected role of a more
traditional Hong Kong "daughter-in-law," most women questioned the
"value" of the kinds of cultural capital to which they were exposed in their
Hong Kong homes. Hungry instead for other kinds of information about
life in Hong Kong, many women searched for jobs that would allow them to
gain some physical distance from their overbearing parents-in-law. Others

visited social service centers to seek help from social workers or found different ways to occupy themselves outside the spaces of their homes.

This distance often led to further problems, causing rifts in spousal relationships and increased conflict acted out within their overly crowded domestic spaces, which—in a cyclical way—contributed to women's desires to seek help outside the home to reconcile these problems. In Chapter Five, I follow immigrant women's initial incorporation into Hong Kong ways of life from their homes to the government-subsidized social service centers, where social workers sought to help immigrant women's adjustment to Hong Kong through lessons about the everyday differences between life on the mainland and life in Hong Kong.

FIVE

Adapting to Life in Hong Kong

Reflecting on their very first impressions of Hong Kong, mainland immigrant wives expressed a range of responses to the city. One woman noted, "As soon as I got to Hong Kong, I thought the buildings were so tall, and everything was so clean. These are the two things I noticed the most." Others, however, had more emotional reactions to the city. One wife told me:

> The first time I came to Hong Kong was to give birth to my oldest child . . . Every day I cried—I regretted coming . . . A few days after [my daughter] was born, I was doing everything myself—buying food, cooking. There wasn't anyone to look after us. It's harder (Cantonese: *chaamdi*) to have [children] here. At home, there are people to help you do everything—you don't have to do everything yourself.

Her concerns—about how to navigate her way around the city and how to take care of herself and her children without caring family and friends nearby—are echoed in May's comment: "There were too many cars. It was really crowded. There were so many cars. If I went out, I didn't know where to go. I had to find someone to show me the way—but no one did . . . I was scared. I didn't dare go out alone." Overall, women's initial comments about life in Hong Kong present a picture of confusion and concern about how to adapt to this intensely vibrant city that was to become their new "home."

In Chapter Four, I discussed immigrants' reactions to their densely inhabited domestic spaces in Hong Kong. However, Hong Kong's "hyperdensity" is not just experienced in terms of living space; it also carries over into all aspects of life, thereby creating challenges of adjustment for immigrant women that extend well beyond the walls of their domestic spaces. Large, broad avenues and smaller streets overflow with pedestrians, cars, minivans, double-decker buses, and taxis. Faceless apartment and office buildings tower high above the crowds, while overhead hang colorful neon signs advertising the locations of the myriad businesses and services lining the streets. At street level, bright and sleek convenience stores and fast-food chain outlets selling hamburgers and fries, noodle-soups, suzhi, or pizza alternate with other local shops—sometimes old and dingy, sometimes shiny and new—whose wares overflow these tiny spaces, often spilling onto the sidewalks. Markets are crammed with rows upon rows, tables upon tables of goods—fruits, vegetables, still-swimming fish, shoes, underwear, girls' dresses, fresh-squeezed juices, fake Louis-Vuitton and Gucci purses, cheap plastic toys, electrical parts and components, and what looks like other people's trash. Air-conditioned shopping malls, always filled with people, provide a range of amusements—ice skating rinks, waterfalls, electronic game parlors, karaoke bars, dimsum restaurants, and in one case, an indoor roller coaster—along with brightly lit shops selling fashionable clothes, shoes, handbags, and housewares. Underground, a vast network of modern and efficient subway trains facilitate movement from one area of the city to another; at rush hour, with platforms so crowded with human life that people squeeze together in unthinkable proximity, trains arrive each minute. Buses are no less crowded, and sidewalks are packed with people waiting in orderly queues for the next bus to stop and disgorge passengers so more can get on to go to school, to go to work, to go shopping, to visit friends, to go *yumcha* (eat dimsum), or to go home.

Hong Kong people make sense of their busy, intensely urban environment in different ways. Most commonly Hong Kong people label their fast-

Figure 5.1   Outdoor market in Kowloon, Hong Kong (August 2001)

paced lifestyle as one that is "nervous" (Cantonese: *ganjeung*; Mandarin: *jin-zhang*), and the everyday ability to navigate the ins and outs of this lifestyle was seen by my Hong Kong informants as an essential marker of "cultural difference" between Hong Kong and the mainland—despite the increased pace of life and the constant transitions associated with the rapid economic development taking place there. In Hong Kong, capitalism is intricately intertwined with all aspects of the region's history, including the relocation of Shanghainese entrepreneurs to Hong Kong following the establishment of the PRC government in 1949, the British colonial government's promotion of a "laissez-faire" economy in the colony, and the city's rise as a major international financial center. Today, in Hong Kong's consumer-driven, capitalist society, it is no exaggeration to say that most people have internalized the oft-heard truism that "time equals money." The fees for public transportation—from the "airport express" train that runs between Hong Kong's newly built, ultramodern airport and downtown in less than thirty minutes to the slow-paced electric trams and cross-harbor ferries that remain as remnants of Hong Kong's less efficient past—cost more the faster the travel time from place to place. When severe typhoon warnings shut down the city, evacuating schools, businesses, and restaurants and sending people home for the day, media reports afterwards invariably attach a specific (and staggering) dollar amount of "loss" to that unproductive period of time.

A second discourse that Hong Kong people use to distinguish their social and cultural life from that of the mainland is the idea of Hong Kong as a place of "order" (Cantonese: *dihtjeuih;* Mandarin: *zhixu*). This discourse, like that of "nervousness," is also rooted in Hong Kong's capitalist economic system and with the routinization and rationalization that theorists have long equated with capitalist bureaucracy (Harvey 1990). This discourse also has strong links to Hong Kong's colonial past and, in particular, to the principles of accountability, fairness, and justice championed by the colonial government and many Hong Kong people as part of the Hong Kong "ethos of belonging" (Lam 2004). Overall, these capitalist and rational orientations to space, time, and everyday social and bureaucratic relations that immigrants experienced in Hong Kong were significantly different from the orientations that women had grown up with on the mainland, where the pace of life is more relaxed, and where women were used to the practice of particularistic (rather than "rational") ties with government and other officials. As a result, mainland immigrant wives experienced numerous difficulties adapting to their new lives in "nervous" but "orderly" Hong Kong, where the fast-paced environment and routinized bureaucratic systems compounded the practical difficulties and emotionally fraught experiences of family reunion that accompanied their moves to Hong Kong.

Figure 5.2   Hong Kong MTR (January 2005)

Mainland wives' needs to get their children settled in Hong Kong schools and extracurricular activities, compounded by their needs to arrange for suitable housing or deal with other pressing family problems, brought wives into contact with many local people, policies, and government agents in "nervous" and "orderly" Hong Kong. Throughout the period of my field-work, my interactions with immigrant women reinforced this picture of women's activity in Hong Kong daily life: wives did the shopping, delivered and picked up children from school, visited social service centers, worked in restaurants or other jobs, performed volunteer work, and dealt with housing and health needs of the family as a whole. Men were generally absent both from informal and organized social activities; in many cases this was because men were out working (while women were out doing other things), but in other cases men preferred to stay at home and watch TV, either alone or in the company of extended family members. These general social patterns among lower-class and immigrant residents of Hong Kong are inter-esting, because they turn the often-held assumptions that attach men to the "public" sphere and women to the "private" sphere on their heads. Activities that are usually considered part of the "domestic" sphere, such as shopping, child care, and schooling, provided women with important opportunities for interacting with, and ultimately integrating with, local communities. As I documented in Chapter Four, the conflicts that took place between immigrant wives and their Hong Kong family members meant that immigrants were not always able to rely on their Hong Kong family members to teach them about the daily habits that differed in practice between life on the mainland and life in Hong Kong. As a result, mainland wives who needed to find schools for children, who needed to learn how to use local transportation, who needed to locate inexpensive sources of food, or who needed to find jobs and places to live or otherwise adapt to living in Hong Kong often turned to social workers for help, both for these everyday problems along with larger problems of serious marital discord and family disputes that commonly resulted when mainland wives joined their Hong Kong husbands after their long years of living separately.[1]

In this chapter, I discuss some of the basic problems of adapting to life in Hong Kong faced by mainland immigrant wives, and how wives' needs were met—or not met—through their interactions with Hong Kong social workers, who are funded by the government to aid immigrants' adjustment to Hong Kong. Focusing on local discourses that place high importance on the tropes of Hong Kong as a "nervous" and "orderly" city, I examine the ways in which the realities associated with these social imaginaries influenced immigrant women's interactions with social workers as one important aspect of their overall adjustment to Hong Kong life. I argue that tensions often accompanied social workers' attempts to aid immigrant women's processes of adaptation to Hong Kong because of the "cultural differences" that resulted from mainlanders' and Hong Kong people's orientations to space, time, and everyday social relations, but also because of the differences in expectations associated with the roles performed by government and other public officials in the Hong Kong and mainland contexts. Thus, although many mainland immigrants often admired social workers and the roles they played in helping immigrants adapt to life in Hong Kong, there were significant limitations to social workers' abilities to aid mainland wives. This chapter is the first of three in which I focus my ethnographic lens on the everyday interactions that took place between mainland immigrants and the Hong Kong government-funded social workers who, with their publicly mandated goals of maintaining social order and stability in Hong Kong, often served as immigrants' primary agents of introduction to the ideal qualities of civility associated with belonging in Hong Kong.

"Nervous" Hong Kong, "Nervous" Social Workers

At the time of my fieldwork, a range of social service organizations existed in Hong Kong to serve immigrant needs. While some were independently funded or housed within religious organizations, most, like the center where I did the bulk of my fieldwork, received at least partial funding through direct subsidies from the Hong Kong government. In the mid-1990s, with Hong Kong's return to mainland Chinese sovereignty just a few years away, the immigration issue between the mainland and Hong Kong had received extensive public attention and, as a result, increased government funding. This willingness to spend public funds to help immigrant adjustment had resulted in a proliferation of social service agencies serving immigrant needs in Hong Kong. The center where I did my research had also been affected by this support. The scope and range of services provided to immigrants had increased substantially to include not only casework, orientation tours, and language lessons for children (which had already been in place pre-1995) but also mutual help groups, family activities, employment seminars, and adjustment programs for immigrant children as well.

This center had been offering services to mainland Chinese immigrants in Hong Kong since the 1960s. While the goals of service provision had always focused on helping mainland immigrants adapt to Hong Kong society, the ways in which these goals were accomplished had changed over time. In its earliest years of operation, the center had mainly served as a "way-station" for Chinese immigrant arrivals needing lodging while attempting to get in contact with relatives in Hong Kong. Over time, increased funding from the Hong Kong government had enabled the center to begin providing educational and adjustment services for immigrants and had allowed for a significant increase in the center's staff. Throughout these changes, the center maintained a close relationship with the Hong Kong government, which, at the time of my fieldwork, continued to provide the bulk of the center's funding for its programs. Moreover, this center's links to the government were reinforced by its history of working in conjunction with the Hong Kong Immigration Department to provide services to newly arrived immigrants. Beginning in November 1969, at the request of Immigration Department officials, workers from the center began helping immigrants at key immigration checkpoints with their immediate needs and adjustment in Hong Kong (IDAR 1970:5). This close cooperation continued at the time of my fieldwork in the form of information desks at the Shenzhen/Hong Kong Lo Wu border crossing restricted area and the Immigration Department's office in Sham Shui Po.

Immigrants approached the social service center after having heard of it through one of several ways: when passing through the Lo Wu border checkpoint on their way into Hong Kong, while waiting for the processing of their ID cards at the Immigration Department, from outreach letters mailed to them at their homes, or from friends. Sometimes clients from previous years would return for help when new family members had just arrived or were about to arrive in Hong Kong. And, on several occasions that I witnessed, clients who had been helped in years past and who were no longer eligible for aid would come out of desperation, not knowing where else to go to get certain information. Sylvia, the center's administrator, was required to check all new clients' one-way permits and ID cards before referring them to a social worker. Funding stipulations not only required that only legal immigrants be served, but also limited service provision to immigrants who had resided in Hong Kong for one year or less. Although clients who could not produce the correct legal documentation were therefore not eligible for service, I was aware, at least once, of a social worker using her own discretion and choosing to "believe" that the client she was serving did in fact conform to stipulated guidelines.

Most clients who came to the center were looking to sign up for free or subsidized educational opportunities. Cantonese, English, and computer classes were always quickly filled, and students six to sixteen years old were also enrolled in the educational and life adjustment classes funded by the Department of Education. When immigrants' desired classes were not available through the center, clients would be given information about other educational opportunities, such as government sponsored training classes or adult education offered through Hong Kong's eight universities. A major concern of parents would be getting their children placed in school, and the social workers would provide as much guidance as they could about Hong Kong's school system, testing and entrance procedures, or advice about accepting certain school placements offered. Besides educational needs, pressing financial and housing difficulties were also common problems faced by clients so that much of the social workers' interaction with clients was spent helping them to resolve these issues of immediate need, either through aid in applying for welfare or advice in looking for jobs or a place to stay. Much less common were situations of family upset requiring counseling, such as bereavement, divorce, or severe disputes between family members, and, because the workers felt that these situations tested their skills as social workers and allowed them to become more deeply involved in the lives of their clients, all the social workers at the center agreed that they preferred working on these kinds of cases rather than just providing "resource" information and immediate aid to clients.

The most common interactions among social workers and immigrants focused around basic issues of service provision, and many of the basic services provided to immigrants by the center were tailored to help immigrants address their most immediate needs—often stemming from the "cultural differences" between local Hong Kong people and immigrants. These "cultural differences" were frequently described as resulting from Hong Kong's "nervous" society and included, for example, learning how to use Hong Kong's complex system of public transportation—where individuals needed to think quickly and yell loudly (in some cases) to be able to get off at appropriate stops. But there were also other markers of difference between Hong Kong people and mainlanders that did not stem from Hong Kong's "nervous" culture. In earlier chapters, I documented the history behind some of the very negative personal attributes associated with mainlanders (and thus with mainland immigrants) in general. These included attributes such as uncleanliness (related to the "dirty" immigrant stereotype personified in the 1980s TV character "Ah Chian"); greediness (associated with the perception that the mainland mistresses and wives of Hong Kong men were "gold diggers"); and backwardness (related to general perceptions that the mainland was less "developed," less "modern," and less "cosmo-politan" than Hong Kong). These perceptions of difference allowed for the association of mainlanders with particular kinds of hairstyles, clothing, and mannerisms, often seen as outmoded, frumpy, or in otherwise bad taste.[2] These sorts of appearance-related differences—which allowed mainlanders to be identified as nonlocals and therefore subject to the prejudicial atti-tudes of many Hong Kong people—certainly served as concrete "markers" that fostered and allowed for perceptions of difference between mainland-ers and Hong Kong people. I only knew one social worker—at a center far removed from the one where I conducted my primary fieldwork—who worked with immigrant wives on these appearance-related issues; however, the social workers I knew were very much concerned with helping their clients identify and change another important "marker" of distinction be-tween themselves and Hong Kong people—their language.[3]

In Hong Kong, the standard form of spoken Cantonese has some differ-ences with the Cantonese dialect spoken in Guangdong Province, where many wives learned Cantonese while waiting to immigrate to Hong Kong. Although most of the immigrants I encountered already spoke Cantonese well enough to make themselves understood in most everyday situations, some immigrants (who entered Hong Kong from northern areas of the mainland or who had lived their lives in very rural areas speaking only lo-cal dialects) did not. Whether an immigrant could speak and understand Cantonese as it is spoken in Hong Kong was an obviously important marker of difference that could be explained in cultural terms. At the social ser-vice center, as was also the case with daily interactions outside the center, all programs were carried out in Cantonese and all written materials used the "traditional," complex form of the Chinese written script used in Hong Kong and in Taiwan rather than the simplified form that has been taught and used on the mainland since the 1950s. Social workers and tutors alike would correct clients' language mistakes, particularly those made by chil-dren, such as one school-age boy who was chided for not knowing how to dis-tinguish between the two different forms of "thank you" used in Cantonese even after he had been living in Hong Kong for several months. (Whereas in Mandarin there is just one word to express "thank you," *xiexie*, in Can-tonese, a speaker must distinguish between *dojeh*, which is used to thank a superior or someone who has given you a gift, and *mgoi*, which is used to thank someone who has rendered you a service.) Even native speakers of Cantonese were not immune to language instruction in the localized, Hong Kong-style Cantonese, which is spoken at a very fast pace and incorporates many English and Japanese loanwords.[4] Most of the immigrants from Guangdong Province had watched enough Hong Kong television before their arrival in Hong Kong to know about and understand many of these local speech patterns, but teaching clients to use local terminology correctly—particularly for younger clients—was an important means of ensuring that they would be less likely to "stand out" as different from local people.

In addition to language instruction, one of the most common basic services offered to mainland immigrants at the social service center was a full-day orientation tour of one part of Hong Kong outside of the poorer, urban areas where many recently arrived immigrants lived. Each full-day tour, which cost only HK$20 (US$2.50) per participant (not including lunch), included stops at well-known tourist destinations around the region and a visit to an important government organization, such as the district police station or the ICAC (Hong Kong's official anticorruption institution). During the tours, a "tour guide" (one of the center's staff members) lectured about Hong Kong services and social life to their captive audience of immigrants as the bus toured from one location to the next. Driving past a university, for example, would result in a lecture about Hong Kong's educational and examination systems. Local housing issues were always addressed, and the distinct design differences between public and private apartment buildings would be used as a starting point for discussing the public housing application process and requirements. Similarly, passing a hospital would produce commentary about health care resources and services in Hong Kong, just as a visit to a temple would result in an introduction to common religious beliefs in Hong Kong. Highway trips entailed pointing out Hong Kong's different forms of public transportation as well as its transportation infrastructure, such as tunnels, and the types and method of payment used when traveling from one place to another. Trips to museums or the Peak on Hong Kong Island included information about Hong Kong's colonial past. Invariably, the districts of the region would be pointed out in passing, general characteristics of the area would be mentioned, and places of note, such as markets where goods could be bought very cheaply, would be commented on. While the information was never exactly duplicated from one trip to the next, the general impetus of this information was clear in every case: immigrants were always introduced to the cheapest and most convenient forms of services and recreation, even as they were meant to be impressed by the cosmopolitan nature of Hong Kong's colonial past, extensive educational system, and modern urban infrastructure.

On the one hand, the bulk of this practical information allowed immigrants to become more familiar with their new city of residence, which, like any big city, had a wide variety of communities, goods, services, and neighborhoods inhabited by people of different class and educational backgrounds. On the other hand, the particular aspects of Hong Kong daily life that were pointed out to immigrants—the universities, the public housing programs, the museums documenting local historical and cultural life, the sikh temple, the world-class hospitals, the racetrack and Jockey Club, and so forth—all reflected the fact that Hong Kong's current institutions and social life are based in a historical past that is significantly different from that of the mainland. Furthermore, that British colonial past is directly responsible for Hong Kong's development into its current form as a cosmopolitan center of international commerce and finance, where the everyday pace of life is "nervous."

Describing the transition from "premodern" to "modern" forms of capital accumulation, David Harvey has linked the particular modes of production associated with capitalism with faster-paced modes of thinking and acting than in the past. He writes:

> There is an omni-present incentive for individual capitalists to accelerate their turnover time *vis-à-vis* the social average, and in so doing to promote a social trend towards faster turnover times. Capitalism . . . has for this reason been characterized by continuous efforts to shorten turnover times, thereby speeding up social processes while reducing the time horizons of meaningful decision-making . . . The general effect, then, is for capitalist modernization to be very much about speed-up and acceleration in the pace of economic processes and, hence, in social life. (1990:229–30)

The words that my immigrant informants used to describe their first impressions of Hong Kong made explicit references to the speed and fast-paced lifestyle that they encountered there:

Everyone is hustling and bustling around (Cantonese: *Chungchung, mohng-mohng*); everyone is always in a hurry; it's nervous (Cantonese: *ganjeung*). (Allison)

On the mainland, if I really need some time to think over something well, there's lots of time to think before you have to do something. After you finish thinking, you still have time to decide if you've made the right decision. But in Hong Kong, there's no time to think over things. (May)

Go to work, get off work, go home, watch TV, eat dinner, go to sleep. But it's not like that where I am from. Work finishes earlier. After work, there are lots of places to be "happy" . . . where you can go and sing, dance, drink, and talk. (Amber)

In Hong Kong, the intensity and rapidity involved in capitalistic business and social relations, and in work output in general, are seen as distinctly different from mainland economic practices, even though businesses on the mainland are increasingly financed and run by Hong Kong and Taiwan businessmen and are currently changing in ways that make them much more similar to Hong Kong's particular brand of capitalism. Nonetheless, for Hong Kong social workers, the lessons that they taught immigrants about adapting to life in Hong Kong were related to Hong Kong's particular historical, economic, and social identity as a big city that is fundamentally different from the "big cities" on the mainland because of its colonialist and capitalist past. Social workers did recognize, however, that immigrants originating from urban areas of the mainland had significantly less difficulty adapting to Hong Kong's particular brand of "big city" life than those immigrants from rural areas.

The "culture of work" in Hong Kong was one aspect of "nervous" Hong Kong life that both social workers and immigrants singled out as differing greatly from that on the mainland. One important job for social workers was to help immigrants find employment in Hong Kong, and immigrants' comments on this subject demonstrated that they were fully cognizant of local Hong Kong ideologies that emphasized the importance of working, compared to the relative lack of value placed on wives' need to work on the mainland. Allison told me, "[On the mainland,] isn't it enough to have your husband support you? In Hong Kong, it's not the same. All young people, men and women, all work. You have to work. Your husband isn't rich, it's not right to not go out and work. So, I didn't want to come to Hong Kong." Another noted:

> There's not much pressure to work on the mainland . . . You think, "If there's work, I'll do it. If not, never mind." But Hong Kong's different. If you don't have a job, you have to keep searching until you find one. You have to find a job. But on the mainland, if you have a job or not, it's all the same. In Hong Kong you have to work . . . In Hong Kong, you have to think of money every minute of the day. On the mainland, you have your own house, there's no rent to pay. You can be more relaxed.

Furthermore, immigrant wives contrasted the style of work that they had experienced on the mainland to that of Hong Kong, where one's performance at work was judged primarily by how busy one seemed. On the mainland the pace of work was slower, English language skills were not required for blue-collar jobs, and employees were not subject to pressures as great as in Hong Kong. Amber noted:

> Working here is much harder [than on the mainland]. Because when I first came, I didn't think that [people in Hong Kong] would work that much. Just to watch them—it didn't seem like they were doing that much. But once I started working, it turned out that one person had to do so very many things . . . So I thought it was difficult (Cantonese: *sanfu*; Mandarin: *xinku*). It was pretty hard to adjust to. And time is so important here. Here, you can't waste time. You can't waste it. Everything is tightly scheduled— and even that's not enough . . . Hong Kong must be the busiest place in the world.

Echoing the same reasoning voiced by Hong Kong employers who refused to hire mainland immigrant employees, Amber and Cybil both told me that working on the mainland had done "nothing" to prepare them with the skills they needed to be successful in their Hong Kong jobs.

This same culture of "nervousness" that immigrants encountered when trying to find jobs in Hong Kong also shaped their interactions with social workers, whose ability to spend time with immigrants was sharply limited by government funding provisions that emphasized "quantity" over "quality" service provision. The funding system in place during the period of my fieldwork was a relatively new system in which the Hong Kong government's Department of Social Welfare provided "lump-sum" grants to service centers to provide particular resources to immigrant clients. This system, which reflected and reinforced capitalist practices in a social service provision environment, allowed the government significant discretion about selecting the most cost-efficient organizations for funding. As a result, this system created a competitive relationship among local service providers and also elevated tensions among the center's staff, many of whose contracts were dependent on this funding for their salaries. This funding system also dictated minimum numbers of clients who had to be served in particular capacities over the course of the year, requiring the center's workers to hold ever-increasing numbers of programs and constantly recruit new immigrant client participants for these programs. In this way, the system discouraged immigrant clients from repeatedly participating in similar types of programs. It also increased the amount of paperwork filled out by the center's workers, who were required to document, through statistical evidence, that the terms of their Funding Service Agreements had been met for each fiscal year. The sheer amount of time and energy spent on this paperwork was a constant source of griping by many of the center's employees, who felt that it would be better to spend their time interacting directly with clients. Longer-term employees complained that meeting the new quotas required not only an increased workload but also that some employees take on important responsibilities for which they had not been properly trained. Throughout the period of my fieldwork, this theme of "quantity" versus "quality," and the concomitant concern that quality interaction with clients was being sacrificed for constant increases in total numbers of clients served, were consistently raised by the center's staff.

On the one hand, this funding policy influenced social worker and immigrant interactions through the creation of incentives that encouraged strict time limits on social worker and client interactions. On the other hand, because service centers won funding agreements based on a "package" of services to be offered to immigrant (or other) clients, the "lump-sum" grant system allowed for the flexible use of resources—which many social workers found valuable.[5] Nevertheless, this government mandated aspect of service provision, which reinforced local ideologies of belonging, equating "fast" and "busy" work with "successful" work outputs, was off-putting to many immigrants who were not used to framing their personal and professional relationships with others at the same level of speed and systemization. Combined with the focus on bureaucratic routinization and rationalization that I discuss in the following section, these two tropes of "belonging" in the Hong Kong context reinforced the discourse of "difference" between Hong Kong people and mainlanders and often prevented the center's social workers from becoming deeply involved in their immigrant clients' lives.

"Orderly" Hong Kong

Besides an increase in the overall pace of life, both at work and in social relations more generally, theorists also commonly associate the rationalization of work and social practices with capitalist economies. Hong Kong people—both social workers and others—prided themselves on the fact that their everyday social and bureaucratic practices were more routinized and less focused on the kinds of particularistic personal ties that were seen as driving economic and social relations on the mainland (see, for example, Yang 1994 and Yan 1996). Social workers also focused on teaching immigrants about local ideas of order, rationality, and fairness, along with how to deal with Hong Kong-style bureaucracy. Learning about these aspects of Hong Kong life was an integral part of many of the basic service programs that I described in the last section and included, for example, knowing where to get the legal documentation that would enable recent immigrants to return to the mainland and knowing how to contact the police—along with other rules for safeguarding one's personal security—particularly from the many hazards (like fire and sexual abuse) common to the tenement buildings inhabited by immigrant women and children. Learning about legality and rationalization also took center stage in orientation visits around Hong Kong, which almost always included stops at the Sham Shui Po Police Station or the ICAC.

The thrust of anticorruption education in Hong Kong was aimed at preventing bribery or other corrupt practices within government departments and public bodies in order to "help keep Hong Kong fair, just, stable and prosperous" (ICAC 2000/01). Hong Kong officials and social workers perceived the common mainland practice of gift-giving (as a means to accomplish a desired bureaucratic goal) as deviant and unlawful, and they were concerned that mainlanders would be overly dependent on such practices in Hong Kong as well. At the ICAC, skits acted out on video by actors portraying both Hong Kong locals and immigrants provided concrete scenarios demonstrating that such mainland practices were illegal in Hong Kong's more "orderly" and "law-abiding" environment. In these skits, well-intentioned mainlanders were shown offering gifts to the authorities involved in order to reduce a local friend's wait at a doctor's office and to thank local Housing Department staff members after being allotted a particularly favorable public housing unit. In both cases, this behavior was chastised by local Hong Kong friends, and these well-meaning but poorly informed individuals were saved from being prosecuted for having committed illegal acts. Following the video, the ICAC's representative was careful to add one additional anecdote, in which an immigrant, who left a large "thank you" gift with a government representative and disappeared before the gift could be returned to the individual involved, was indeed reported to the authorities as having broken the law. In this case, the moderator highlighted the fact that all Hong Kong residents need to know, understand, and comply with all local laws. Should individuals unwittingly break the law, either through unhappy circumstance such as being tricked by locals who know better, or through ignorance, they are just as guilty under Hong Kong law as someone who knowingly commits a crime.

The message at the Police Station was similar: "Hong Kong is a place of well-regulated order and principle" (Cantonese: *Heunggong haih yat go yauh kwaigwei ge deihfong*), and it is the duty of Hong Kong people to help maintain that order, through their knowledge of and compliance with local laws. In this case, knowing traffic rules and regulations, the violation of which can endanger others as well as oneself, the acceptance of police authority, and the right of Hong Kong police to perform random ID card checks, were emphasized. Immigrants were told that all Hong Kong residents over the age of 15 must carry their ID cards with them at all times, thus facilitating police efforts to find and repatriate illegal residents of Hong Kong; and, as the representative made clear, this responsibility supersedes any familial or individual concerns.

These legalistic ideologies of belonging that championed rationality, fairness, and efficiency, like the ideologies of "nervousness" that I described in the previous section, were also reflected in the daily interactions that took place between social workers and their mainland immigrant clients. Clients were dealt with systematically, as new clients were first screened to make sure they met the center's service agreement requirements by Sylvia, the center's administrator, before being asked to wait for intake with a social worker. Calls to the center were handled efficiently, usually answered after the first or second ring, with any social or welfare worker available answering. This efficiency and systemization of worker/client interaction lent a certain air of mystique to the regular duties performed by the social workers and intimidated seated clients waiting for their turn to meet with a social worker. On any given day, only one worker in the office would be assigned to meet with new clients, so that many clients and their families had to wait for periods of up to (or exceeding) an hour to meet with a social worker. I always had trouble accepting such wait periods, which not only reflected the everyday practices of rationality and routinization that fit part and parcel with Hong Kong's overall work ethic but also seemed to be part of a built-in mechanism to ensure social distance between each worker and her client—part of the "fine line" that social workers walk between developing a level of trust and closeness with their clients while not sharing their own personal information with these clients. Nevertheless, the social workers' efficiency in dealing with clients was not just a product of Hong Kong and social work cultural practices; it was also a necessity, because of the sheer number of immigrant clients that social workers were responsible for helping.

With an average monthly intake of almost two hundred clients a month during the period of my fieldwork, the center's four social workers remained extremely busy (in actuality, and not just appearance) at all times. In addition to rotating office duties, such as client intake, the workers all had a number of individual case files they were following at any given time, as well as programs and activities to plan and run and paperwork to complete. Nonetheless, the social and cultural distance imposed by social workers on their immigrant clients during their meetings strongly contrasted with the friendly informality of the center's employee interactions within the office. The close spatial proximity in which everyone in the office worked, and the loose patterning of structure among employees within the office, encouraged friendly collaboration among employees who were often dependent on each other to fill in important details about the lives of clients. Social workers often relied, for example, on client updates from welfare workers and tutorial class teachers, whose daily contact with clients placed them in better positions to determine when a particular client might be at risk. Likewise, when a case was unusually troublesome, or a social worker was looking for guidance in a newly encountered situation, she would volunteer certain details for general discussion, which would then engage all office members. In this way, the internal workings of the office were characterized by an openness that, for immigrant outsiders, remained masked behind routine bureaucratic endeavors.

Routinization Without Standardization

Social workers at the service center cultivated a bureaucratic demeanor of efficiency that served to delineate their relationship with clients as "professional" rather than personal, and social work conventions, funding stipulations, and cultural norms in Hong Kong worked together to reinforce the aims of social workers in their professional interactions with clients. Immigrant clients, on the other hand, approached their interactions with social workers from their own socialization experiences on the mainland, which led them to expect more personal and particularistic relations with social workers, while also hoping that such meetings would lead to the resolution of important problems and, perhaps, to friendship. As a result, first meetings between social workers and their immigrant clients were at times upsetting for mainland wives already experiencing emotional and practical difficulties associated with immigrating to Hong Kong. These meetings often established a barrier of cultural difference between immigrants and social workers, whose "efficiency" upset immigrant clients who had not expected that their first meetings with social workers would be characterized with such bureaucratic "indifference" (Herzfeld 1992). Cybil, for example, described her first meeting with a social worker as having "broken her heart" (Cantonese: *dagitgwo ngohge sum*). Noting that she had only been in Hong Kong for two weeks when she first entered the center to approach the workers for help, Cybil felt that Emily, the social worker doing intake that day, was brusque with her. In particular, Cybil said that Emily disapproved of the fact that Cybil's husband had accompanied her to the center and indicated that Cybil should not be so dependent on him. Cybil, however, had felt that her husband's willingness to accompany her to the social service center was an important sign of support and a positive indicator of the strength of her and her husband's relationship. In all, it took over six months for Cybil to excuse Emily's response to her that day—a response in which Emily said things that, according to Cybil, "a social worker should not say."

Cybil was not my only immigrant informant who had a particular reaction—either positive or negative—to one of the social workers at the center. Many of the women I got to know during the period of my research developed a strong bond with one social worker in particular. These positive relationships were often described by my informants as having been the result of "fate" (Mandarin: *yuanfen*, Cantonese: *yuhnfahn*), while negative relationships were tainted by the suspicion that a certain social worker felt herself to be too important, busy, or culturally superior to treat these women with the attention they felt they deserved. There may have been a grain of truth to some of these suspicions; the social workers at the center were not only susceptible to Hong Kong people's biases against mainlanders in general but also—like most Hong Kong employees—faced serious time and financial pressures in their work environment that shaped the interactions they had with their immigrant clients. Nevertheless, the interactions among immigrants and social workers in Hong Kong's routinized, bureaucratic social work system were not completely standardized. As I describe below, social workers' individual personalities and immigrants' expectations about social workers—which differed strongly from Hong Kong social workers' views of their roles—meant that immigrants had widely varying experiences with and responses to the "orderly" system of social work provision once in Hong Kong.

Immigrants who came to the center looking for help in adapting to Hong Kong would necessarily have to interact with at least one of the center's four social workers. Although the four social workers at the center shared a strong commitment to meeting the needs of their clients in straightforward, positive, and efficient ways, they had nonetheless been motivated by different reasons to become social workers, and their individual personalities very much influenced the kinds of interactions they had with their clients. Elizabeth, the social worker in charge of the center, always struck me as being very respectful of her clients, and, with her calm, quiet, and polite tone, she managed to convey a sense of sincerity about her work that impressed her clients. As a teenager, she had been positively influenced by social workers who helped provide diversion and entertainment for residents living in the public temporary housing estate where she had grown up, so when she applied to university she chose social work as her field of interest. She had been working at the social service center for the six years or so since she had graduated from university, and she was both thoughtful and insightful about her work and her interactions with her clients. Comparing her manner of instructing clients to those of the other social workers in the office, she noted that she preferred to give her clients the "tools" to work a problem out for themselves. For example, if Elizabeth knew that a client would not qualify for social welfare but was still begging her to help apply, rather than simply saying she would not help, Elizabeth would indicate that the client did not seem to fit the guidelines for approval. If the client continued to insist that she help, then Elizabeth would provide the client with all the necessary information to apply and tell the client to go ahead and apply if she really wanted to, expecting that somewhere along the way the client would hear from enough sources that she didn't meet the qualifications that she would eventually accept her position. Elizabeth's interest in encouraging self-discovery among clients was fostered by her diplomacy, making her a generally successful mediator between both co-workers and clients.

Elizabeth's personal style with clients stood out in strong contrast to the manner exercised by Siu-saan, one of the other social workers, with her clients. Siu-saan had decided to become a social worker only after she had already been employed by the center's umbrella organization in an administrative capacity. Thus, she had spent ten years working at the organization, but only about half of that time as a social worker. Job stability had been one of Siu-saan's most important motivating factors in her pursuit of this career. In Hong Kong, social work is considered to be a stable, respectable, and well-paid profession. In 2001–02, social workers in Hong Kong earned from US$2,000 to US$5,000/month depending on their educational background and level of experience; even entry-level social workers received a higher salary than the Hong Kong average monthly salary of approximately US$1,500. Furthermore, the popularity of social work as a local profession was explained to me by one social work professor who noted that there are not many professions in Hong Kong where one gets to "have fun" and also "help people" at the same time. Although social work as I was familiar with it was not a profession that I had associated with "having fun," I was repeatedly cited examples of the kinds of family- and child-centered programs led by social workers as including elements of "fun" off-limits to most local white-collar workers.

Since Siu-saan had already been working alongside social workers when she decided to become a social worker, she was more aware than many new social workers of the hard work involved in the job. Nonetheless, she was less prepared to give up the idealism about helping others that she developed during her social work schooling for the practical realities of the daily grind of providing resource information and aid to new arrivals. Perhaps for this reason, Siu-saan most enjoyed working with children and occasional adult clients whose particular creative interests (and, in her words, "unspoiled" nature) she found attractive. With other clients, however—particularly those wanting to receive welfare benefits—Siu-saan's attitude was often abrupt and judgmental. Unlike Elizabeth, who had the patience to encourage clients to work out problems for themselves, in situations where Siu-saan knew that clients would not qualify for welfare or other benefits, she would tell them so bluntly and refuse further help. Several of my informants complained to me about Siu-saan's refusal to help them resolve their economic difficulties and then turned to social workers in other organizations for help instead. But Siu-saan's unfailing support of her favorite clients was equally extreme. One afternoon, when I sat down next to her to ask some questions, I saw that she was busy researching the United Nations regulations on the rights of the child. She planned (and did) use this research to petition the Social Welfare Department to provide money to an impoverished client who needed to buy formula for her infant. The petition was not successful, but the example is typical of the initiative and creativity which Siu-saan routinely applied to helping clients.

Siu-saan's straightforward nature and direct approach to telling clients exactly what she was thinking was emulated to some degree by Emily, the youngest worker at the center. Working with the immigrants at the center was Emily's first job out of university, and, as a result, she was concerned about seeming "too young" and was also impressionable, searching for models in the office to help her form her own philosophy for social worker/client interaction. Although she told me that she had been motivated to become a social worker both through a desire to address problems of social inequality and in the interest of job stability, other comments she made indicated the truly pragmatic way in which she had decided on her choice of profession. Despite the fact that her mother had immigrated to Hong Kong from China in the 1970s, Emily told me that before working at the social service center she, like the majority of Hong Kong's population, looked down on recent immigrants; nonetheless, realizing that she would have more job opportunities with this population, she purposefully chose to work with this client base. Her thinking about mainland immigrants had matured during the time she had been working at the center, however, and after a year of work there, she felt that she no longer harbored such prejudices. Emily's style of interaction with clients had also changed during that time: in contrast to her eagerness to help any client in any way just after her arrival at the center, eighteen months later she was primarily interested in challenging clients' thinking, wanting them to demonstrate their understanding of Hong Kong life and how to ameliorate their living situations in Hong Kong. In particular, her thoughts on clients' overreliance on government welfare benefits echoed those most often expressed by Siu-saan (for an in-depth discussion of this topic, see Chapter Seven). But like Elizabeth, she was also aware of struggling with the apparent contradiction of needing to develop a trusting relationship with clients without revealing much about herself or her own prejudices about their life choices.

Despite the sincerity with which Emily approached her profession, my immigrant informants reacted negatively to their interactions with Emily more than with any other social worker. It was not only Cybil who complained that Emily did not convey an attitude encouraging trust or caring during their initial meeting. My immigrant informant Allison also had a similarly negative reaction to the way Emily talked to her, feeling that Emily was simply performing a job that was required of her and that Emily did not respect her—treating her conspicuously differently than Allison felt she would have treated someone else from Hong Kong. In both cases, these mainland wives complained that, among other things, Emily did not smile at them during intake and that she seemed strict. Emily, in turn, told me that because she was so young—often considerably younger than her clients—maintaining an attitude of sternness was the only way she could impress upon her clients that she knew what she was talking about and that they should take her seriously. Perhaps, however, clients sensed a change in Emily as she became more comfortable in her job, or perhaps Emily loosened up with long-term clients in her interactions with them over time. Months after their initial upsetting interactions with Emily, both Cybil and Allison independently told me that they had revised their negative impressions of Emily and attributed their earlier impressions about her as unfriendly to the fact that Emily must have been having a "bad day" when they first met her.

In contrast to criticisms about their interactions with Emily, my immigrant informants almost unanimously praised Alexa's attitude in her relationships with them. Alexa was a woman who had taken a less conventional approach toward her education and career than many Hong Kong professionals do. Her adult working life had taken several different twists and turns, although the underlying theme of her work life was always that of helping others. Before starting at the social service center, where she had been working for two and a half years when I left, she had spent many years working with handicapped children; she had been certified to teach young children before going back to school to get a degree in social work. Her previous jobs had allowed her to interact with many different kinds of people, children and adults, handicapped and healthy, in China, Hong Kong, and Western countries, and the maturity and insight that she had gained from these interactions shaped her views in dealing with the center's immigrant clients as well. She had, she told me, chosen social work as a career because it is a profession, not just "a job." And her professional attitude carried over into her interactions with immigrants, who repeatedly told me that they felt Alexa to be sympathetic to their needs and concerns, that they liked the quality of her voice, and they felt that she treated them as "equals." Indeed, Alexa characterized her style of interacting with clients as that of "collaboration," working together with each individual client in order to develop that client's strengths. She also emphasized the sincerity with which she approached each client and that client's problems. Unlike most Hong Kong people who were intent on delineating their differences from the immigrants as part of the "othering" process inherent in the legal and social exclusion of this group from locals, Alexa noted that these immigrants were, above all else, "people," and, as such, deserved the respect and equality with which she treated them.

Overall, the center's close relationship to the Hong Kong government, its dependence on the government's "lump-sum" funding provision, and the personal importance placed by the center's social workers on maintaining professional relationships with their clients through their systematic and efficient daily routines, meant that immigrants needed to "adjust" to social workers and Hong Kong government methods of service provision, just as they had to adjust to other aspects of life in "nervous" and "orderly" Hong Kong. Yet their adjustment to social workers' attitudes and social work provision in Hong Kong was crucial, because immigrant wives relied upon these individuals and services for help obtaining many of their basic needs, including learning how to get around Hong Kong, how to find schools for children, how to find and keep jobs, and how to speak Cantonese and English. On the mainland, immigrant wives had not had access to social workers; moreover, the interactions they were used to having with officials (government or otherwise) were often based on particularistic ties rather than the ideologies of "rationality," "fairness," and "law and order" that characterized Hong Kong bureaucracy and daily life. As a result, immigrants' interactions with social workers were also strongly influenced by their reactions to the individual personalities and attitudes of the social workers they met. In these cases, the local funding climate—which had caused the proliferation of many centers offering some form of services to recent immigrants in Hong Kong—worked to immigrants' advantages. Like savvy shoppers who search for the best "deal" on certain goods, my immigrant informants picked and chose which resources they felt best served their needs among multiple social workers and service centers. Searching not only for the services that would help them adapt but also for social workers whose personalities they liked, many immigrants seemed to have little difficultly navigating Hong Kong's complex world of service provision, where they did sometimes find what they were seeking.

Personal Ties Versus Rationalization:
Immigrants' Views of Social Workers

What were immigrants' views of the social workers they met? What were the expectations that mainland wives had about the roles that social workers would play for them in Hong Kong? Overall, immigrant women—perhaps because of their expectations of particularistic ties, or perhaps because they really lacked other networks of support in Hong Kong—seemed to expect a level of potential constant support usually associated with friendship. These expected roles contrasted strongly with those assumed by Hong Kong social workers, with their focus on professionalism, routinization, and efficiency. While one important goal that social workers had was to increase immigrant women's networks through encouraging women to form ties among themselves, these goals were not necessarily realized, creating an even greater desire on the part of immigrant wives to have social workers fulfill this role. One informant, for example, explained: "I've met some friends by coming [to the center] here . . . But we don't often talk on the phone . . . I never know what to say . . . I'll take out my phone—I have their phone numbers. I could call, but it seems like there's nothing to talk about. I don't know what to talk about." Although social workers supplied many other kinds of support to their needy immigrant clients—such as helping them receive basic language training, introducing them to Hong Kong social and cultural life, and aiding them in finding jobs—social workers never intended to act as "friends" to their clients, whom, consciously or not, they rarely even treated as equals. As a result, the potential for misunderstanding about these roles between Hong Kong social workers and their immigrant clients remained significant.

My immigrant informant clients who did develop closer relationships with at least one of the social workers at the center praised the general role of social workers in society, tended to see their work as important and busy, and said that they felt encouraged by the help they had received from them. One woman, for example, told me, "I think it is great that Hong Kong has this kind of [social work] service available. If there's something that you can't solve yourself, social workers can help you. And if you need to find something, find a school, social workers can help you." At the same time, however, women also demonstrated some ambivalence about the extent to which they would actually involve a social worker in the details of their private lives. Another informant explained:

> I don't have a good impression of the social worker I've talked with. Her attitude is bad, and—when you look at her face—it looks as if she has many problems weighing on her. For example, if you are already feeling unhappy and you go talk to her—when you see her face, and you see she looks even more unhappy than you are, then you don't want to tell her anything.

Although many of the immigrant women, like Amber, noted that there were no "social workers" on the mainland, they indicated that they had heard about social workers either from friends or by watching Hong Kong television programs on the mainland before coming to Hong Kong. One of the tutors at the center, an immigrant from the mainland who had arrived in Hong Kong just months before my research at the center began, identified the old women, or "aunties," of mainland neighborhood committees as serving a role similar to that of social workers in Hong Kong—with one main difference being that these women would approach neighborhood residents rather than rely on being approached, as in the Hong Kong professional social service model. As a result, some immigrant women may have been uncomfortable with the need to initiate this interaction. One informant, who confirmed this view, said: "Some social workers are really friendly and will ask you, 'Is there anything you need help with? How are things going? Are you adjusting to Hong Kong?' . . . Some of them are more reserved and won't actively start a conversation with you. I prefer it when someone actively talks to me. If she doesn't say anything, then I don't want to say anything either." None of the immigrant clients at the center, however, made a connection between these "aunties" and their Hong Kong social workers in their conversations with me. Whether this was because many of the women clients I knew had originally come from rural areas where they had not experienced such neighborhood committees, or because they viewed these professional Hong Kong social workers with a certain degree of awe, I am not sure.

During the period of my fieldwork, I commonly heard Hong Kong locals refer to the work performed by social workers described as "great" or "mighty" (Cantonese: *waihdaaih*). My immigrant informants also used this word to talk about social workers and their important work of helping others and maintaining social order and stability. May, for example, likened the services performed by social workers to those of the martyr Lei Fung, whose heroic feats of self-sacrifice for the good of others were promoted by the CCP as an example to be followed by all citizens. She told me:

> Before I came to Hong Kong, I hadn't thought about [social workers], because we don't have social workers on the mainland. After I came to Hong Kong, I thought Hong Kong social workers reminded me of a song we sang on the mainland—have you heard it? About Uncle Lei Fung? A really,

really long time ago, even before we were born, there was a person who always went out of his way to help others. He helped anyone who needed help. No matter what problem, he would help you. You probably haven't heard it—it was a long time ago before we were born . . . But this is what Hong Kong social workers are like. In the end, if you have a problem, they are willing to help you. Unless you aren't willing to talk to them. As soon as you talk to them, it's ok.

Amber also described social workers in glowing terms: "I've really seen that social workers can really help you. When I've talked with [one of the social workers], she's helped me see that some of my thinking is wrong. She's showed me how to think about things from a different point of view. [Social workers] can think of ways to comfort you, to help you. I think social workers are great." She also told me that being a social worker required certain qualities that not just anyone could fulfill, since to be a social worker one needed to be well-educated, patient, sincere, warm, and able to explain something carefully and persistently over a long period of time. Nonetheless, to my knowledge, Amber never fully confided in any of the center's social workers about her unhappy living situation with her husband, whom she was contemplating leaving when I left Hong Kong in July 2002. Content to limit her interaction with social workers to the garnering of practical local knowledge learned through her participation in some of the center's language classes and volunteer activities, Amber felt the need to resolve her problems personally rather than through reliance on social workers.

Cybil, likewise, valued the information she learned through her discussions with some of the center's workers, but she also remained cynical about the degree to which a social worker could actually help her resolve her personal feelings of upheaval resulting from her interactions with her Hong Kong family members. Noting that the social workers were "on vacation," out of the office, or otherwise occupied most of the time, Cybil felt there were real obstacles to initiating and maintaining an in-depth discussion with any of the center's social workers at a time when she would be most upset. She cited, in particular, the fact that she could very much have benefited from a social worker's advice following some serious arguments she had with her Hong Kong in-laws late at night during the Lunar New Year holiday. Had she been able to reach a social worker at that time—which was impossible on two counts, because of the lateness of the hour and because of the holiday—she would not have felt the need to "run away" to the mainland. Had she been able to reach a social worker at that time, she might have stayed in Hong Kong for the holiday and dealt with the problems she was experiencing with her family members in a more coherent way.

Unlike Amber and Cybil, other clients with specific needs would frequently use the center's resources to their advantage but continued to search for a more meaningful relationship with a social worker at another organization. May, for example, had developed a close relationship with a social worker at another center. May treated this social worker both as a personal friend as well as her primary source of local information and problem solving. Another immigrant, A-Chun, participated in organizational activities in at least five different community and church-affiliated centers in the poor, urban area of Hong Kong where she lived. A-Chun was conscious of the important contribution that each organization had made to her overall adjustment in Hong Kong, such as providing after-school tutoring help or recreation for her children, volunteer activities and opportunities for her to learn about different aspects of Hong Kong life, and access to women's groups and language learning. Nonetheless, she had also found one particular social worker with whom she had developed a close relationship. She told me that she felt really free to talk to this person—more so than any of the other social workers she had encountered. This particular social worker made her feel comfortable, took time to answer her questions, filled out forms for her when needed, and called her frequently to check up on her. A-Chun remained grateful for the support and kindness that this worker had shown her, feeling that this interaction, combined with the advantages of making use of the different resources offered at multiple local centers, had substantially contributed to her "successful" adjustment to her new life in Hong Kong.

In many situations, immigrant clients were genuinely grateful for the support they received from their social workers during the initial period of their adaptation to life in Hong Kong. Many of the basic services provided by social workers were also perceived as helpful by the clients, particularly the basic Cantonese and English language skills and other local resource information recognized as relevant to the successful accomplishment of their everyday life needs. Yet even immigrants' acceptance of such practical advice depended on their impressions of and trust in the particular social workers with whom they interacted. In cases where the personalities of the social worker and client were not mutually agreeable, clients were more likely to ignore the information given to them by their social workers or simply omit details of their lives that they were reluctant to share with their social workers. Immigrants' conscious refusal to engage with social workers may have stemmed from the realization that their social workers were, like the rest of Hong Kong's population, often "typecasting" them into certain cultural, social, and economic niches that reinforced their positions as marginalized members of Hong Kong society—positions which, although often true, were particularly difficult to accept because they conflicted with immigrants' dreams and desires for their new lives in Hong Kong.

The Limits of Social Work

Many immigrant wives were less successful in adapting to Hong Kong life than A-Chun, May, Amber, and Cybil. The long waiting periods endured by women before they were able to immigrate to join husbands in Hong Kong, coupled with the downward mobility, prejudice, and social marginalization that they faced once in Hong Kong, created serious family rifts that social workers, however hopeful, might not be able to solve. These problems were compounded by the cultural differences that women encountered through their interactions with their Hong Kong social workers, including the rationalization, routinization, and efficiency of social work provision; the emphasis on "quantity" versus "quality" provision; and the disappointment that resulted when social workers did not act as "friends" or provide the particularistic service provision expected by immigrants. With some of my informants, it was clear that the busy nature of the office, or the perceived brusque manner of the social worker they met for intake, put them off from telling much detail about their lives, even when social workers encouraged them to say more.

In cases where immigrants disagreed with, or simply did not accept, what their social workers told them, they would often "disappear" from the range of social worker involvement. Immigrants did this in several ways.

Like Cybil and Amber, they could continue to interact with workers at the center but not reveal the real problems they were experiencing. In other cases, they would reject information given to them by social workers. In one case, for example, a social worker had opened a case file for a woman and her six-year-old son who had some, as the social worker said, "very small" problems, such as the child refusing to feed himself and occasionally hitting his mother. But this same social worker was unwilling to help this mother with any financial-related problems, saying that the family was "well-enough" off and not eligible for welfare benefits. The child's mother, who was both upset and angry that the social worker would help her with one problem but not the other (more pressing, in her mind) issue, gave vent to her frustration one afternoon after a meeting of my English class—after first taking the precaution of closing the slim door between the classroom where we were meeting and the rest of the office—and immediately solicited her classmates for the contact information of social workers they had found helpful. Women often looked for social workers at other centers who might be more inclined to help them or with whom they could develop a better rapport. In extreme cases, however, women might completely refuse to engage with social workers and would return to the mainland—either temporarily or for a longer time—leaving confused family members with problems to sort out in their wake.

A few months into my fieldwork, it became clear there was something seriously worrying one of the young women who frequented many of the center's programs. Tall, with an engaging, open smile, this woman had recently joined her husband and young son in Hong Kong after having lived in Shenzhen—where she had migrated as a teenager—for ten years. Originally an engaged and communicative member of my English class and another mutual help group in which I was participating, this woman became quiet and morose and refused to say what was bothering her, even when Cybil once asked her directly what was wrong. The last time I saw this woman, she was sitting in one corner of the service center, visibly crying while talking with one of the center's social workers. Following this meeting, she left the center and did not return, despite repeated attempts by the social worker to encourage her to do so. Because I knew this woman, her social worker told me that she was upset because her husband had left her and had taken their son with him. Although he had called her, and she could also reach him on his cell phone, she did not know where he was. The social worker had tried to get her to explain why her husband had left, but the woman had not responded.

Over the next few days, the social worker was able to learn more about her client's situation. The woman had returned to Shenzhen to be with her friends and her "support network," but she had also called the social worker and had left a message asking her to help contact her husband. After speaking to both the woman and her husband several times, the social worker had heard both their stories—which contained few (if any) points of agreement. The woman claimed that her husband never gave her spending money and that he wanted a divorce. Her husband, on the other hand, said that she had asked him for an unreasonable sum of money, HK$1,000,000 (US$129,000), and that she had asked for a divorce. When asked why he had taken the son away and left the house, he said that his wife was so unhappy that he had taken the boy away out of fear for his safety. Later, both the husband and son came up to the office to talk with the social worker, although the woman refused to return from the mainland to speak with her husband in person, saying that she was afraid that he would hit her. The social worker continued to urge her client to return to Hong Kong to work her problems out with her husband in person, but her client never came back and eventually stopped calling the social worker.

In this situation, the social worker was primarily concerned that the parents should try to reconcile their differences without harming their child. She told me, however, that it was common in this kind of argument to use children as "pawns"—although a more usual scenario entailed one parent taking children back to the mainland where they could not be reached or found by a Hong Kong parent. There was never a question of this particular incident being a kidnapping, which would require it being reported to the police, since the husband had his mobile phone and could always be reached even though his wife did not know exactly where he was. On the other hand, the woman's mobile phone did not connect once she returned to the mainland, and she never gave the social worker another phone number to reach her, so that the social worker could not reach her client. Although the social worker remained concerned about her client, she was realistic in accepting the limitations involved in helping her: she could not locate her client if she did not want to be located, and, as the social worker had no means of initiating communication with the client, she could not open a case file for her.

In later conversations, this social worker told me that one of the biggest differences between "social work" as she had experienced it as a student and as a professional social worker lay in the realization of the limitations involved with helping clients and in her acceptance of these limitations. In some situations, such as the one just detailed, these limitations stemmed from a client's refusal to participate in mediation with the social worker. In other cases, however, these limitations resulted from the code of ethics adhered to by all social workers, which includes not passing judgment on others and not imposing individual values on clients. She noted another case she had encountered several years earlier as an example of the kinds of personal dilemmas social workers can face in their interactions with clients. In that case, an older woman who had come to Hong Kong with two children had been abandoned by her husband in all but their actual legal tie of marriage. Although they lived in the same apartment, he refused to support her or help in any way with their two children. After almost two years of helping this client adjust to her difficult living situation, the social worker had formed the strong opinion that this woman would be much better off, both emotionally and financially, if she divorced her husband; however, her social work code of ethics barred her from actively advocating that her client divorce her husband. Over time, her interactions with this client became increasingly difficult, until her client came to the conclusion herself that she should get divorced—at which point the social worker was able to help her with the formalities involved. This client continued each year to send this social worker a Christmas card thanking her for her help in greatly improving her life.

There were, however, other reasons that affected social workers' abilities to help their immigrant clients, and these often stemmed from conflicts between social workers' and clients' assessments of what problems immigrants had and how those problems might be resolved. At times, these differences were related to the "cultural differences" between Hong Kong people and mainlanders; in other cases, they stemmed from the different expectations and empirical orientations of immigrants and social workers. Social workers' goals for defining and solving everyday problems in adapting to life in Hong Kong often stood in stark contrast to the goals that immigrants had before coming to Hong Kong, when "dreams" had figured large in women's calculations about their future lives in Hong Kong. "Dreams" did not, however, fit into social workers' conceptions of immigrant needs. As a result, tensions often developed between immigrants and social workers, whose practical approaches to learning about and understanding local life were not always valued by their clients. In particular, social workers often assumed that immigrants' personal difficulties in marriage and family life in Hong Kong were directly related to the "cultural differences" that existed between mainlanders and Hong Kong people. Since social workers assumed that such problems would gradually resolve themselves as women became more accustomed to Hong Kong ideologies of belonging, marital problems were not always treated with the priority that immigrant women felt they deserved. Such was the case with May, whose otherwise supportive social worker disagreed with her over the subject of divorce.

Several months after immigrating to Hong Kong, May told me that she was upset because she wanted her social worker to help her obtain a divorce from her Hong Kong husband, but her social worker would not help her do this. May felt that her husband was unhelpful, noncommunicative, and unhappy, and the family's recent move into a public housing flat had not seemed to help. Moreover, May was worried that her husband, who had lost his job shortly after her arrival in Hong Kong, was still not working, nor would he help out around the house while May was at work. May's social worker, attempting to address May's concerns, met with May and her husband on one home visit. On that visit, May's husband was, in May's words, "uncharacteristically" communicative, and May's social worker gained the impression that he was "not that bad." In talking with me later, May's social worker justified her refusal to consider May's reasons for divorce by explaining that the main problems facing May and her husband were the result of "cultural differences." These "cultural differences" included, for example, May's inability to understand why her husband was not willing to sell his valuable stamp collection, even though the family was in desperate need of money, and the fact that May's husband was Protestant, while

May's religious background was the more "traditional" worship of gods and ancestors. Unlike some other women in similar situations, May continued to rely heavily on her social worker for advice and support even though she disagreed with her social worker's assessment of her and her husband's problems. More important in May's eyes was the fact that she had found with this social worker the opportunity for personal engagement that eluded so many of the relationships between social workers and their mainland immigrant clients in Hong Kong.

Adapting to Life in Hong Kong

At the time of my fieldwork in Hong Kong, the population was officially listed as 95 percent ethnically Chinese—making that population—at least on paper—significantly more "homogenous" than most cosmopolitan world cities.[6] Nevertheless, there were indeed strong delineations of social and cultural difference—not only between Hong Kong and mainland Chinese, but also among Chinese of different regional backgrounds and other minority groups, particularly the Filipina and Southeast Asian domestic helpers and European and American expatriates. Despite this ethnic diversity, mainland immigrants certainly faced pressures from the majority of Hong Kong's population to conform to "mainstream Hong Kong" idealized qualities of civility—which included, for example, conforming to local ideologies of work and busyness, obeying all laws, and refusing to engage in bribery and gift giving—and which were often articulated through the discourses of "nervousness" and "order" that I have described in this chapter. In many cases, social workers also shared these goals for their immigrant clients. Social workers not only worked to help immigrants adapt to the cultural differences they encountered in Hong Kong; they also hoped to influence the ideas and behavior of their clients to allow them to fit into these particularly Hong Kong ways of thinking and being in the world.

Although the social workers I knew in Hong Kong ultimately hoped that mainland immigrants would become integrated (Cantonese: *yungyahp*) with the local Hong Kong population, the funding and time constraints imposed on their work meant that, in reality, in a best case scenario they could only hope to help their immigrant clients adapt (Cantonese: *sikying*) to their new lives in Hong Kong. One social worker explained to me what she meant by these terms. Adaptation involved getting used to living in a new environment. To say that a person had "adapted" meant that she or he had begun going to school or work in Hong Kong and could function on a daily basis—buying food, riding local transportation, making sure the family's daily needs were met, and communicating with locals. On the other hand, this routine involvement in local life did not necessarily mean that a person had integrated into a place. Social workers' definitions of *integration* meant that a person had changed attitudes and behavior to fit more in line with local ideologies of belonging. In other words, by integrating locally, an immigrant went a step beyond adapting; in addition to just being able to get by and function on an everyday level, the person had local friends, interacted on a daily basis with a variety of local people, and became involved in local networks and organizations in a meaningful way. This in-depth interaction worked, on the one hand, to change individuals' ways of thinking and acting so that they appeared more like locals and less like "others." On the other hand, integrating into local life in this way did not necessarily entail a shedding of previous values and beliefs.

This social worker drew on the example of her family to illustrate the practical distinctions among these terms. She noted that her father—despite having lived in Hong Kong for over twenty years—had adapted to life in Hong Kong without ever having integrated into local life. Although he worked in Hong Kong, he had no local friends outside of his co-workers, and he spent all of his time with his family when not working. She contrasted his situation with that of her own, in which she had been educated in local schools, and all of her professional and personal interactions were involved with other Hong Kong local people; indeed, she considered herself to be a local person. Overall, this social worker felt that many men who had immigrated to Hong Kong from the mainland in past decades had lived lives similar to that of her father and had never fully integrated into Hong Kong life, despite having lived and worked there for twenty years or longer.

The social workers I knew all shared goals of helping their immigrant clients integrate to Hong Kong life. In particular, they hoped to facilitate the integration of immigrant wives, who spent much of their days interacting with Hong Kong people, administrators, and officials while shopping, arranging for housing, looking for educational opportunities, and otherwise meeting their own and their children's everyday needs. Instead, the limitations of social work provision in Hong Kong meant that social workers had to focus the majority of their attention on merely helping immigrants adapt to their new lives. Ever practical, social workers knew that the only way for immigrants to cease being targeted as "different" from the remarkably homogenous general local population was for these immigrants to be taught the particular skills linked to local ideologies of belonging— including the discourses of "nervousness" and "order"—that would enable them to interact unobtrusively with local Hong Kong people. Such skills included the ability to deal with everyday bureaucratic norms, to navigate the city's complex infrastructure of public transportation, to understand traffic regulations, to speak Cantonese with Hong Kong "characteristics," and to find and maintain jobs. These practical skills, along with the everyday knowledge relating to these most basic aspects of Hong Kong life, were not only emphasized in the most routine encounters between social workers and their immigrant clients but were also reinforced through the routinization, efficiency, and busyness that characterized social service provision.

The limitations of social worker involvement in immigrant women's lives were ultimately inseparable from the larger issue of "political difference" between the mainland and Hong Kong, where capitalism and colonialism had helped shape a local culture of work that emphasized rational and routinized professional interactions over personalistic ties, along with fast-paced outputs, efficiency, flexibility, and the value of "quantity" over "quality." These ideologies of belonging in Hong Kong were linked to more abstract concepts of the qualities associated with membership in the Hong Kong polity, but they also created very real differences of "culture" between Hong Kong and the mainland, where citizens living in these two places had developed different orientations to space, time, and expectations for encounters with bureaucratic norms. These ideologies and actualities of difference, which were reflected in women's struggles to adapt to Hong Kong, also shaped immigrant women's everyday experiences of adaptation. Some women were more able than others to adapt to these conditions of difference, perhaps because of their individual personalities, attitudes, and life experiences, but also because they were able to establish personal—and particular—relationships with social workers who provided them with the support and practical skills women needed. In other unfortunate cases, the limits of social work provision in Hong Kong meant that some desperately needy women were not able to get the support they required.

In Chapters Six and Seven, I continue to explore how ideologies of membership and belonging in Hong Kong shaped the immigration experiences of the mainland wives of Hong Kong men. In these chapters, I focus on two significant themes—parenting and responsibility—that informed immigrant and social worker interactions over the period of my research. Through these themes, social workers sought to teach their immigrant clients more than just the practical skills that women would need to adapt to Hong Kong life. Instead, social workers hoped to help immigrants actually begin to integrate into Hong Kong life.

SIX

Fashioning (Reunited) Family Life

For over one thousand years, China's political culture linked effective and peaceful state governance to Confucian principles idealizing the harmonious regulation of family relationships (Glosser 2003). These principles established rules outlining the interactions among family members as hierarchical, with fathers and husbands dominating over children and wives. Respect for elderly family members, in the form of filial piety, was of paramount importance.

One result of this strong philosophical connection between "family and state order" (ibid. 5) has been that Chinese reformers in the late nineteenth and twentieth centuries consistently targeted "the family" as an important site for engineering social change. Chinese "self-strengthening" movements in the late 1800s, which were aimed at "modernizing" China's citizenry and thus enabling the country to withstand political assaults from both Japanese and Western imperialism, focused in part on reforming women's roles in Chinese family and social life (Judge 2002). Women were encouraged to contribute to China's social development, and one important part of this contribution entailed the formative influence of mothers in raising their children—the next generation of "citizens" (ibid.). After the fall of the Qing dynasty in 1911, political activists in Republican China:

> seized upon family reform as the key to unlocking the potential of China's youth and rebuilding their shattered nation. They accused the traditional patriarchal family of sacrificing China's youth on the altar of filial obligation, teaching them dependency, slavishness, and insularity, and robbing them of their creative energy. In its place they advocated the Western conjugal family ideal . . . , an ideal that promoted free marriage choice, companionate marriage, and economic and emotional independence from the family [which] had made the countries of the West strong because it encouraged productivity, independence, and civic virtue. In short, they hoped to restore China by destroying the traditional family and rebuilding it according to Western blueprints. (Glosser 2003:3–4)

The "family" has continued to be a political target in China since the founding of the PRC in 1949. Political movements to effect major social change in the PRC have included the dismantling the nuclear family in favor of the creation of a national socialist "family" during the Great Leap Forward (1959–62), sending urban youth to the countryside to perform hard labor and attacking "bourgeois" family forms during the Cultural Revolution (1966–76), and controlling population growth through the "one-child" policy (1981–present). Despite these major and sustained attacks on the "traditional" Chinese family concept, I found that both Chinese immigrants and social workers in Hong Kong all subscribed to a shared set of values that idealized "traditional" Chinese family life. Such views remained contested at the level of the everyday interactions between social workers and their clients, whose mutually contrasted life and educational experiences necessarily influenced their perceptions of this ideal. Nevertheless, this ideal served as a presumed sense of unity among these two groups of PRC citizens, even in the face of the many other actual and discursive differences among these citizens that otherwise excluded mainland immigrants from idealized conceptions of membership in the Hong Kong polity.

In this chapter, I focus my discussion around this assumed presumption of unity centering on idealized conceptions of Chinese family life as one means of highlighting the disjunctures that existed between Hong Kong social workers' and mainland immigrants' goals for socializing children in

Hong Kong. Both immigrants and social workers had certain hopes for immigrant children's socialization in Hong Kong, but immigrants' and social workers' ideas about what that socialization should entail, or how it should be achieved, did not always coincide. In particular, mainland wives placed their hopes and dreams on their children's future success and, most notably, on children's scholastic accomplishments in Hong Kong. Social workers, on the other hand, were much more focused on changing mothers' ideologies of parent/child relations—ideologies judged by social workers to be overly "passive," in which mothers "managed" their children's behavior through reliance on "traditional" concepts of obedience and authority. Focusing on their concerns that reliance on these kinds of parenting behaviors would exacerbate family conflict and threaten the social cohesion, harmony, and well-being of immigrant families—and, by extension, Hong Kong society as a whole—social workers drew on Hong Kong government-sponsored "Family Life Education" programs to encourage immigrant mothers to adopt Western-influenced models of parent/child relations that advocated the empathic and "open" communication between parents and children that were championed by many Hong Kong people and government representatives as part of the social imaginary of belonging in Hong Kong. In this way, Hong Kong social workers sought to reinforce the "traditional" Chinese family values of harmony and cohesion while concomitantly helping immigrant mothers and children to integrate into Hong Kong-based ideologies of Chinese "family values" that differed in important ways from immigrants' and older Hong Kong residents' understandings of these values. Overall, I argue that Hong Kong social workers desired to implement change in "traditional" Chinese familial and interpersonal relations—changes that they linked to Hong Kong's continued social stability and prosperity and which they believed would lead to improved familial relationships among all Hong Kong people, not just their immigrant clients.

Separation and Reunion in Chinese Family Life: Actual Hardships, Imaginary Ideals

In his analysis of Chinese individuals living on the mainland and Taiwan, Charles Stafford has linked the strong focus on the underlying symbolic ties of family unity in the Chinese cultural context to the mitigation of difficult life experiences and other problems arising from separations among both the living and the dead (Stafford 2000:163). For my informants, separations from their husbands, children, and other family members were indeed problematic for them in actuality, and most immigrants I knew in Hong Kong voiced considerable emotion about the separations they had endured while waiting to immigrate to Hong Kong. Allison, for example, had made the difficult decision to send her adopted five-year-old daughter back to Sichuan to live with her parents so that she could move to Hong Kong and live together with her husband there, rather than having him continue to commute back and forth between her apartment in Shenzhen and his work in Hong Kong. May and her children continued to feel the effects of their periods of separation as well. May's seven-year-old daughter, who was born in Hong Kong and was thus a Hong Kong permanent resident, had been living in Hong Kong with May's husband's family for five years, since she was two and a half. Without her mother, however, May's daughter received little support, supervision, or guidance, and her grades at school were very poor—a source of concern for both May and her daughter. May also experienced a period of separation from her three-year-old son after she received her one-way permit and moved to Hong Kong to look for work and take care of her daughter. During this separation, May's son exhibited many health and emotional problems—including bed-wetting, frequent bouts of crying, and intense insecurity—all of which worried May terribly and affected her ability to make level-headed choices about employment and other daily life necessities in Hong Kong.

Even my informants who had enjoyed the freedom they experienced while living alone on the mainland after their children had already immigrated to Hong Kong still suffered feelings of upset when, after arriving in Hong Kong, they subsequently discovered that their husband's family allowed them little place in their own children's lives. Amber, for example, described with frustration her attempts to spend time alone with her young son. She told me that when she sat down with him—to talk or to help him do his homework—her mother-in-law would call him over for snacks and entice him away from her. Amber was consistently excluded by her husband and mother-in-law from "family" decisions regarding her son's welfare, and her opinions on how he should be educated and fed were either ignored or superseded. Cybil, likewise registered similar complaints about the relationship her parents-in-law had with her daughter, even though in her case she had only been separated from her daughter for one year. For both of these women, the long periods of time during which they lived separately from their husbands and their husbands' families allowed their in-laws to establish patterns of interaction with their children that precluded the need for their own involvement. Thus, mainland wives like Amber and Cybil were often denied the opportunity to perform their social roles as mothers in Hong Kong, just as they had been denied the ability to perform those roles when children had preceded them to Hong Kong. Following on the many years that they had lived apart from their husbands on the mainland, shouldering the burden of caring for their children while waiting to immigrate to Hong Kong, the denial of their roles as mothers—an integral aspect of their roles as wives (cf. Evans 2002:348)—was particularly distressing.

The realities of the familial problems caused by mainland and Hong Kong immigration policies—which kept families separated for years during their attempts to reunite in Hong Kong—were made more poignant by the fact that both the social workers and immigrants I interviewed identified the "traditionally Chinese" emphasis on "family reunion" as one important point of similarity between mainland and Hong Kong Chinese residents. This ideal is celebrated in most major Chinese festivals—including Spring Festival (also known as Lunar New Year) and the mid-Autumn Festival. Furthermore, as I pointed out in the introduction to this book, this concept was also championed in the discourse deployed by the Chinese Communist Party celebrating Hong Kong's "reunification" with the mainland in 1997. One of my informants, a man in his twenties who had waited for over twenty years to be reunited with his parents and siblings in Hong Kong, described his happiness at finally achieving his family's long-awaited goal: that of living together in one place, in Hong Kong.

> For a period of time our family had been split up—living in four different places. My father and mother were in Hong Kong, my younger sister was a student in our hometown, I was working in Guangdong Province in Jiangmen City, and my older sister was in Guangzhou. So, our family was split-up in four different places. In one year, there wasn't more than one time when we could all get together in the same place. . . . It was such a happy time [when we were all reunited in Hong Kong].

This focus on family reunion was just one of several "Chinese family values" deemed to be held in common by both Hong Kong and mainland Chinese residents. Although everyday discourse in Hong Kong almost always focused on delineating the differences between these two groups of Chinese citizens, most of my informants (immigrant women and children as well as Hong Kong social workers) considered the importance placed on family reunion, filial piety, respect for the elderly, and harmonious interactions among family members as hallmarks of a general "Chinese identity" shared by both long-term and New Arrival residents of Hong Kong.

Chinese family life, and the ideals associated with this life, have long been rich subjects of study by anthropologists and other scholars of Chinese society (see, for example, Wolf 1972, J. Watson 1975, Cohen 1976, and R. Watson 1985). Although recent ethnographies have problematized prior conceptions that treated the family as a unified entity characterized primarily by its "corporate" interests,[1] even these works demonstrate the power of the traditional Chinese family concept as it is imagined by Chinese individuals (Yan 2003; Fong 2004a). For example, Yunxiang Yan notes "the following eulogy to the ideal family" written on his front gate by one of his informants in 1990:

> The family is a harmonious whole
> that is created by the universe;
> containing the personal happiness of family life,
> it is the origin of well-being
> and the symbol of warmth. (2003:1).

Similar sentiments about the value of maintaining close familial relationships are expressed in this 1999 Chinese state-sponsored song, "Return Home Often" (Mandarin: *Chang Huijia Kankan*) quoted in Vanessa Fong's ethnography documenting the coming of age of the first generation of Chinese "only children":

> Find some time,
> Find some time.
> Take your child,
> And return home often.

Wear a smile,
Bring good wishes.
Together with your spouse,
Return home often.
Mama has prepared some nagging;
Papa has prepared a table of good food.
The troubles of life
Discuss with Mama.
The things at work
Discuss with Papa. (2004a:133-34)

Like Yan, Fong provides detailed discussions about contemporary Chinese urban family life that also demonstrate that the ideals of family harmony and filial piety are contested on an everyday basis at the level of the individual. Nonetheless, these accounts, like those of my Hong Kong and mainland Chinese informants, highlight the continuing saliency of an ideal which, although problematic as an analytic construct, must nevertheless be considered as a major factor in people's assessments of their own lives. This perspective is further rendered more complex by the strategic deployment of this discourse on idealized Chinese family values as a method of "subject formation" (Ong 1996) by state representatives who hope to foster such qualities in their citizen populace. The song, "Return Home Often," for example, not only "brought tears to [the] eyes" of many individuals when first introduced (Fong 2004a:133), but it also influenced the daily interaction of adult children and their aging parents. As Fong writes: "[t]he song resonated powerfully with the sentiments of many listeners who actually did try to 'return home often,' rushing from one spouse's parents' home to the other every holiday, every weekend, or even every day" (ibid. 134).

Writing about the role of the family in Hong Kong's tremendous economic growth during the second half of the twentieth century, Aihwa Ong criticizes Hong Kong social scientists—both Chinese and Western—for "ignor[ing] the effects of state discipline and a highly competitive marketplace on refugee families" (1999:118). Ong notes instead that these social scientists have often explained the economic success of Hong Kong immigrants in terms of local ideologies that place central importance on "Chinese family" life. She provides, as one example, "the term 'utilitarian familialism,'" which Hong Kong social scientists have used "to describe the everyday norms and practices whereby Hong Kong families place family interests above all other individual and social concerns" (ibid. 118; see also Greenhalgh 1994). Ultimately, Ong's concern rests on the fact that "these writers seem to identify these family practices as something inherent in 'Chinese culture'" (ibid. 118). Ong's point is a valid critique—not only of a local academic literature that has often neglected to consider the "disciplinary" (Foucault 1979; Ong 1999) role of political and economic practices that have shaped Hong Kong's striking commercial success—but also of British government practices that have historically cited the cultural norm of the "Chinese family," with its focus on harmony, obedience, and filial piety, as justifying certain omissions in social service provision in Hong Kong (see, for example, Draft White Paper 1990:13). Nonetheless, what Ong overlooks in her critique is the fact that this "imaginary" of the primacy of Chinese family life remains a model for behavior for many Chinese individuals in both Hong Kong and China, who continue to define themselves in relation to certain idealized views of the "Chinese family" that are rooted in "Confucian tradition."

For both my immigrant and social worker informants, the concrete focus on the ideal of "family reunion" took on even greater meaning as the justification both for immigration to Hong Kong as well as for hardships endured during years of waiting to immigrate to, as well as after arrival in, Hong Kong. Although mainland Chinese residents waiting to immigrate to Hong Kong were prevented from being able to "return home often" by the enforcement of Hong Kong immigration policies, family reunion remained a firm goal of these immigrant split-families, who hoped to be able to achieve this ideal behavioral model in Hong Kong—a location they believed would enable their children access to future success.

Immigrant Mothers' Western Dreams

The belief that life in Hong Kong offered substantially better future opportunities for their children than life on the mainland was a major motivating factor in my immigrant informants' willingness to put up with the family separation and other hardships they encountered both while waiting to immigrate as well as following their moves to Hong Kong. "For the children" is a reason commonly cited as a prime motivating factor to explain why people move from one location to another, and it should not be surprising that it was also an important factor driving mainland wives' desires to migrate to Hong Kong. Yet migration "for the children" was just one of the complex factors that influenced women's decisions to go ahead and move to and stay in Hong Kong after their years of living separately from husbands on the mainland. Other factors included access to rights, and, in particular, the right of mobility (Chapter Two); access to Hong Kong's "modern" and "cosmopolitan" lifestyles, along with the perceived social and economic advancement that would accompany moves to Hong Kong (Chapter Three; also see below); and women's desires to be "good" wives and daughters-in-law (Chapter Four). Although the social and economic realities of life in Hong Kong meant that many immigrant wives were not able to realize all of their migration-related desires for themselves, they could still hope to reap some benefits of Hong Kong social, economic, and political life through their children, who—in perception as well as in reality—would integrate to Hong Kong's "westernized"[2] lifestyle more easily than they would.

Hong Kong's westernized lifestyle—its cosmopolitanism and internationalist orientations in social and economic life—is one of Hong Kong's many legacies as a former British colony. Hong Kong identity is closely bound up in Hong Kong's transnational outlook (Mathews 1997); indeed, James Watson has even argued that in Hong Kong, the "transnational *is* the local" (Watson 1997:80). Access to international news, travel, and educational opportunities is much more circumscribed for residents of the mainland—even for those individuals living in the "semi-transnational" (Latham 2000) regions of Southeast China directly bordering Hong Kong. Immigrants of both rural and urban backgrounds were drawn to the international opportunities for their futures and their children's futures in Hong Kong.

Discussions with my immigrant informants highlighted the apparent contradictions between immigrants' goals for their children and the possibility of realizing these goals in Hong Kong's internationally focused community. For example, several of my informants wondered at the relative value of having children educated in Hong Kong rather than on the mainland—noting that extracurricular activities (like piano lessons) that they could have afforded on the mainland were not affordable in Hong Kong. Women also debated the relative merits of enrolling their children in one of Hong Kong's elite "international" schools, even though these women had no realistic means of paying the high costs of tuition for these schools. These articulated goals for their children's advancement and future success were not easily separated from goals that women immigrants had for themselves. At one dimsum outing several immigrant wives in their mid-twenties briefed the others at our table on the finer details involved with applying for visas to travel to the United States. Most of these women had only been living in Hong Kong for several months; before even adjusting to life in Hong Kong, they were already contemplating how to leave Hong Kong for other international destinations. Nonetheless, none of these women could even begin to realize their dreams of emigrating still further away from the mainland until they had lived in Hong Kong for at least seven years—the minimum required period for application for permanent residency and thus access to a HKSAR passport. Echoing the desires to go abroad held by many young people in China today (see Fong 2004b), many of my immigrant informants clearly held out hope that their immigration to Hong Kong would ensure them access—if not for themselves, then through the achievements of their children—to a future including the possibility of moving from Hong Kong to other, even more westernized, parts of the world.

Immigrating to Hong Kong did ensure that children would benefit from one aspect of Hong Kong's westernized lifestyle that immigrants knew was crucial to the future success of their children—English. Although Cantonese is the spoken language used in Hong Kong schools, many of the textbooks—even at the lowest grade levels—are in English, so that mainland children (along with the Hong Kong locals) often struggled to learn basic math, science, or other skills presented in English, rather than in Chinese. The widespread use of English in the Hong Kong educational system and in society more generally has been a locally contentious issue for many years (see, for example, E. Chan 2002). Many local people pride themselves on their English abilities, linking English proficiency to a cosmopolitan Hong Kong identity separate from that of the mainland (ibid.). Furthermore, Hong Kong people stress the importance of their familiarity with English as crucial to Hong Kong's continued dominance in the international financial community (ibid.). During the period of my research, many of my informants and other Hong Kong people focused on the opportunities provided by English usage rather than a more "fashionable" postcolonial interpretation that would identify English-language use as an unwelcome by-product of colonial rule (see Lau 1997 and Mathews 2001). Nonetheless, general levels of English proficiency in the former colony remain low. One local commentator writes (in English):

> Visitors to Hong Kong can be excused for wondering whether Hong Kong had been a British colony for over 150 years, if only because they cannot make themselves understood in English. Although the territory has a sizeable English-speaking community and one bumps into English almost everywhere—street signs, posters, bill boards, menus, price lists, and the like—tourists often encounter difficulties asking for directions from the man in the street and giving instructions to taxi drivers in English. Expatriates working in the territory complain that telephone operators and secretaries cannot catch English names or understand simple enquiries in English . . . As English has been Hong Kong's language of administration, law, and commerce since 1842 and taught to every child from kindergarten through university, the inability of most Hong Kong Chinese to communicate in simple English must be considered unusual. (Lau 1997:101)

While well-educated Hong Kong Chinese remain concerned about the overall low levels of English language proficiency, most locals remain convinced that English-language education remains an important factor in local identity and future commercial success.[3] For mainland immigrants, ensuring their children access to the opportunities provided by Hong Kong's English-language-based educational system was one of their primary motivating factors behind their immigration.

As a result, the immigrant mothers I knew were consumed with worry over their children's difficulties in transitioning to Hong Kong's school system and agonized over their children's initial low grades—routine scores of 0, 20, or 30 (out of 100) on their almost daily English quizzes, for example—fearing that such scores would not improve over time and would jeopardize their children's ultimate academic and future success. Other reasons for children's low levels of performance in schools during their periods of adjustment included the Chinese language differences between mainland and Hong Kong schools: whereas the mainland immigrant children were used to learning in Mandarin, they now had to learn in both Cantonese and English. The transition to using the traditional, or "complex" form of written Chinese instead of the "simplified" form used on the mainland posed less of a problem overall than the persistent problem of English. Mothers of young children were also concerned about the number of hours required each night for their children to complete their homework assignments—at least two to three hours per night for first graders. In contrast, some of the older children I knew—teenagers who had done very well in school on the mainland—would instead note that they had less homework in Hong Kong and that the local system was based even more rigidly on rote memorization than what they had previously experienced on the mainland. Several of the social workers at the center also echoed these views, noting that mainland students were different from local Hong Kong students in that they had more reasoning ability. Such criticism was likely to be ignored by many Hong Kong people and immigrants, however, who maintained the steadfast belief in the superiority of the Hong Kong educational system to that of the mainland, primarily because of the emphasis on English as part of the Hong Kong system.

English-language learning was not the only legacy of colonial Hong Kong that immigrant parents hoped would benefit children. Immigrant mothers also demonstrated a keen awareness of differences in parenting techniques between Westerners and Chinese people in general, and I was asked many questions on this subject as women debated the relative merits of each system. During these encounters, I enjoyed a unique position, since I was a Westerner who was also the mother of a blond-haired, blue-eyed, three-year-old son, whose exuberant energy, active imagination, and "healthy" physique were often the subjects of commentary by both Hong Kong social workers and their mainland immigrant clients.[4] Throughout the period of my research, social workers and immigrants remained steadfastly curious about the choices I made in raising my son. Other anthropologists have documented ways in which the concept of the "West" in East Asian locations has been reified in local parlance to refer specifically to white, upper-middle class, English-speaking communities (see, for example, Kelsky 2001 and Fong 2007). Such was the case with my informants as well, who viewed me as a "case study" in Western parenting techniques. While social workers consciously incorporated "content" about my interactions with my son in their discussions about parenting with their immigrant clients and held me up as an example to be emulated, immigrant women were also never shy about asking me about how I handled behavioral and disciplinary issues. Through these interactions, it became clear that my informants, like other mainland Chinese parents (see, for example, Fong 2007), essentialized Western goals for child development as centered around the ideals of creativity and independence; at the same time, they remained suspect of these goals, sometimes associating them with higher "quality" children, but at other times questioning how the adherence to such values might conflict with their preferred goals of children's scholastic achievement.

One curious mother, who had been reading a book explaining Western-influenced views of child development, asked me what I thought about the following anecdote that she had read, summing up the differences between Chinese and Western ideologies of child development. In this example, Chinese and Western parents each buy their children a new suit of clothes, but then place very different strictures on their children's behavior while wearing these clothes. The Chinese parents tell their child to be careful not to soil his new clothes and scold him if he dirties them while playing. The Western parents, on the other hand, dress their child in new clothes and then tell him to "have fun" on the playground, not caring whether the new clothes get dirty or not. Despite the obvious oversimplification of this example (which ignores, among other things, issues of generation, social class, and the cost of clothing), it nonetheless addressed a fundamental perception of difference between contemporary Western and traditionally Chinese goals of parenting: while Westerners were believed to encourage their children to be independent and creative, many Chinese parents, both in Hong Kong and the mainland, were thought to be more concerned about encouraging obedient behavior in their children. Immigrant mothers, whether they agreed or not that Western methods of child development were better than Chinese methods, still hoped that the introduction of their children to Hong Kong's Western-influenced ideologies of belonging and cosmopolitanism would benefit their children in some way.

Women's views, and their focus on their children as one means of realizing their personal desires, can be better understood within the context of understanding their moves to Hong Kong as "investments" in their children's futures. From this point of view, women's moves to Hong Kong seem to be in keeping with the late twentieth-century focus on the market economy and urban culture in China, in which "an individual's ability to make money is now considered most important" (Yan 2003:185). Describing the ways in which this materialistic focus has changed intergenerational power relations in rural China, Yan argues that children, not parents, now exercise more control within the family, largely because of their abilities to earn money (ibid.). This pragmatic orientation toward the world made Hong Kong a seemingly ideal destination for mainland Chinese, who were drawn by stories of high wages and TV images of a comfortable middle class. The reality of the very difficult living situations faced by most mainland Chinese immigrants in Hong Kong did not nullify the fact that, at the time of my research, even the lowest salaries in Hong Kong were still ten times more than the relatively high wages (by mainland Chinese standards) earned by factory workers in Guangdong and Shenzhen. For mainland parents, especially those of "only children," their moves to Hong Kong held the promise of even greater expectations for their children and, consequently, for themselves.

Both Fong (2004a) and Anagnost (1997b) have documented the regimentation and discipline enforced on Chinese urban children in the 1990s by parents who believed that access to a college education and "First World knowledge" (Fong 2006) would provide the only sure route to the high salaries that their children will need to help support them in their old age. Furthermore, Anagnost describes the process whereby the Chinese state discourse on "quality"[5] (Mandarin: *suzhi*) is inscribed in children's bodies through the careful selection of educational activities, consumer products, and other outside influences to which Chinese children are exposed. In this discourse, "everyday practices of consumption mark out certain commodities as contributing to the improved mental and bodily quality of the child: chocolate, dairy products, even potato chips" (Anagnost 1997b:216–17). From this point of view, access to the myriad, international consumer products available in Hong Kong, coupled with the city's internationalist possibilities and English-language-based educational system, represented for mainland Chinese parents the pinnacle of potential sources of perceived high quality "nourishment" for the minds and bodies of their children, and immigrant parents in Hong Kong may have believed that all Hong Kong-based products and services would contribute to their children's (and thus their own) future success. Hong Kong social workers, however, had different concerns about the futures of these immigrant children. On the one hand, social workers hoped to alleviate some of the tensions faced by immigrant families, whose potential for conflict and misunderstandings were certainly exacerbated through their long periods of separation before being reunited in Hong Kong. On the other hand, social workers aimed to cultivate Western-influenced ideologies of child development and parenting skills in their immigrant clients. In this way, social workers sought to ensure that parents would raise children whose thinking, behavior, and actions—along with their patterns of consumption—reflected their integration into the norms of civility and belonging in the Hong Kong polity.

Colonial Legacies: Family Life Education and "Parenting Skills"

Writing about the emergence of a distinctive Hong Kong identity separate from that of the mainland "other" in Hong Kong's historical past, Grant has argued that the British colonial government in Hong Kong was a key actor in this process of identity construction (2001:160). He cites a number of programs implemented by British colonial officials in the early 1970s to promote a "sense of belonging" to Hong Kong as one means of staving off actual and potential social upheaval both in reaction to Cultural Revolution-era riots that had "spilled over" into Hong Kong and amid growing concerns over increasing social inequality in the colony (ibid. 161–64, see also Heaton 1970). Grant identifies "Family Life Education" as one of "the key areas in which the colonial state intervened to reinvent culture during [Hong Kong's] industrialization process" (ibid. 159). Family Life Education (FLE), which was established at approximately the same time that the City District Officer Scheme, the first "Keep Hong Kong Clean" campaign, and the effort to organize area residents into Mutual Aid Committees (MACs) were launched, was aimed at "the reinventing of identity values around the nuclear family" through the propagation of "a new ethos of 'modern' marriage, child rearing, and harmonious individual human relationships" (Grant 2001:164). Promoted with annual mass publicity campaigns that encouraged increased family interaction and better emotional health, FLE programs "became part of an all-embracing social imaginary" (ibid. 164). Grant explains: "Young couples were instructed in the meaning and responsibilities of love in marriage; the elderly were taught how to adapt and change and get along with the younger generation. The aim was for a controlling yet supportive family, taking care of the old and disabled, as well as the young, regardless of who was actually living at home" (ibid. 164).

From this period until 1997, the British colonial government in Hong Kong, acting in its own interest to strengthen security and social stability within the colony, consistently targeted "family life" as one key element of reform. Likewise, the post-1997 Hong Kong government continued to link this principle of "utilitarian familialism," in which families are encouraged to act as cohesive, self-sufficient units, to the current and future economic prosperity of the region.

During the period of my fieldwork, Hong Kong social workers and government representatives identified the "family" as an important site for educating parents and children about state-sponsored norms of health, behavior, and social harmony. In 2004, the Hong Kong Department of Social Welfare website defined FLE in the following way:

> Family Life Education is a form of community education, both preventative and developmental in nature, intended to arouse the awareness of the public on the importance of family life. The main objectives are to prevent family and social problems, and to promote harmonious human relationship [sic] and to help families function effectively. In Hong Kong, family life education is one of the major services rendered by the Social Welfare Department in conjunction with non-governmental organizations since 1979. (www.family-land.org/life/ser_brief.htm)

In describing FLE's philosophy, the website further noted: "The basic philosophy in providing FLE Service arises from the recognition that family is the primary socializing agent through which an individual grows into adulthood, and that the integrity of the family has significant effect on the healthy development of individuals, both physically and mentally. *A stable and progressive society is composed of such healthy and responsible individuals who are nurtured and brought up in happy families*" (ibid.).

Now an integral feature of social work programs in Hong Kong, the continued emphasis placed on this subject by the government has been fueled by concerns that Hong Kong's rapid development has led to increasing numbers of divorces, single-parent families, and at-risk youth (ibid.). The reunited immigrant families in Hong Kong were also an obvious target of concern: of the 50,000-odd mainland immigrants entering Hong Kong each year for the purpose of family reunion, most were women and children who were likewise prone to these social ills because of their long periods living as split-families and the social and economic marginalization they faced once in Hong Kong. Thus, as I documented in Chapters One and Two, from the point of view of many policy makers and other individuals, these immigrants were seen as posing significant threats to Hong Kong's social and economic well-being by compromising Hong Kong's continued prominence as a center of global economic activity (through their low levels of education) and by causing severe strains on Hong Kong's social welfare infrastructure (by their large numbers). Furthermore, Hong Kong people's overall negative perceptions of mainlanders, and mainland women in particular, were also an important driving force behind the urgency with which lessons on FLE and "parenting skills" were promoted among mainland immigrants in Hong Kong. As I described in Chapter Three, Hong Kong people not only assumed that all mainland wives were "gold diggers" who had married their husbands for purely material gain, but they also tended to equate mainland wives with mistresses ("second wives") or prostitutes (Shih 1998). These associations were particularly problematic for immigrant wives, since mistresses were not only viewed as uneducated, backward, profit-seeking mainlanders but were also largely blamed for the destruction of local family life (Wu 2003); for obvious reasons, the association of mainland wives with prostitutes was equally undesirable.

Social workers were less likely than most Hong Kong people to think of mainland wives as threatening local social and economic mores, but they did worry about immigrants' "passivity" (associated with their [often] rural and lower-class mainland backgrounds) and their reliance on obedience and the assertion of parental authority in disciplining their children as obstacles to the development and maintenance of "healthy" family life. Social workers also worried that the relatively low levels of education among many immigrant women, coupled with mainland norms that locate women as the primary actors responsible for maintaining "harmonious" family life through wives' subordination of interest and subservience to husbands (Evans 2002:338–40), meant that many immigrant wives might subscribe to some of the less than ideal qualities of civility associated with the "traditional" Chinese Confucian family system. These ideals included the focus on patriarchal authority, women's relegation to the family sphere, and household and child-rearing activities as being solely women's responsibilities. These ideals presented a challenge to contemporary Hong Kong ideologies of belonging by contrasting with the more liberal views of conjugal equality and women as independent social actors that were associated with younger and better educated members of Hong Kong's westernized society (Law et al. 1995:90–91; see also Ho et al. 2000). As a result, they were seen as undesirable social practices that had the potential to cause serious family tension while also undermining immigrant women's and children's attempts to integrate with cosmopolitan Hong Kong society. In identifying immigrant women as the targets of lessons aimed at "modernizing" their views of family life, social workers aimed to influence not just immigrant wives but also their husbands and in-laws, since these more "traditional" values were also identified with older, male members of Hong Kong society. As a result, social workers targeted immigrant parents, and mothers in particular, for education about the government-sponsored FLE norms about proper disciplinary techniques, effective communication, and children's growth and development. This ideology has its basis in Western models of interpersonal family relationships and conflicted both with immigrant parents' views of child rearing as well as with the socialization experiences of social workers who had grown up in Hong Kong with mainland immigrant parents.

Through the implementation of the government-funded FLE programs aimed at fostering "healthy" individuals and families (www.family-land.org/life/ser_brief.htm), social workers worked to engineer Hong Kong government goals of achieving a "healthy" (and therefore stable and prosperous) social body. Social workers' concerns focused both on practical issues of adaptation—the fact, for example, that children were more likely to adapt to Hong Kong's cosmopolitan and "nervous" and "orderly" environment more quickly than parents, thus leading to the increased possibilities for conflict between family members of different generations (Ho et al. 2000:18)—as well as on more abstract principles that identified "families [as] the primary socializing agent" (www.family-land.org/life/ser_brief.htm). Similar to social workers described by Ong who worked to facilitate the incorporation of Cambodian refugees into American ideologies of belonging (1996, 2003), Hong Kong social workers also strongly believed that immigrant parents' interactions with their children must be considered of primary importance in determining what kinds of "citizens" their children would become. These goals, which strongly link family life with the future strength of the nation (or, in this case, the SAR), echo those espoused by late Qing and early Republican Chinese social reformers, who stressed the important socializing roles of mothers and advocated for women's education in order to ensure that mothers would raise good "citizens" who not only knew how to act in "civilized" ways but also shared a set of nationalistic, ideological beliefs (Judge 2002; Glosser 2003). Theorists writing about citizenship and family life in the West have also made the connection that the training of "citizens" begins at home. Yuval-Davis and Werbner, for example, explain that:

> The familial space is one where important aspects in the biological and cultural reproduction of collectivities takes place. Making a home includes fostering relations across generations, cooking and nurturing, playing and educating. Familial relations thus seem to constitute the "essence" of national culture, a way of life to be passed from generation to generation. Equally, however, training to be a citizen, to respect the rights of others, begins at home. (1999:14).

In this view, like those of the Republican reformers, the creation of citizens —those individuals who share certain ideologies of belonging, entitlement, and duties that define the possibilities of inclusion and exclusion in a community—is a gendered process, in which women, as mothers, are key agents in effecting changes in family life, and, thus, in the socialization experiences of their children (see also Wikan 2002).

For Hong Kong social workers, educating immigrant children's parents (and mothers, in particular) in "healthy" parent and child relationships therefore served two fundamental social and political goals. First, it educated both mainland wives and, to a lesser extent, their husbands (and, by extension, children), in local norms, thus facilitating the integration of both parents and children to Hong Kong ideologies of belonging. Second, it fostered the growth and development of children into "healthy" local citizens, particularly through attempts to cultivate cohesive and harmonious families. Most of the FLE programs that I observed addressed certain common issues related to these goals. For example, themes prioritized awareness about women's and children's physical safety; methods of "open" communication between family members; Western-influenced ideologies of child development, which privileged goals for raising independent and creative children; and "parenting skills" that sought to teach mothers to be empathetic, rather than authoritarian, disciplinarians of their Hong Kong citizen children.

A Case Study in Family Life Education:
The "Happy and Relaxed" Parenting Program

The FLE programs in which I participated during the period of my research often combined their lecture or educational component with a half-day of recreational activity; alternatively, these programs often took the form of a two-hour long weekend afternoon program. One representative program with which I helped was a two-hour program on parenting led by one of the center's welfare workers, an unmarried woman named Abby who had been working at the center for about five years. Abby had often protested during staff meetings that she felt "unqualified" to lead parenting groups, since she had never had any formal educational or practical experience in counseling or parenting. To improve her knowledge of "parenting skills," Abby had spent a considerable amount of her personal time (including one two-week "vacation") consulting magazines and books that dealt with issues related to parenting. She also discussed the topics that she planned to address in her programs with Elizabeth, the head social worker at the center, to compare what she had learned with what Elizabeth had been taught during her social work training. In this case, Abby told me that the goals of her program were to encourage parents to think about their interactions and communication with their children, to teach parents to praise their children, and to try to get parents to appreciate and think about their children's points of view. The by-line of the program recruitment flyer read: "Parents—hectic lifestyles, busy work, and intense homework pressure all mean that you don't have time to communicate with your children. Participate in this parenting activity, improve your communication skills with your children, and increase your affection for each other!"

As with many of the other FLE programs I observed, the three main components of this program included (1) general discussion about the kinds of communication and other problems that immigrant mothers had with their children; (2) a role-play skit in which different problems and their interactions were acted out for the immigrants to watch; and (3) interactive games played by competing teams of women and their children. For the discussion, the participants, about twenty mothers, were divided into small groups to talk about problems they had with their children. Overall, immigrant mothers were concerned about how to manage difficult behaviors and how to get children to obey them; many mothers were also particularly concerned about how to control children's difficult emotional outbursts. Some mothers complained, for example, that their children would often cry or otherwise cause trouble when they wanted to buy something and were told they could not. Another mother worried that her daughter had become unmanageable since coming to live with her in Hong Kong. The middle of three daughters, this eight-year-old girl had been left on the mainland to live with her grandmother when her mother and sisters had immigrated to Hong Kong. Since recently joining her mother in Hong Kong, the girl frequently cried, asking for her grandmother and clutching her grandmother's picture in her hands. Frustrated with trying to deal with her daughter while also single-handedly raising two other children in Hong Kong's stressful environment, this mother, like many immigrant women, was at a loss about how to deal with her daughter's distress. Another of my informants described the distance between her husband and six-year-old son, who steadfastly refused any interaction with his father even though his father clearly adored him. These immigrant mothers were clearly interested in sharing their stories and in participating in the group, and many were willing to explain how they reacted when they became upset or frustrated with their children. Yet they also indicated—through their repeated questions of "what can I do?"—that the group format was not necessarily furnishing them with any suggestions that they found helpful.

Following this discussion was a skit, planned and scripted by Abby as an important part of the content of her course, during which an immigrant volunteer and I pretended to be a mother (she) and her child (I) dealing with a number of issues that a parent might find trying but where a child might need comforting. Through the different resolutions that we presented to three different scenarios of potential mother/child conflict, our skit was planned by Abby to introduce mothers to Western-influenced models of mother/child communication, in which mothers were exhorted to empathize with their children's feelings and negotiate with them to create desirable outcomes for undesirable situations. The scenarios that we acted out included the death of a favorite pet, getting a shot at the doctor's office, and, last, an argument that takes place between a mother and child when the child refuses to put on her coat before going outside. In each case, following Abby's instruction, we first performed the role-play using a scenario where the mother makes no attempt to listen to her child or empathize with her child's point of view, resulting in tears, upset, and finally, some punishment for the child who had "misbehaved." Next, again under Abby's direction, we would reperform the same scenario, invoking instead a mother who talked with (rather than at) her child, who listened to her child, and who offered some form of positive "reward"—either praise that she was being brave or a more tangible present such as a trip to McDonald's—for her child's understanding of and compliance with the situation at hand. At the time of the performance, there was no discussion among immigrant parents about the skit's outcomes (other than agreement that getting children to stay warmly dressed was indeed a common problem). In part, I suspect this was because Abby hurried the group's participants into the final game-playing component of the program without leaving time for further group discussion.

Earlier in the week, however, while practicing our lines for the skit, the other volunteer, an immigrant mother of three girls, had talked to me about her reactions to the skit's scenarios. In responding to the first scenario, she agreed that, of course, a child would want to be comforted upon the loss of a pet. For the second scenario, however, she disagreed with Abby's "improved communication model," and she frankly stated that she did not see the need to explain to a child why shots are necessary or to reward a child afterward for her "brave" behavior at the doctor's office. Like the other women who participated in this program, this mother was most interested in the third scenario, feeling that she often encountered the situation of fighting with her children over wearing warm clothes, and that it would certainly be useful to find a way to work this problem out more easily with her daughters. Unlike the other two scenarios, however, our performance offered no clear solution to this conflict. Nonetheless, she refused to accept Abby's suggested means of negotiating for a positive outcome with her children on this topic, and she remained unable to "empathize" with "her child" in this scenario. From her point of view, this mother believed that her capitulation to her children's desires to wear less clothing would make her an "irresponsible" parent who endangered the health of her children and caused them to catch cold. In this case, as in the case of getting a shot at the doctor's office, the child's point of view was seen as immaterial; in these situations of health and well-being, children should be expected to obey—and not question—parents' judgment. Later, this volunteer told me that one of the games, in which mothers had to dress their children in clothes that they fashioned out of old newspapers, was the most interesting part of the entire FLE program. For her, this game was the only tangible result of the program that she could easily repeat with her children at home.

"Hong Kong" Versus "Chinese" Family Values

In emphasizing "communication skills" as a means to create and maintain "healthy" parent/child relationships, Abby had drawn on one specific content area that FLE programs were supposed to target (www.family-land.org/life/ser_brief.htm).[6] According to Abby, effective parent/child communication included the ideas of explaining parental logic to children rather than ordering them to obey; attempting to gain children's compliance and reinforce their positive behavior through the offering of positive rewards rather than threatening children with punishment or hitting them; and encouraging parents to empathize with their children. Yet immigrant parents' interactions with their children, which often included yelling, demanding obedience, and slapping (as I frequently witnessed), were based on a "traditional" Chinese cultural script of "shaming" children into respecting the authority of parents and teachers (Fung 1999). This focus on obedience, with its roots in Confucian philosophy, is still practiced by parents in many Chinese locations despite the conflict that exists between this cultural script and the ideals of sociality, self-reliance, and excellence that many Chinese parents also expect from their children (see Fong 2007). These contradictions, encountered by Vanessa Fong in her research on Chinese only-children in Dalian (ibid.), were also common among both Hong Kong and mainland Chinese lower-class ideals of parenting that I encountered during the course of my fieldwork. In Hong Kong, these "traditional" (and thus undesirable) models of behavior—despite their continued practice throughout many sectors of society—were identified in particular with older generations of Hong Kong residents (Law et al. 1995:90), who were likely to be either the husbands or in-laws of mainland immigrant wives. As a result, social workers targeted immigrant women for training in these westernized parenting skills that were more in keeping with the ethos of belonging in "modern" and "cosmopolitan" Hong Kong not only because social workers hoped to influence wives, but also because wives served as the only possible means to get these messages across to other family members as well.

Abby was aware of both the low educational levels of the majority of the immigrant wife participants of her program as well as the serious time constraints they faced on a daily basis. As a result, she told me that she was content that parents would simply take the time to come and listen to the program, whether or not they learned anything from it. Thus, from Abby's point of view, her program was successful: not only did a number of women show up for the program, but they also participated to the extent that they voiced concerns that they were currently experiencing with their children. But comments made both by my immigrant covolunteer as well as by other immigrant clients in different contexts led me to conclude that many immigrant women remained dissatisfied with the overall content of this course and others like it. Despite her efforts to provide communicative models that mothers could emulate in attempting to resolve the disciplinary problems they encountered with their children, Abby did not succeed—on the strength of this one program—in providing effective models (either Western or Chinese) that mothers understood or could easily adopt to resolve their disagreements with their children. Ultimately, Abby's failure stemmed from the divergence between her goal of challenging women to reevaluate their "traditionally based" models of parent/child interaction and immigrant mothers' parenting goals, which focused instead on learning simple techniques for disciplining their children.

Abby's conversations with me on the subject of her own upbringing made it clear that she was herself a product of a more "traditional" Chinese childhood that included, among other values, absolute obedience to her parents (and to her father in particular). Not only did she never have the option of "communicating" openly with her parents in the more meaningful ways that she was attempting to introduce to these immigrant Chinese mothers, but she was also the frequent recipient of that traditional form of deterrence, the slap—a form of punishment that the social workers tried their best to discourage among their clients despite its continued, widespread use in Hong Kong society at large. In our discussions, Abby never addressed the issue that Chinese parents would not have seen these forms of interaction with her and her siblings as signs that they were not loved—indeed, this attention to children's behavior and molding them into obedient and filial children would have been felt as demonstrating their parental concern for their children (see also Cheah and Rubin 2003). Instead, Abby said that, as a child, she would have preferred these westernized models of interaction with her parents. She hoped, in addition, that by introducing such concepts to these immigrant women, she might in some way influence their behavior so that their children could experience happier relationships with their parents than she had. Nonetheless, because she had never experienced the Western-influenced models of parent/child communications that she was introducing on a personal level, either in her own interactions or as a parent, she found it difficult to mediate between the kinds of behaviors represented by these models and the socialization processes that she herself had experienced and that were still being practiced among her clients.

Other Western-trained Hong Kong social workers, like Abby, were torn between models of parent/child relationships to which they had been introduced through their Western-based educational process and the more "traditionally Chinese" relationships (rooted in the Chinese "family values" discussed previously) which had informed their upbringings and that they continued to share with their own family members. For example, frequent complaints were made by the center's social workers about the extreme pressure placed on children by their parents and the rigid nature of the local educational system, in which, like that of mainland China, success was judged by uniformity and memorization rather than by creativity and ability to reason (see Fong 2004a). Another stereotype that I frequently heard expressed by the center's social workers was that rural Chinese children were thought to be less well-behaved than those with parents who came from urban Chinese locations. Despite their vocal criticisms of the strictures placed on children by Hong Kong's rigid social and educational system, the social workers I knew viewed the freedom experienced by rural Chinese children in a negative light compared with the more structured upbringings of urban Chinese children. The social workers did not seem to equate this "freedom" with the kinds of encouragement toward independence and creativity that they so admired in their conceptions of the Western educational system for children (see also Fong 2007). Instead, their views on child rearing in actuality remained much closer to the mainland Chinese discourse which treats "creativity" as leading to uncontrolled, undisciplined, or "naughty" behavior (see Anagnost 1995 and 1997a). In these cases, social workers' ideologies highlighted the championing of Western goals for child development even as they remained rooted in the "traditional" Chinese family ideal.

Points of Disjuncture: Social Workers' and Immigrants' Parenting Goals

Immigrant parents, worried about their children's well-being in Hong Kong, often approached social workers for help with their children. In many cases, parents were tired and frustrated because of the everyday hardships they experienced as split-families and as socially and economically marginalized members of the Hong Kong polity. As a result, they had little patience to cope with their children's disobedience or emotional outbursts and hoped that social workers would teach them concrete methods they could employ to improve their children's undesirable behaviors. Social workers, however, saw these same problems in a different light. While they were concerned about helping to reduce parental stress that might lead to serious rifts in parent and child relationships and thus endanger the health and harmony of the family as a whole, social workers nonetheless often targeted immigrant parents—rather than children—as the agents of changing negative family dynamics. For immigrant parents who were used to more "traditionally" authoritarian models of parent/child relationships, this lesson was difficult to accept. One of my informants complained:

> [L]ast time when I talked to [my social worker] about my son's problem—because my son is difficult—he doesn't like to do what others tell him . . . So I went to talk to her about this. *She started asking me lots of questions about what I was doing to help him* . . . On the other hand, my son has a teacher now, and when she tells me he has been naughty, she also tells me exactly what I should do with my son . . . , what method I should use to teach him better.

As with many other immigrants, this mainland wife preferred to learn about how to manage her son's behavioral problems through concrete means, such as those suggested by her son's teacher, who did not challenge her ideology about parental roles and authority. In contrast, she told me that she had stopped relying on her social worker for help with her son.

During a taped interview, Siu-saan, one the center's social workers, explained to me why she disagreed with immigrants' goals of "managing" their children's behavior. Overall, her concerns echoed many of those that were also articulated by Abby, and they demonstrate the conflict between immigrants' goals for their children's success and social workers' goals that immigrants and their children integrate into a Western-influenced ideology of child development that promotes "open" and empathetic communication between parents and children and allows children more independence and creativity in their developmental process. Yet, Siu-saan also acknowledged that some immigrant parents did change the ways in which they tried to discipline their children, but that these changes did not always occur in ways intended by social workers:

> Lots of Chinese people hope that their children will be the best. Or, if not the best, that at least their children will get really good jobs. This way, [the parents] will feel that their lives will become less difficult. They are very nervous about their descendants. But sometimes, this nervousness does not help children. It hurts them. And, sometimes, [parents'] concept of educating children is to manage them. But I think that leads to not giving kids any personal space to develop. So, this is the point that I am constantly

arguing about with parents. They don't agree. They come here hoping that I will help them manage their children. But I usually tell them that they shouldn't be managing their children. But then you have to explain to them what they should do. And some of them really learn well. They want to learn new methods for teaching their children. They see that we can use some methods of behavioral modification. [That is,] if [a child] does something good, then we praise him to reinforce that behavior. If [the child] does something bad, we punish him. And [the parents] learn this. But their punishment is to threaten to take away their love for their children, and so we always have to teach them: this method is good, but there are some things that you cannot use as punishment . . . They say, "If you do that, I won't love you! I'll throw you away!" Their intention is good, but they use the wrong things as punishment.

One of my informants, who had difficulty accepting Siu-Saan's advice, stopped showing up for meetings set up by Siu-saan to discuss the "behavioral problems" that she had experienced with her twelve-year-old son. Oscar, an active boy, had trouble sitting still during class and was not performing well in the rigid setting of the Hong Kong school in which he had been placed. Ironically, the only class that he felt was interesting was the class in which his grades were the poorest. This class was an English class taught by a native English speaker who, Oscar noted, was more dynamic than his other teachers. Oscar was an only child, and my informant and her husband—although they adored him—were dismayed at their son's active and curious nature, felt that he lacked direction, and worried that his affable and outgoing social qualities, which allowed him to make friends easily, prevented him from concentrating on his studies. In reaction, they had become increasingly strict with the boy, to the point that Siu-saan felt that the relationship between these parents and their child was becoming strained. As a result, she had begun meeting with my informant and her husband and son to try to resolve the situation.

My informant had clearly listened well to Siu-saan's advice before she stopped coming to their scheduled appointments, as she was able to articulate clearly Siu-saan's point of view about Oscar. Nonetheless, she seemed to feel dissatisfied, as if she did not know how to act on this advice or as if it was not what she really wanted to hear. She told me that Siu-saan complained that my informant and her husband did not give Oscar enough personal growing space and, by "lightening up" on the rigid structures they imposed on him, they could facilitate a closer relationship that would help them all work through Oscar's schooling and behavioral difficulties together. Furthermore, she noted, Siu-saan had suggested they try to find a different kind of school environment for Oscar—if not an international school, at least a local school more influenced by Western concepts of teaching, where Oscar's desire for interaction with his teachers and constant questioning would not be seen as aberrant and undesirable behavior. My informant claimed that she and her husband, with their more "traditional" notions of child rearing, did not feel comfortable changing the kinds of demands they made on their son, nor did they accept the idea of placing him in a more westernized school. Like some of my immigrant informants, Oscar's mother remained critical of the often-expressed idea that Western schools were necessarily "better" than local Chinese schools. Likewise, she questioned what the differences in these educational systems really were, and what kinds of parent/child relations might result from the independent and "creative" attitudes encouraged in less "traditionally Chinese" schooling environments.

Despite her rejection of Siu-saan's advice about her son's schooling needs, Oscar's mother did take away some lessons about modifying her own methods of parenting from her encounters with the center's social workers. She explained that she had changed some of her parenting techniques, and she gave me an example of one way in which she had revised her thinking on this subject:

> For example, [one social worker] talked about what to do if your child is not writing neatly. You shouldn't say, "Wow! Your writing is really awful today." You shouldn't say that. Instead, you should ask, "What do you think about your writing today?" [and have the child compare today's writing with an example of writing that was neatly done, so that he can see for himself whether he has written neatly or not]. But most of the time at home, when [my son] writes messily, we'll say, "What's wrong with you? Why is your writing so ugly today? Write everything again!" But this isn't a good method [for teaching children] . . . I've already changed lots of things I did before that weren't good.

As this quote demonstrates, the FLE-based discourses employed by social workers did serve to make the center's immigrant clients increasingly aware of internationally influenced patterns of child development and problem resolution between parents and children. On the other hand, the lack of a supportive social and cultural context required for the implementation of such changes in clients' daily life interactions prevented the implementation of all but the most concrete of suggestions in the everyday events of client parents and their children. Elaborating on the difficulty of influencing individual behaviors that go against such deeply held community norms and beliefs, Siu-saan told me:

> Parents will sometimes place all of their personal hopes and aspirations on their children. As far as they are concerned, a completely obedient child is a good child. But this concept is misguided. So you have to talk to them, help them. But this can be very difficult, because parents' thinking has been like this for a very long time, and it is not just [the parents]—school principals and teachers will think this way as well. So, it is not so easy. Actually, there is no way to change this whole situation. I can only say so much. Usually, after I've said this much, [the client] won't come back to see me again. They think that I am not helping them . . . But this unhealthy thinking, it is not just the parents. It is a social problem, and teachers also think this way. Sometimes parents say that it is not that they don't want to change, but after they have changed, they would have to deal with teachers and relatives saying, "What! Your child is so naughty," or "Your child is not studying!" It's hard. Hong Kong has a special characteristic, which is that you have to study and you have to do really well in school to be considered a good child . . . In Hong Kong, there is no space for children to develop in other ways, with other strengths.

Ultimately, some immigrant parents—like Oscar's mother—did modify some aspects of their communication and disciplinary interactions with their children in ways that were encouraged through their involvement with social workers and the values associated with FLE. Nevertheless, some goals promoted by social workers—particularly those focused on promoting children's creativity—were so divorced from the reality of everyday values placed on children's obedience and scholastic performance by both mainland and Hong Kong Chinese that there was no possibility that immigrants could accept them. In this way, despite the many perceptions of difference between mainlanders and Hong Kong people, the everyday thinking and behavior of both groups of Chinese citizens indicated their continued reliance on the discourse of "traditionally Chinese" family values as the basis of their interactions with children.

The Underlying Tension of Chinese "Family Values"

At the beginning of this chapter, I argued that the realities of the familial problems caused by the mainland and Hong Kong government immigration policies were made more poignant by the fact that both social workers and immigrants I interviewed identified the "traditionally Chinese" emphasis on "family reunion" as one important point of similarity between mainland and Hong Kong Chinese residents. As a result, in Hong Kong a tension existed among the local population—to which the social workers were most certainly not immune—that forced individuals to acknowledge that they shared certain Chinese cultural traits and beliefs with the otherwise vilified mainland immigrants. This brings up the question of what it means to be Chinese, and how mainland immigrants' and Hong Kong people's ideas may have varied on this subject.

Despite the many complexities involved with trying to define what it means to be Chinese, there is definite consensus among scholars that individuals of Chinese descent do widely believe in a Chinese, or pan-Chinese "identity" to which they belong (see Tu 1994; Wu 1994; Cohen 1994). This identity, which includes both "geopolitical and cultural dimensions" (Tu 1994:2), is rooted in a mythologized and historical past that pinpoints the Wei River Valley as the origin of "Chinese culture" (ibid). Throughout the centuries that followed, being Chinese was defined primarily through the practice of mutually reinforcing sets of rites and relationships that linked "proper human behavior" to "cosmic principles" (Cohen 1994:88).

> [By] late traditional times there was in China a common culture in the sense of shared behavior, institutions, and beliefs . . . China's common culture was also a unified culture in the sense that it provided standards according to which people identified themselves as Chinese. Taking this

Han or ethnic Chinese culture as a whole there can be no doubt that the historical trend in pre-modern times was towards increasing uniformity. By the end of the traditional period the Han Chinese had hardly attained a state of total homogeneity, but the extent to which the Han Chinese shared a common culture was considerable in comparison with many traditional empires or states, and all the more impressive given the size of the Chinese empire and the very small proportion of non-Han within it. (ibid. 89)

James L. Watson has identified what he calls "orthopraxy"—the shared, but malleable, ritual practices and their accompanying beliefs throughout this common cultural area—as the means through which individuals could continue to "be Chinese" while simultaneously adhering to local practices and ideologies that were encompassed within the larger Chinese geopolitical region (1988). Thus, Chinese identity draws on historically and culturally embedded states of being that allow individuals to subscribe to their Chinese identity by way of a local identity—which does not diminish the overall importance of being Chinese even as one's "Chineseness" remains rooted in the importance of the place to which one belongs. For social workers in Hong Kong, the cultural traits they shared with mainland Chinese immigrants represented an important avenue through which the social workers could engage their clients in dialogues about how to be Chinese the "Hong Kong" way. As I have described in this chapter, conceptions of Chinese family life—which included the idealized focus on family reunion, filial piety, respect for the elderly, and harmonious interactions among family members—were central to these dialogues.

In Hong Kong, I found that despite the importance of the family concept (or, perhaps, because of it), there was extensive contestation over which Chinese society—Hong Kong or the mainland—subscribed more faithfully to the "traditional" Chinese family ideal. Both mainland immigrants and Hong Kong people seemed to identify "traditional" Chinese family life with being more "authentically" Chinese, and each group strove to gain the recognition of being more "authentically" Chinese, even as mainland immigrants and Hong Kong people both sought to distance themselves from the association of "tradition" as linked to the rural, "backwards," and underdeveloped Chinese mainland and desired instead to be recognized as members of Hong Kong's modern, cosmopolitan, and capitalistic society.

Comments about children's behavior reflected these ambivalences, demonstrating the difficulties of untangling how to evaluate what is more (or less) "authentically" Chinese. Both social worker and immigrant informants would sometimes state that mainland children were better behaved and more studious than Hong Kong children, while others would state the opposite. In terms of parental control and the instilling of values in children, I heard similarly conflicting statements, although Hong Kong people were more likely to criticize mainlanders on this point than the other way around. I heard defenses that social relations and family life on the mainland were more "traditional." One immigrant informant noted, for example, that "young Hong Kong people" who had been very influenced by Western ways of thinking might not adhere to "traditionally Chinese" familial beliefs, just as their methods of speaking and communication had become significantly different from those more respectful patterns still practiced on the mainland. He felt that the directness of Hong Kong people who "said what they thought" "whenever they wanted"—even interrupting others—seemed unacceptable in comparison with what he characterized as the "more respectful" mainland practices of waiting for one's turn to speak or never voicing anything that would be considered impolite. On the other hand, I heard defenses (often from older Hong Kong residents who had lived their entire lives in Hong Kong) that Hong Kong family life (and individuals' "traditionally Chinese" values) were more authentically rooted in idealized past models, because in Hong Kong families had not undergone continuous state-sponsored attacks as they had through PRC educational, political, and economic campaigns.

Despite these contestations, Siu-saan and the center's other social workers had identified certain problems shared by all Chinese parents in their interactions with their children. These problems included the overmanagement of their children's activities, control over their children's interests and behavior, and the lack of personal space for the growth and development of children. Hong Kong social workers, who desired to change these problematic relationships, were frustrated by the disjuncture between the reality of parenting practices in Hong Kong and widely held social norms that identified Hong Kong as a "cosmopolitan" and "modern" society. The social workers had no ability through their daily interactions to influence the majority of the non-Western-educated local Hong Kong people whose actions as parents and educators reinforced such strong social values as the definition of "good" children as those who are filial, obedient, and studious. Nonetheless, this did not stop them from attempting to influence their immigrant clients into more flexible, communicative, and sympathetic parents who would encourage, rather than only punish, their children, and who would not impose such rigidly conformist guidelines on their children's actions and behavior. Social workers—echoing government concerns—viewed these qualities as essential in fostering harmonious social relations, creating a "healthy" social body, and creating and sustaining a stable and prosperous society overall.

Noting that whether Hong Kong culture is "Chinese" or "Western" is still "an open question" (Mathews 2001:295), Mathews has likened Hong Kong identity to that of a "cultural supermarket," in which individuals are free to pick and choose aspects of different cultural values in constructing their own identities (1996, 1997, and 2001). Mathews cites the local Hong Kong use of English names as one example of this concept, noting that individuals often choose English names for themselves during their schooling and use these names among school and work acquaintances while maintaining a more traditionally "Chinese identity" at home—where their Chinese names continue to be used by parents who may have no knowledge of their children's English names (1996). Perhaps a similar analogy can be made with contemporary "family values" in Hong Kong, where many well-educated individuals and government officials hope to combine what they view as the strengths of "traditional" Chinese family values—such as family cohesion and respect for elders—with Western-influenced views of "modern" family life—including the focus on conjugal family life and the independence of women—in ways that both contribute to harmonious and cosmopolitan Hong Kong society (see Law et al. 1995).

My immigrant informants had, in part, immigrated to Hong Kong to take advantage of the greater access to internationally influenced ideas and options that they knew to be available in Hong Kong; however, the methods used by social workers in their attempts to help immigrants integrate to Hong Kong ideologies of belonging did not always achieve social workers' desired effects. As a result, such ideas and options seemed likely to remain peripheral to many aspects of immigrants' daily lives, including interactions with their children. In Chapter Seven, I focus on a similar disjuncture that resulted from social workers' attempts to influence immigrants' integration into Hong Kong social and economic life by teaching them to be "responsible" citizens. In both cases, while social workers succeeded in introducing mainland wives to Hong Kong idealized discourses of civility—as empathetic and communicative mothers and parents, and also as "entrepreneurial" and "self-reliant" social actors—mainland wives did not always realize the possibilities that social workers imagined they would by engaging in these discourses of membership and belonging that distinguish and define everyday life between the mainland and Hong Kong.

SEVEN

Acting Responsibly

Emily, the youngest social worker at the social service center, had been working there for just a few months when I began my involvement with the center's staff and clients. By the time I interviewed Emily almost one year after first meeting her, she had begun to form clear opinions about the center's clients and her work with them. In particular, her interaction with numerous clients and the influence of the more experienced social workers had left her with the point of view that many of the recent immigrants who came to the center were not particularly responsible, either in terms of their expectations for their lives after arrival in Hong Kong or in terms of their planning before arrival. She told me about the interaction that she had with one immigrant client, who was pregnant, which had been especially memorable for her.

She [the client] wanted to know if after she had the baby the [Hong Kong] government would give her any money to help support the child. I thought it was really strange to ask in this way! You should have a plan before having a baby. You should have financial support before having a baby. If not, you will be a very "irresponsible" mother! But she just answered me: "Why wouldn't the government help her raise her child?" And then I asked her: "After you have the baby, will you look for a job to help support the child?" And she said that she couldn't, because she didn't have anyone to help her look after the child. So, I suggested that by working, she would make enough money to hire someone to help her look after the child, or to place the child in a daycare or creche. And then her answer was even stranger. She said, "No, that is not possible, because my baby must drink breastmilk. The baby cannot drink formula, because it will not be nutritious enough and is not really good for the baby." I thought this answer was really strange, really "irresponsible." She had completely no sense of "self-help." That's why, after meeting more and more cases like this, it seems like you really have to look and see if a client is worth helping. I just thought that this example was really odd.[1]

Unlike the PRC's state-led educational campaigns that promote breastfeeding in urban Chinese hospitals, there had not been any such campaigns in Hong Kong, where, at the time of my research, mothers rarely breastfed.[2] As a result, Emily's refusal to acknowledge the health benefits of that practice to both mother and infant was understandable. Nevertheless, I was still struck by her apparent inability to empathize with a mother who obviously wanted the opportunity to be with her child rather than working at a job that would probably not even provide enough money for living expenses after her child's day care expenses had been paid. Emily's remark that this immigrant wife was not interested in "self-help" conveys a sense of the context of local values in which we can more easily make sense of her reaction. Immigrants' efforts to learn and act "independently" were consistently valued over inaction or "laziness." Immigrants who proved their own worth through active involvement in resolving difficulties were "worth helping," whereas immigrants who continued to demonstrate a dependency on social workers or other means of support, without any attempt to make any sort of personal "contribution" to society through their paid or unpaid work, were judged to be less "worthy" of help. This theme of "responsibility" pervaded much of the interaction that I witnessed between social workers and their immigrant clients during my period of participant observation at the center. Referred to just as often in the English, *sense of responsibility*, as in the Cantonese, *jaahtyahmsum*, this common referent for clients' behavior was never a topic of conversation among clients themselves. While often addressed indirectly, through discussion about self-reliance, learning, planning, consideration for others, volunteering, or making a contribution to society, "acting responsibly"—the Hong Kong way—was clearly an important lesson that immigrant arrivals in Hong Kong were expected to learn.

In this chapter, I investigate the concept of responsibility as it was promoted by social workers in Hong Kong to their immigrant clients. I argue that, for Hong Kong social workers, the demonstration of economic and social responsibility was an important local norm, intricately linked to ideals of civility and, thus, the social imaginary of belonging in the Hong Kong polity. As a result, lessons on mundane, daily matters, such as budgeting for a party and reporting on homework assignments, provided the framework for Hong Kong social workers and (sometimes) government representatives to socialize mainland immigrants into a Hong Kong-based ideology of governance hinging on concepts of "self-help," "entrepreneurial" action (Ku and Pun 2004), and "voluntarism" that were seen as necessary for maintaining the social stability and prosperity of the SAR. By focusing on developing their immigrant clients' attitudes and behavior to conform to these ideals, social workers ultimately hoped to aid immigrants' integration into local Hong Kong social life. Immigrant clients, as mainland citizens of the PRC, had been socialized to expect different goals and privileges for relating to state and society, and did not always agree with or accept the lessons about the roles, rights, and duties defining local norms of belonging that social workers tried to teach them. In particular, their conflicting reactions to these lessons about acting "responsibly" resulted from immigrants' socialization to value social rights over political and civil rights and from the tension that existed between Hong Kong values of "self-help" and "entrepreneurship" (ibid.) and the socially and economically marginalized immigrant wives' needs to provide for their children and families.

The Responsibilities of Citizenship

Often conceptualized as a contract between individuals and the state, citizenship describes the political and social condition in which individuals gain certain rights and agree to certain responsibilities in return for the

Mainland residents' ideas about "responsible" citizen behavior have also been strongly shaped by Chinese socialist state practices, which continue to influence the actions and behaviors of mainland residents even during the postsocialist period. Writing about power and the shaping of citizen subjectivity in the PRC, Ann Anagnost has argued:

> In China we see many technologies of power that appear at first glance to be fully "disciplinary" in Foucault's sense of this term—the placing of persons onto a grid which makes even intimate areas of practice visible to a panoptic gaze [, . . .] the meticulous rituals of criticism and self-criticism, . . . and the dossiers, which record each person's political history . . . The goal is not so much the orthopedic refashioning of the individual so that deviance is made to conform to a norm presumed to be already present in the social body as a whole but *the radical re-formation of that very social body, in which old practices are displaced by new, in the utopic projection of a new social reality.* (1997a:115–16, emphasis added)

In effect, Anagnost posits that the "disciplinary" effects of governmentality in the PRC are focused on producing individual citizens whose actions all contribute to a greater collectivist vision of social and political reality. That these "realities" may or may not have achieved their "desired" effects is not the point of her argument; rather, Anagnost contrasts this goal of fashioning citizen subjectivity to align with collective interests with the ideologies of freedom and the pursuit of individual interests in maintaining and sustaining social, political, and economic life in the liberal tradition. Ong likewise notes a tendency to focus on the security of the collective rather than on the individual in other East Asian countries besides China, and she argues that this "Asian model of pastoral care" aims to foster "citizens with the human, social, and cultural capital that will allow them to thrive in a global economy" (1999:212).[4]

Ong contrasts her "Asian" model of "pastoral care" governance to the "Western" model of neoliberalism, in which states encourage citizens to achieve similar levels of competence through encouraging ideologies of individual effort and responsibility. Although principles of "responsibility" or "duty" in discourses of citizenship have often taken a backseat to discourses of rights in the liberal context, they have always been integral to conceptions of citizenship because of the strong association between the "social standing" of citizens and citizens' abilities to "contribute" to national life (Narayan 1997). This focus on the language of citizen "responsibility" and on the role of "contribution" as significant forms of community membership has been reinforced in recent years by the neoliberal ideologies that have increasing influence over official state discourses of belonging—in contrast to the social welfare discourses that dominated in the past (Turner 2004). Within this neoliberal discourse, contribution to the national interest most often takes the form of working (that is, earning an income), but it can also include other forms, such as volunteer work (ibid.). In other words, in the "Western" neoliberal context, "responsible" citizens are expected to contribute to the provision of many public amenities, such as "schooling, policing, welfare, and maintenance of physical infrastructure," that, in the past, were provided by the state to all citizens (Hyatt 2001:206).

These "rational" attitudes, which both derive from and reinforce the social practices needed to sustain a thriving capitalist economy, apply to Hong Kong as well. As Ku and Pun argue, Hong Kong people have been encouraged by government actors to be strong social actors who are "enterprising individuals," competent in an ideology of "self-enterprise" and "self-help" (2004:1) that places the burden of economic growth and social stability on the shoulders of individual citizens rather than the state. Actively promoted by Hong Kong's former chief executive, Tung Chee-Wah (ibid.), these visions of state-society involvement, like the political and civil rights-based ethos of belonging in Hong Kong that I described earlier, hinge on the role of individual citizens in maintaining Hong Kong's stable and prosperous economy and society. This discourse of "self-enterprise" and "self-help" persists despite the availability of important sources of social welfare for Hong Kong citizens. These sources include access to state-subsidized housing, medical care, and public education, all of which are becoming increasingly expensive and difficult to obtain on the mainland, particularly for rural or less-well-educated mainland residents like many of my immigrant wife informants. The potential for mainland immigrants to access these important social rights through their moves across the Hong Kong/mainland border exacerbates tensions among immigrants and Hong Kong citizens, many of whom seek to deny immigrants access to these social rights on the basis that even legal immigrants, as "mainlanders," do not "belong" in the Hong Kong polity. As a result, discourses on social rights in Hong Kong are often uncoupled from discourses on political and civil rights and are also superseded by the discourse of citizen responsibility, which hinges on the duty of "citizens" to contribute to the social stability and economic prosperity of the region overall.

Thus, Hong Kong's system of governance, which remains closely aligned in ideology (if not always in practice) to Western neoliberal models of governance, aims to create a competent citizenry that will contribute to national and international economic growth. Despite the fact that these goals echo those outlined in Ong's "Asian pastoral care" model practiced by governments—like that of the PRC—emphasizing social rights over civil or political rights, the means of actualizing these goals are substantially different in postcolonial Hong Kong than in postsocialist mainland China. Drawing on these discursive views of membership and belonging, Hong Kong social workers (and government representatives) sought to encourage mainland immigrants to develop a Hong Kong-based ideology of achieving these competencies in order to maintain Hong Kong's current and future social stability.

Focusing on the ways in which nineteenth- and early twentieth-century social reformers in the United States sought to change the thinking, habits, and behavior of certain disadvantaged segments of the population to align better with the goals of state-sanctioned projects, Barbara Cruikshank has argued that "the social confuses and reconstitutes the boundaries between the personal and the political, the economy and the state, the voluntary and the coercive" (1999:6). She elaborates: "once the social became the object of reform, agitation, and science, the political lost its spatial association with sovereign power and the state" (ibid. 7). In her analysis, Cruikshank describes the ways in which social reformers adopted a discourse of "self-help" to teach impoverished citizens how to act as independent agents who could work to fix problems such as their own joblessness. This discourse, framed by social workers in past eras yet strongly reminiscent of current neoliberal ideology, puts the responsibility for solving problems like citizens' welfare squarely on the shoulders of the individuals who suffer most (ibid. 54). As I describe in the remainder of this chapter, immigrant wives in Hong Kong faced similar lessons at the hands of Hong Kong social workers. Through programs focused on teaching immigrants how to adopt Hong Kong standards of self-regulatory, independent (that is, not dependent on social welfare), self-enterprising, and contributory behavior, social workers sought to turn "uncivilized" mainlanders into "civilized" individuals who could better integrate into Hong Kong life.

Civility, Responsibility, and Social Worker Motivation

Emily's concerns about her client's "irresponsible" behavior may well have been affected by the center's three other social workers, who all voiced similar concerns to me during formal questioning about their views of their immigrant clients. In all cases, the social workers distinguished between different kinds of mainlanders: those who were well educated, from the cities, or the more northern areas of China, versus the mostly rural women and children from Guangdong who formed the core of the center's client base. Very few of the center's female clients had not spent at least several years in Guangdong, often in Shenzhen, where they might have migrated from other parts of China to work in factories or where their husbands might have bought apartments for them to live close enough to Hong Kong to be visited on the weekends. But the rural women from Guangdong tended to be both the least cosmopolitan and least educated, and this group in particular was often described by the social workers as "uncivilized" (Cantonese: *yehmaahn*).[5] Siu-saan, another of the center's social workers, explained what she meant by "uncivilized" in the following way: "The way that they are 'uncivilized' is [that they think]: 'You gave me legal permission to immigrate here, so you should take complete responsibility for taking care of me in every way.' They 'blame' all of their problems on others. They won't think that something is their personal problem. It's everyone's problem." Other "undesirable" behavioral characteristics, such as poor hygiene, off-putting personal habits (including not always wearing shoes), and impoliteness, were also associated with both mainlanders and mainland immigrants in Hong Kong, but these kinds of quality[6] "defects" were more likely to be interpreted by Hong Kong locals as the kinds of cultural differences between mainlanders and Hong Kong people that I discussed in Chapter Five. Thus, what is noteworthy in Siu-saan's quote is that definitions of "civilized" behavior in Hong Kong were also fundamentally linked to larger social and political ideals that characterized Hong Kong people as having particular kinds of state/society relations that differed from mainlanders' ideologies of goals and privileges for interacting with state and society actors. In this case, "civilized" clients (that is, clients who fit local ideologies for membership in the Hong Kong polity) were willing to take charge of their lives and support through work or other community involvement rather than "passively" relying on acceptance of government aid.

Whether immigrant clients acted in "civilized" ways not only determined how social workers evaluated their clients' progress in adapting to life in Hong Kong, it also strongly influenced social workers' feelings about their individual clients. According to Siu-saan and Emily, many immigrants— like the woman quoted at the beginning of this chapter—arrived in Hong Kong with a sense of "entitlement" to government aid.[7] Fieldwork conducted on the mainland during the 1990s has indicated that most mainland "respondents believe that either the central or the local state should be responsible for providing the social security provisioning to which they believe they are entitled" (Croll 1999; see also Smart and Smart 2001 and Wong and Lee 2000). The mainland immigrants arriving in Hong Kong may well share this view, compounded by certain expectations about other state forms of welfare (such as housing, in particular) which should be provided as well. But the social workers I spoke with never mentioned socialization to certain PRC government-sponsored practices as a possible factor in the negative qualities they associated with their clients. Instead, social workers remained frustrated by their immigrant clients' feelings of "entitlement," which they often interpreted as a "personality" problem resulting from their clients' failures to conform to Hong Kong values espousing the importance of an individual's "contribution" to society.[8]

In most cases, the social workers qualified any negative feelings they expressed about clients by indicating that the more "considerate" mainlanders were less likely to bother the workers or approach them to help solve problems. Nonetheless, over time it became clear to me that many of the employees at the social service center distinguished between immigrants who had come in previous time periods, who were seen as hard-working, and the current wave, who were characterized as coming to Hong Kong in order to gain access to government resources without any intention of providing for themselves. It was Siu-saan, the social worker who had been working with immigrant clients longer than the other workers, who first voiced this viewpoint to me, noting that the immigrants she had known ten years previously had been extremely hardworking—willing to work up to three jobs at once to help support their families—in contrast to the majority of immigrants she had been servicing recently, whom she felt would rather not work. As Siu-saan was clearly going through a period of disillusionment, wanting a change to a different kind of client base after ten years of working with immigrants, I initially interpreted her statement about these differences in earlier and later immigrants' characteristics as exaggerated by the current discontent she was experiencing. When questioned, however, others at the center also indicated that they shared this view—a view in turn held by many long-term Hong Kong residents and that is similar to the kinds of stereotyping about immigrants prevalent in other societies, such as in the United States (see, for example, Steinberg 1989).

In earlier decades, immigrants from the mainland arrived in Hong Kong with stronger markers of difference—in the form of their simple, blue and gray Mao suits—which clearly indicated their inclusion in the PRC's socialist economy of the time. These previous generations of immigrants were seen as more deserving of immigration, given the difficulties they experienced living on the mainland during the Cultural Revolution. As I described in Chapter Two, however, one result of the economic and political liberalization that took place on the mainland in the 1970s was the mass influx of (mostly illegal) immigrants into Hong Kong, which resulted in a significant negative shift in Hong Kong people's perceptions of these immigrants—and of mainlanders in general. In 2000–02, mainland immigrants in Hong Kong continued to suffer from this stigmatization, and, as citizens who now share the benefits of the PRC's liberalized economic and political policies and whose lifestyles on the mainland are much more comfortable that they were in the past, they were no longer seen as "deserving" members of Hong Kong society. Such thoughts were exacerbated by Hong Kong residents' insecurities over their own futures, given the straightened economic circumstances they had experienced since 1997, but gender may also have played an important role in the biases against mainlanders arriving in Hong Kong at the time of my fieldwork. As I discussed at length in Chapter Three, the mainland wives of Hong Kong men were portrayed in the Hong Kong media as "gold diggers," searching to come to Hong Kong for the primary motive of relying on Hong Kong resources—including state-provided welfare, jobs "belonging" to locals rather than immigrants, or husbands' incomes. As a result, immigrants were vilified both as relying on government welfare that should be used instead to help unemployed locals and as stealing potential jobs away from locals who had lost their jobs during the long period of recession.[9] This strong public opinion affected the social workers at the center, particularly in their interactions with clients who were seen as able but unwilling to work.

When I mentioned this bias among center workers to Elizabeth, the social worker in charge of the center, she was surprised. Although she acknowledged that many immigrants did come to Hong Kong with the intention of drawing on government resources, she was also optimistic in pointing out the hardworking nature of many more recent clients as well. Noting the importance of clients' personalities in her ability to get along well with some more than others, she distinguished between the really positive feeling she got from working with some clients compared to the frustration she felt in working with others. Elizabeth cited the case of one long-term client, an older, widowed woman with two sons who had really "encouraged" her in her own life.

> She didn't know anything [when she came to Hong Kong]. Because before she had depended on her husband for everything. I think that her husband must have been one of those very traditional Chinese husbands. Very chauvinistic. He had to do everything himself. He made all of the decisions, and so on. So because he made all of the decisions, she didn't have to think about anything, or pay attention to anything. All she knew how to do was work in the fields, she didn't know how to do anything else. She told me that usually women who live in rural areas know how to kill chickens and ducks, but she didn't even know how to do this because her husband would help her do all of these things. And then her son got older, and he did these things. And she was illiterate. Later, her husband died, and she came to Hong Kong all by herself. She had to learn how to do everything from

scratch. I feel that the way that she encouraged me is that without knowing even one word, she has slowly begun to learn [to read]. And she has also been learning English—beginning from ABC, she's now already at a Third grade level. She is really diligent. There was a period of time when she was on CSSA [welfare], and she would still go and volunteer. She would spend lots of time volunteering, and she would work hard to help other people. So, you think: here's a person who didn't know anything, who continually works to improve herself. You can see that she has already improved in such a short period of time. Hong Kong is a city that is well-off, so you have to make more effort here, and here are people who will work so hard to be involved. The feeling that you get from these people is really positive. But there is another group that you see quite often, who don't have any plans to work hard to get involved with society. You can't deny that there is a group of people who come here to take resources. [They say:] "I don't know how. You teach me. You help me do it." This kind of thing. "Give it to me. Give me money." Sometimes, with even very simple things, like filling out forms, the client will depend on the worker. And then we'll say: "Why don't I teach you how to fill it out instead of filling it out for you, because afterwards you will still have many opportunities to fill out other forms." And then you can see that the expression on their faces has changed—their attitude will be awful—they'll think: "You won't help me fill it out. You won't help me. Forget it." When you see these kinds of people, it makes you feel very frustrated.

The "model" immigrant of this anecdote was indeed just that—after being nominated by Elizabeth, she was given an official award in a public relations ceremony sponsored by the Sham Shui Po District Office, in which her hard work and efforts at adjustment into local Hong Kong life were acknowledged. In this case, her inspiration for emulation stemmed from two particular qualities: First, she was not a passive recipient of state welfare, but instead spent full days volunteering to help others (including working in the kitchen of a home for elderly people) when she was depending on state welfare to pay her living expenses. Second, she worked hard to learn new things and "improve herself." This concept of "improving oneself"— a hallmark of Hong Kong culture that I experienced in my interactions with the local social workers and others there—was intimately tied to local discourses of belonging grounded in the Hong Kong-brand of neoliberal governance discussed in the previous section of this chapter. "Learning" was a big business in Hong Kong, and absolutely every employee at the center, as well as each of my other local Hong Kong contacts, were all enrolled in at least one evening class during the period of my fieldwork. In some cases, these courses were directly related to their work, so that they could further their knowledge of certain aspects of social work. Many employees also took advanced level English composition classes. One employee admitted that the class he was taking—and did not enjoy—on Hong Kong popular culture was not in any way pragmatic. Nevertheless, when I questioned him about his motivations for taking this class, he noted the necessity of maintaining the appearance of "improving himself," which would be valued by his boss and keep him on equal footing with his co-workers, none of whom wished to "fall behind." This fear of being "outmoded" was reinforced by the center's tight funding situation and the accompanying concern that employees could be laid off at the end of each fiscal year (see also Ku and Pun 2004)—part of the culture of "nervous" Hong Kong life that I described in Chapter Five.

Thus, this model client's openness to learning made her not just laudable for her hardworking attitude, but it also demonstrated that she had adopted a Hong Kong (rather than mainland-based) ideology of thinking and behavior that ensured her integration into Hong Kong social life. Overall, her actions and responsible attitude continued to set her apart from many other clients who were less open to the challenges they experienced in their Hong Kong lives. Social workers' interactions with clients who clearly needed to be taught how to accomplish certain everyday tasks, like "filling out forms," along with broader concepts of acting as responsible citizens in society, directly influenced the planning and content of many of the center's programs. Mutual help groups, in particular, were tailored to help teach different kinds of "responsibility" to the clients who participated in these groups. Prompted by success stories, such as that told by Elizabeth, social workers used a variety of methods to convey key concepts about Hong Kong hardworking and responsible attitudes to immigrants while simultaneously trying not to be too discouraged by the "failure" of other clients to grasp these concepts. In the next section, I provide an in-depth look at two mutual help groups and one social work case, in which an important aim of each social worker involved was to help increase her clients' sense of individual and social responsibility as an important means of aiding immigrants' socialization into Hong Kong life. Through these examples, I explain in more detail what exactly it means to "act responsibly" in Hong Kong and how Hong Kong social workers' views of acting responsibly often conflicted with immigrants' perceptions of their own (and their families') needs.

Lessons in Individual Responsibility: The Teenage Drama Group

The Teenage Mutual Aid Drama Group was run under the supervision of social worker Emily, who was personally interested in working with teenage clients. This group was comprised of ten teenagers, ranging in age from thirteen to nineteen, all of whom had to meet the center's participation requirement of having been in Hong Kong for less than one year. In most cases, the teenagers had arrived in Hong Kong several months before the group began, and all but one spoke fluent Cantonese. The premise for the group was to compete in a Traffic and Road Safety Drama Competition for New Arrival children and teenagers, which was sponsored and funded by the Sham Shui Po Police Department. Having identified traffic safety, and violations of traffic rules, as one of the most common offences committed by immigrants in the Sham Shui Po District, the Police Department hoped with this competition to elevate the level of awareness of proper traffic safety precautions among young immigrants. In addition to providing prizes, in the form of trophy cups for the three best skits, the Police Department funds provided a hot boxed lunch and a small gift for all participants as well as allowing for a budget of HK$500 (US$64) for each group to help pay for props and costumes.

The group was originally scheduled to meet over four weekends in November 2001 for two hours each meeting. However, the high level of interest by the teenage participants and their commitment to producing a viable skit for the drama competition in which they were involved led to a total of ten meetings overall, each lasting four hours on average. Despite the program's long hours, and heavy home and school commitments by the participants involved, there was almost perfect attendance at every group meeting. In this level of participation, the group was more successful than any of the other groups that I encountered during my fieldwork at the center.

Although one of Emily's aims for the drama group was to introduce her clients to some basic concepts about drama and playacting, her primary goal was to increase the participants' knowledge and awareness about communication—both their own and in their interactions with others. In particular, she hoped they would become more comfortable and confident in expressing themselves in various situations. Through these skills, Emily hoped to help these immigrants adapt to their new Hong Kong lives by allowing them to gain confidence about themselves, by encouraging them to express themselves clearly, and by teaching them—through these means—to "help" themselves. While "responsibility" was not openly stated as a goal to the program's participants, it remained an important theme in all of my discussions with Emily about the group.

Following an almost "set" formula that I experienced in other mutual help groups as well, the first two sessions focused primarily on "ice breaking" games, so that the participants could begin to get to know each other and feel comfortable in their interactions with one another. In this case, the games were modeled around "acting out" expressions or other drama-related concepts, with particular attention paid to the many ways in which nonspoken communication occurs. The next four meetings were spent preparing for the drama competition. Two meetings were dedicated to thinking up and deciding on possible plotlines for the skit, as well as voting on which participants would play which roles. (For most of this time, I was more of an observer than a participant, as Emily and I had both noticed a tendency by the teenagers to rely on me for the problem solving that Emily wanted the teenagers to work out on their own.) After much wrangling, the following plot was endorsed by all concerned. Two triad[10] members stood by the side of the road to hail a taxi. After the taxi driver, much to his horror, accidentally noticed the extremely large knife being carried by one of the triad members, one triad member panicked, killed the driver, and threw his body out of the taxi. Unfortunately for the triad members, they had forgotten that they did not know how to drive, and in trying to control the taxi, they ran over a pedestrian who happened to be crossing the street. This young, handsome victim was too busy listening to his walkman, reading a comic book, bouncing his basketball, and simultaneously trying to attract the attention of the beautiful woman across the street, so that he did not notice the taxi swerving down the road toward him. After he was hit, the young man and the two triad members, who had also been injured in the crash, were taken to the hospital, where they were examined by a doctor and a nurse. Meanwhile, the patients were visited in turn by an angel and a devil, each demanding obeisance. When the two triad members refused to kowtow to the angel, their lives were effectively over, with one dying and the other becoming a human "vegetable." The student escaped with a lighter sentence—he was only paralyzed from the waist down. Finally, the whole cast reappeared on stage to announce that road safety is important.

The lengthy process involved in proposing and agreeing on this plotline became the content through which Emily instructed her clients in the skills associated with communication that she wanted them to learn. Because of Emily's desire not to become overly involved in her clients' efforts at decision making, each decision made by the group took on a tortuous quality, lasting hours, until Emily would finally point out certain flaws in the students' reasoning and take enough charge to result in a completed decision. The finalization of the plot, the casting of the characters, and the process of deciding upon props and how they would be made and procured each took hours to resolve. The discussion about the props carried with it the added dimension of budgeting, as Emily had planned for the HK$500 allowance to cover not just the cost of props but also the cost of refreshments to be served at the final meeting following the competition. Although the allocation of responsibility of the procuring and making of each prop was finally decided more by Emily than by the group participants, the introduction of each new prop entailed a reminder from her about the need to plan carefully how the allowance monies would be used. Thus, planning, and the relationship between planning and responsibility, became a central lesson introduced to the group participants, as this lesson was repeated yet again during the long process to decide what refreshments would be served at the final meeting. The students, of course, desired both props and foods that would have easily carried them over budget, but as none of them had enough money to supplement the allowance provided by the Police Department, Emily was adamant that the students needed to learn the importance of working within the limited means available to them.

The following weekend, at the competition, it became apparent that the group's efforts in joint decision making had distracted them from producing a well-polished product. Despite offering a more creative plotline than the other skits, the actors' unpolished dialogue and shyly delivered lines apparently did not suitably impress the judges of the competition. Although there were three prizes and only seven skits, the teenage drama group did not place, and the participants were clearly very disappointed—complaining to Emily that they would have "tried harder" if they had realized there would be official prizes. Emily, however, reflected that the loss of the competition was an important lesson for the group participants and perhaps a more fitting conclusion to the group's content than if they had won. In particular, Emily explained to me that dealing with this loss had forced the group's participants to learn about ways of coping with failure. The participants, however, did not seem to make this connection, as they instead focused on the planning of the final party as a way to assuage their hurt pride. Yet not even the planning of the party refreshments escaped being integrated as an important "lesson-learning" mechanism. Several of the teenagers had never eaten pizza before, and most could not usually afford the HK$100 (US$13) cost of buying a large pizza at a local Domino's shop. Thus, it was a big decision to spend two-thirds of the final allowance money budgeted for the party on a pizza as a rare treat. At that time, I was a vegetarian, as I had been for the previous ten years. Although Emily knew this, the participants did not. Despite my objections—after all, I said, I had eaten pizza many times—Emily forced the participants to order a vegetarian pizza, since she considered that they needed to think about my needs as well as their own.

This final lesson in responsibility—the need to consider the feelings of others—was in keeping with the other means with which Emily had integrated the topic of responsibility into the group's content. Individually, the group participants were held to their word: if they said that they would come to the next meeting on time, they were expected to be on time and were chastised if, for any reason, they were late. As a group, they were responsible for planning their involvement in the competition and budgeting accordingly, but they were also held responsible for the fact that their failure to communicate effectively led to their loss in the competition, even though they had worked hard on the skit and its props. As an observer, I found the means with which Emily delivered her lessons on responsibility to be heavy-handed, considering that when quizzing the participants on their anticipated arrival time for the next meeting, she never seemed to consider that many of them had substantial responsibilities associated with their own families, such as looking after younger siblings while parents worked on the weekends. In one case, a teenage girl of fourteen was chastised for not having called to say that she would be late when she had been kept at a family gathering longer than expected. In another case, one of the thirteen-year-old participants always showed up on time, often accompanied by her seven-year-old sister and eight-year-old brother. At the time, it struck me as inconsistent that Emily never recognized these young teenagers' commitments to family responsibilities, and instead focused only on their responsibilities to group activities. In retrospect, however, it seems that since these teenagers already understood the importance of being "responsible" family members, Emily hoped instead to encourage their sense of responsibility to other kinds of social communities outside of their families. As with other programs at the center, her lessons met with mixed success. In comments made to me months later, Emily unhappily acknowledged that many of group's participants had often failed to appear for the volunteer duties to which they had been recruited as "willing" participants by the center's social workers.

Responsibility to Family: The Case of Siu-ping

When I had been at the center for only a few weeks, Alexa, one of the social workers, told me about a young teenager who was part of a family case file she had been following. This teenage girl, Siu-ping, had recently come to Hong Kong to live with her father, her stepmother, and her several step-siblings. Siu-ping's handicapped stepsister was Alexa's primary client, but one afternoon Alexa also spent over two hours talking with the family's father, trying to give him "support." Siu-ping's father was upset that he had lost his restaurant industry job because he had taken time off to help his recently arrived mainland wife and children. His wife refused to learn to use local transportation, he said, and could not get around and take care of the children without his help. In particular, she was unable to take their handicapped daughter to her physical therapy appointments at a local charity hospital. Siu-ping's father was worried about money, and he was tired of trying to do everything for everyone in the family. Knowing that he was at his wit's end in trying to get by, Alexa was helping him to apply for social welfare and also to look for another job. A few days later, Alexa asked if I would be willing to provide some private English tutorial classes for Siu-ping, whose English level was particularly low—less than a local first grade level—because Alexa felt she needed some symbolic token of support. Siu-ping's relationship with her stepmother was not good, her father did not seem to take her "side" in any family disagreements, and she was often not even given any money to buy lunch at school.

Alexa did not know the whereabouts of Siu-ping's mother, and it seemed that Siu-ping had been living with her boyfriend's family on the mainland for several years before immigrating to Hong Kong. Siu-ping's attendance at the Induction Program class for mainland immigrant children ages six to sixteen was sporadic, and several times during the fall of 2001 she left Hong Kong to go back to the mainland without asking permission or telling her father how long she planned to be gone. Sometimes Siu-ping would "disappear" to the mainland after a disagreement with her father, and on school holidays she would regularly leave home without telling him where she was going. Throughout this time, Alexa tried to mediate between the two of them, although the focus of her interactions with Siu-ping and her father reflected an important difference. Despite Siu-ping's father's need to rely, hopefully only for a short time, on social welfare, his dedication to helping his recently arrived immigrant family deal with their adjustment to Hong Kong cast him in a favorable light as being responsible in his interactions with his family members. Siu-ping, on the other hand, was viewed as acting irresponsibly toward her family—both in terms of her lack of respect for her father's position within the family and in terms of her failure to contribute to the care and well-being of her stepsiblings. From Alexa's point of view, Siu-ping's marginalized position within the family did not justify the fact that she felt no need to help ease her father and stepmother's burdens in the family's adjustment to the arrival of the wife and children in Hong Kong. As a result, Siu-ping remained the focus of Alexa's efforts aimed at getting her to act in a more responsible manner toward her Hong Kong family members.

Alexa's attempt to arrange the extra tutoring for Siu-ping was viewed as "preferential" and was not well received by other office workers, who felt they knew of clients just as bad in English who were not getting individual attention. Quite a lively debate ensued on this subject among several center employees, during which time Alexa held her ground and reiterated that in lieu of not being able to offer Siu-ping any real long-term support, she hoped this "gesture" would provide some sort of symbolic "support" for a young woman otherwise totally lacking in support on every level. Over the next couple of months, I met with Siu-ping four or five times, each time taking over one hour to help her learn maybe ten basic English vocabulary words, such as *table, plate, orange,* and *bicycle.* Her progress was agonizingly slow, and she constantly told me about the frustration involved with always getting a "o" on her school English assignments. She told me very little about her family, but she did say she was very moved that Alexa had arranged this extra tutoring for her. Very quickly, however, a problem surfaced: it became apparent that Siu-ping had begun to cast me in a role as "best friend" rather than tutor—a relationship I did not want to encourage given her youth and the extent of her serious family problems. Concerned about how to handle the situation, I turned to Alexa for help.

Alexa had also been surprised by Siu-ping's rapid embracing of me into her current and future plans, and she explained Siu-ping's attachment to me as indicative of the kinds of "self-centered" (that is, "irresponsible") behavior that had led to the difficult relationship that Siu-ping continued to experience with her father and stepmother. Commenting that "nine times out of ten" Siu-ping's accounts of family quarrels were so completely biased as to be unreliable, Alexa considered most of Siu-ping's comments and complaints to her to be untrustworthy and described to me a number of instances when she had had to "untangle" what Siu-ping was saying. (In other words, Alexa had to guess at a more objective account of events to try to understand what had really been going on.) Noting Siu-ping's difficult family background, her history of limited contact with her father, the general unhappiness of her living situation, as well as the fact that she was a teenager and teenagers are normally self-involved, Alexa told me that: "You could say that this behavior is natural." Nonetheless, Alexa was not prepared to pardon Siu-ping's "self-centered" behavior by relying on such excuses. Alexa very much believed that Siu-ping needed to be more responsible for her own actions and their repercussions, and their talks together frequently focused on this subject. In particular, Alexa wanted Siu-ping to improve her interactions with her father, whose authority as her legal guardian she continued to ignore completely. Alexa also began to encourage Siu-ping to become more involved as a volunteer with center activities, so she could learn that she, too, could help others, rather than always be the recipient of others' help. In the end, Siu-ping's school schedule changed, and Alexa made use of the opportunity to end our tutorial sessions. Several months later, I asked Alexa how Siu-ping's adjustment to Hong Kong was going. Alexa's attempts to get Siu-ping involved in center activities had not been very successful, as she had only participated as a volunteer on one or two occasions. Likewise, her encouragement for Siu-ping to begin acting more "responsibly" toward her Hong Kong family members seemed to have failed as well: Alexa told me that Siu-ping had moved out of her father's house and was living with an uncle in another part of Hong Kong. Given the mutual distrust with which Siu-ping and her Hong Kong father and stepfamily viewed each other, responsible, respectful behavior was apparently not possible between them.

Responsibility to Society: Voluntarism

Bryan Turner has identified the "voluntary sector" as one of the most important means for providing meaningful opportunities of social participation and democratic involvement at the local level in a modern world based on global capitalist practice (2001:200). Reflecting this belief—that the way to foster social meaning and involvement lies with the participation of individual Hong Kong residents—the Hong Kong Department of Social Welfare launched a "volunteer movement" in 1998. With the aims of "maximizing community resources" and "enhancing a sense of social belonging," this movement attempted to involve Hong Kong people "from all walks of life to participate in building society so as to develop a caring and harmonious community" (www.volunteering-hk.org). Under the sponsorship of Betty Tung, the wife of former SAR Chief Executive Tung Chee-wah, this movement was formed, in part, as a response to the economic downturn that took place following the Asian financial crisis in 1997 and was based upon the assumption that involving citizens in volunteer activities would increase individuals' personal sense of responsibility as well as enhance their commitment to social responsibility. Despite seeing advertising posters all around the city, I was not aware of Hong Kong people in general participating in this program. Nevertheless, the ideas that it represented were seized upon by government representatives and social workers as one means of integrating mainlanders to the ideal qualities of civility in the Hong Kong polity. Backed by specific funding requirements that encouraged the introduction of volunteer work to recent immigrants, social workers focused on the concept of voluntarism as one of the most common ways to introduce and promote ideas about social responsibility to the clients at the center.

Alexa was the social worker who planned and held a "learning to volunteer" mutual help group, which met over three weekends in January 2002. Although immigrant clients already participated as volunteers in many of the center's activities and programs, the center's social workers were motivated to train a core "group" of immigrants to serve as volunteers in helping to perform a variety of social work-related tasks. Their reasons for doing so were related to the daily functioning of the center as well as concern about immigrants' socialization. First, the social workers wanted to get their clients more involved in community affairs. Second, social workers thought that increased voluntarism at the social service center could enhance service provision to clients. Third, volunteering in center activities was one valuable way clients could continue to interact with social workers even after they had exceeded one year of residency in Hong Kong. Finally, recruiting volunteers from their immigrant client base was actually one of the stipulations required by the center's Funding and Service Agreement with the Social Welfare Department. As a result, the workers' inability to involve sufficient numbers of clients as volunteers would actually jeopardize their primary funding source for the following year. Making use of the rhetoric and materials supplied by the Hong Kong-wide "volunteer movement" that had been begun in 1998, social workers gave all volunteers "log books" to record their hours of community service. Those individuals reaching milestones of 100 or more community hours served per year were automatically recognized in a special ceremony and awarded a prize by the Social Welfare Department. Nonetheless, as I relate below, few immigrants of my acquaintance ever adopted the practice of voluntarism as more than a temporarily meaningful activity.

The participants of Alexa's "learning to volunteer" group were recruited primarily from the basic-level English class that I had begun teaching in December 2001, and the group's overall interaction was helped by the fact that at least half of the thirteen registered participants already knew each other from their twice weekly attendance at my class. Alexa also pointed out that perhaps their interest in English indicated personalities predisposed to an open-mindedness of expression, such that she was both pleased and surprised at the "active" participation of the majority of members in the group. Most of the sessions were organized along similar lines. Meetings began with a report on the previous session's "homework" assignment, followed by one or two "ice-breaking" or "getting to know each other" games. Next came a brief component on the topic of being a volunteer and the theme of "contribution to society." The majority of each session was then spent learning about a topical subject related to Hong Kong life and immigrant adjustment. Finally, each session concluded with a "sharing time," in which all participants were free to converse while eating the specially prepared sweet soup dessert that had been cooking while the earlier part of the meeting was in progress. The sixth and final session was meant to serve as these women's "volunteer" activity, and it was organized to allow up to forty immigrant women to participate in an information session to learn more about housing and health care resources in Hong Kong. Although led by Alexa, the women (including myself) who had participated in the mutual help group were incorporated into the presentation through the performance of skits on housing and health care situations, the quizzing of clients on their understanding and retention of the talk's content, and the handing out of snacks at the end of the session. For most of the women involved, this was their first "volunteer" experience, and they found it fun and interesting enough to sign up for a five-day volunteer workshop held in conjunction with a local home for the elderly one month later.

Alexa's goals for the group were multifaceted. On the most basic level, her goals were for the participating clients to learn about the local resource availability for housing and health care, so that they could participate as volunteers at the information session based on these subjects at the conclusion of the group. On a more complex level, she hoped through discussions about these topics to address issues of communication and voluntarism with these women so that participation in this group would represent the first step in their greater participation in Hong Kong community life and activities. As with any mutual help group, one main purpose was to introduce a number of clients to each other in the hope that their shared meeting and experiences would allow them to further their own personal social networks, thus reducing their dependence on social workers to help them solve their problems. Furthermore, Alexa hoped these immigrants would actively share their newly gained knowledge about local resources with other friends needing such information, thus improving their self-confidence while also demonstrating their ability to understand and engage with local valuation systems. As was the case with Emily's teenage drama group, the theme of "responsibility" was incorporated into the group's content both through discussion and practice, and the practice of everyday mundane activities provided the concrete means through which to introduce the group to larger lessons about ideologies of belonging in the Hong Kong context. Alexa gave the group's members individual "homework" assignments, which they were required to report back to the class. She also assigned the task of preparing a soup for each meeting and put one person in charge of all planning regarding soup preparation, which included budgeting and buying the necessary ingredients. These tasks provided the lesson that carrying through with a task was one easy way of "acting responsibly" and also demonstrated the applicability of this concept to everyday life. But the issue of "contribution" remained the central theme addressed, and the group's participants were actively encouraged to contribute to the larger community as a matter of personal and social responsibility.

Alexa's structuring of group learning sessions encouraged the involvement of the group's members, who all told me that they judged the program to be successful, since they had all "learned something" (Cantonese: *hohkdou yeh*). To learn about health service provision and resources in the Sham Shui Po area, the group visited a public women's and children's health clinic located nearby. To improve our understanding of housing options and eligibility for applying to public housing, we also took a "fieldtrip" to the Housing Authority's local office. Alexa always assigned lessons for the group's participants to complete during these visits. As a result, the women were required to wait for available service representatives and then ask them questions, the answers of which would then be reported back to the group. At the Housing Authority's office, for example, the women had to find out how they could check on an application for public housing in process; whether there were special application procedures for households with senior citizen members; whether only permanent residents could apply for public housing; and how the name of a child newly arrived in Hong Kong could be added to an existing application. By addressing the gathering and presentation of topic materials as a group effort, Alexa ensured her clients' involvement and interest in the discussions that were held on these topics, and complicated bureaucratic information became less "dry" with more personal involvement. Equally as important, the visits to these offices and the clients' need to find out the answers to particular questions at each office served to "demystify" these local bureaucratic practices. Serving the same principle as teaching a client how to "fill out a form" rather than filling it out for her, these visits were meant to teach these women the basic protocol necessary to gain information from any Hong Kong government department or service representative. Finally, these exercises also required that the women practice their general communication skills with Hong Kong locals. When Amber, one of the group's immigrant participants, reported to the group the highly detailed response she received in answer to her questions at the women's clinic, Alexa praised her for her ability to elicit information from others, and turned her response into a lesson on how to develop successful communication skills through the cultivation of a polite attitude and the proper etiquette of interaction with others. Overall, learning to communicate well was seen as an important way for immigrants to achieve the goals of "self-help" integral both to Hong Kong social work practice as well as local ideologies of belonging.

Most of the participants from this "learning to volunteer" group were recruited for a five-day program the following month, which was jointly sponsored by the social service center and some social work student interns working at a local home for the elderly. The goal of this second "voluntary" program was to learn about common ailments and behavioral difficulties experienced by the residents of the home and to plan an hour-long "party and social gathering" for the home's residents. After visiting the home and learning about suitable activities that had been planned for the home's residents in the past, we agreed on a social program that included the following elements: two games requiring very simple motor skills to be played with the group as a whole; the performance of two popular and old-fashioned Cantonese songs; and a snack session of dumplings with conversation afterwards. In planning the program, the needs of the elderly were emphasized: the games allowed the residents to remain seated and did not require good sight or sudden movement; the songs were picked to appeal to people of an older generation; and the food, both dumplings and "prizes" awarded at the games, were soft and easy to chew. The immigrant women seemed to enjoy both the planning of the party's details and their interaction with these elderly members of Hong Kong society, who were clearly in need of "help" and entertainment. The day of the performance went well, and there were no surprises. Attendance for the group's meetings and final performance was high; the immigrant women were happy to spend additional free time chatting with the home's residents after the conclusion of the party; and all the center's clients (including me) were awarded "certificates" of training to work with the elderly by the organization running the home. Thus, the "learning to volunteer" group had performed according to Alexa's hopes: the women in the group were seemingly well on their way to becoming a corps of volunteers active in participating and contributing to community involvement in different situations.

To judge both from comments collected by Alexa after this party, and from my conversations with the women involved, the women's feelings about their volunteer experiences were, by and large, positive. One participant concluded: "My personality opened up, and my life became more meaningful. I was able to learn communication skills and how to get along with other people. And also learn interesting things that I had never seen or heard before. For this, I say thank you [Miss Alexa] for giving me this opportunity to learn and hear and see more. I am very happy. Thanks again." And Amber wrote: "After doing this volunteer work, I feel really happy. I think that by helping other people I can hope to reach my goal of making other people happy. Helping others is really just helping oneself." These comments and others indicated that the women felt they learned new things, improved their communication skills, and had an opportunity to interact with local people, which they valued. Amber's comments about learning and helping others, and the fact that she had been able to become "happier" through this involvement, were also echoed in other conversations I had with her. Months later, she told me:

> Before, I would always hear you say "volunteer," but I didn't know what that was. After [the social workers] told us, taught us what it means to volunteer, then I knew what it was. So I learned something. Before I didn't know: What is a volunteer? What does a volunteer do? Why be a volunteer?

I didn't know that a volunteer must act professionally, must have a plan for helping others appropriately. Before I didn't know this . . . I like to volunteer. I like to help people. When you help others and you see they are happy, then you feel happy, too. You can think, "Oh, I am a useful person. I can help others, bring them happiness." I think this is a good thing. And you can learn lots of things . . . and teach others what you have learned.

Another participant, Allison, was also very enthusiastic about her volunteer experience. Indeed, she was so excited that she supplemented the prizes and treats that we had gotten for the home's residents with snacks that she bought with her own money. This volunteer training and experience came at a time when Allison had just had the serious disagreement with her elderly mother-in-law that led to her and her husband's move to their own apartment (see Chapters Three and Four for a more detailed discussion about Allison and her disagreement with her in-laws). As a result, Allison found the training about dealing with the ailments and behavioral difficulties of the elderly to be relevant to her own life. She also voiced a personal interpretation about the experience that was not expressed by any of my other informants:

I think that doing volunteer work can help me regulate my temper (Cantonese: *peihei*; Mandarin: *piqi*). My temper is usually not good—[and at my expression of surprise, she emphasized the point again]. My temper is actually not good. But I don't lose my temper when I am outside—I usually just get mad at my husband . . . But when you are doing volunteer work, you have to take care of other people. You have to have a good temper, explaining things to other people, taking care of elderly people. Your status is like being a son or a daughter to them, [to] take care of them, give them things to eat. If you don't have a good temper, it's useless.

Focusing on the patience involved with learning and caring for others, Allison singled out this experience as helping her adjust her attitudes and behavior to cope with the ongoing conflicts she had with her in-laws since her immigration to Hong Kong.

Judging by these comments, it would seem that the women involved had certainly accomplished some of the goals that Alexa had initially hoped to accomplish with her mutual help group. However, one immigrant, Cybil, was less impressed with both the message involved and the program that resulted:

> Actually, I was really nervous that day because I was late. But I don't think that we really helped anyone . . . It was such a short period of time, and there were so many elderly people. Those people who were happy didn't really need the program, and those who weren't happy won't have been changed by such a small program. Because it was a really small thing. I even sang badly . . . I felt like I didn't really make a contribution. But I was sincere [in my participation]. If I was going to go, I didn't want to be late. I rushed to the bus stop because I was afraid that I was going to be late.

Like the other participants, Cybil picked up on Alexa's goals for the group, using the word *contribution*, and explaining how she had "rushed to the bus stop" and worried that she would be "late." Nonetheless, and unlike the others, she seemed not to have derived any greater meaning from this experience. Cybil's appraisal of the group's project demonstrated that she had gained a greater understanding of the local norms valuing responsibility; at the same time, however, it seemed that she rejected the value of these ideologies, opting instead to criticize these forms of participatory social behavior and individual responsibility to which she had been introduced. Cybil's criticisms were compounded by the fact that she had not sung well, which she found particularly bothersome on the grounds that she had formerly been an amateur singer of Chinese opera. Perhaps, however, Cybil's feelings resonated more with the overall reactions of the others than the remarks they offered made apparent. Within a month, Alexa was expressing her frustration to me that the women of this volunteer corps were too caught up in the busy details of their everyday lives—working, socializing, and raising children—so that they were rarely available to participate as volunteers in other activities.

On the one hand, Alexa's failure to engage these women in a "voluntary" work ethic highlights the disjuncture that existed between Hong Kong government and social work-sponsored projects promoting this concept and the lack of a public discourse acknowledging the importance of voluntary contribution as a means of social engagement. Writing about voluntarism in contemporary Japan, Nakano found that "the decision to adopt a volunteer identity is historically specific, institutionally constrained, and grounded in local contexts" (2000:97). For mainland women immigrants in Hong Kong, there was little historical support for participating in voluntary work: their socialization experiences on the mainland had not prepared them for such work nor was there strong local support for such work in Hong Kong outside of the social service center. Furthermore, such work was likely to conflict with the paying jobs and child-care activities that formed the most important aspects of women's lives in Hong Kong. On the other hand, these women's "disappearance" from the range of social worker involvement indicated that these immigrants' increased levels of local knowledge and self-awareness may perhaps have made them more successful than most in adjusting to the Hong Kong world around them.

Contribution, Empowerment, and Ideologies of Belonging in Hong Kong

The importance of "responsibility" was a central aspect of the local norms of belonging in Hong Kong life promoted by the social workers at the center, both in terms of their interactions with their clients and with regard to their decisions about their own lives and work. Siu-saan, in particular, had been heavily influenced in evaluating her responsibility to her clients by an encounter that she had with a local grassroots leader. While still a student, Siu-saan had taken part in a "community development" internship in which she and other young social workers were sent out to different grassroots organizations to help encourage participation in social and political events by individuals at the local level. This leader, who Siu-saan described (using colloquial Cantonese) as very clever or "sharp" (*lek*), questioned her involvement in community development in a way that Siu-saan had never forgotten. As Siu-saan recalled, this woman said: "You social workers only know how to push us forward. In the end, who takes responsibility? For this behavior, for these things that we do? In the end, who bears the burden [of our actions]?" Siu-saan was so struck by the strength of this woman's argument that her personal beliefs about the roles of social workers in society changed. As a result, she has worked since that time in service-provision work rather than the riskier and more demanding community development work.

In fact, there is very little social work of the community development variety in Hong Kong, and one social work professor estimated that perhaps only 1 percent of government social work funding is spent on community development, the key tenet of which is based on "empowering" local individuals to act in more "political" (that is, from the point of view of the government, "controversial" and potentially "destabilizing") ways. Unlike the social service center where I conducted my research, some organizations in Hong Kong were involved in political issues that the government would rather not address, such as the right of abode issue and the "cage dwellers"—those individuals who are so poor that they live in cages rather than apartments. At the time of my research, popular opinion in Hong Kong linked the violent protests and arson attacks that occurred in August 2000 at the Immigration Department, which I discussed at the beginning on Chapter Two, with one of these organizations.[11] Citing this incident as a prime example, Siu-saan cautioned that social workers should find socially responsible ways of interacting with their clients and make sure they have taught their clients what the outcomes of their actions will be. From her point of view, a "safer" way of encouraging "empowerment," for both worker and client, was represented by the concept of "self-help," which could teach immigrants to interact in a self-confident way with the local people and situations they encountered on a daily basis. To this end, Siu-saan was not only a strong supporter of the concept of "individual responsibility"—as detailed earlier—but she was also actively involved with inculcating immigrants in a hegemonic Hong Kong identity based on models of self-entrepreneurship (Ku and Pun 2004).

As I discussed in this chapter, local understandings of "responsibility" were complex and meaningful in the interactions that took place between Hong Kong social workers and their mainland immigrant clients. As demonstrated by the requirements outlined for participants in the teenage drama group, individual responsibility was judged according to one's ability to plan and budget, to have thoughtful and considerate interaction with others, and to keep one's commitments. In the case of Siu-ping, responsibility to family was defined as being respectful of elders and maintaining a "traditionally Chinese" hierarchy of power and command within the family, as well as by contributing to the family's overall functioning and well-being. Finally, the emphasis on voluntarism and active community involvement focused on the idea of needing to "contribute" to society. Through such involvement, individuals could improve their own skills of interaction and communication, while also learning about the social world around them. In all cases, clients' integration to local Hong Kong life was judged on the basis of immigrants' abilities to demonstrate that they had understood, and could also act, in ways that were deemed "responsible" by the social workers at the service center. These views of responsibility echoed the views expressed by Hong Kong government employees, who, as I discussed in Chapter Five, employed a similar discourse of "responsibility" to inculcate in recent immigrants an appreciation and understanding for the principles of "law and order" in Hong Kong society.

While both social workers and government department representatives emphasized the need for Hong Kong residents to act responsibly as individuals, their concern was not always aimed at protecting the individuals themselves. Rather, acting responsibly was deemed an important factor of overall social and community functioning and success. To act responsibly as an individual also signified that one was acting responsibly toward society as a whole and thereby contributing to the overall well-being, social stability, and economic prosperity of the region. One woman's desire to receive government support to stay at home with her child instead of working might not threaten the orderly running of society, but should large numbers of women—like the client Emily discussed at the beginning of this chapter—begin expecting or demanding such support, this situation would result in a significant drain on government resources and potentially undermine the confidence of working mothers who might resent the unfair advantage they perceived nonworking mothers to enjoy. This definition of social responsibility—couched within the language of individual rights and responsibilities—is clearly distinguishable from the idea of collective responsibility that many mainland immigrants learned through PRC government propaganda campaigns which, as I explained at the beginning of this chapter, have instead championed the importance of working together for collective, rather than individual, goals.

By attempting to socialize mainland immigrants as "civilized" and "responsible" Hong Kong people, social workers and government representatives in Hong Kong sought to change the negative ideologies and behaviors that they assumed all mainlanders to hold. These ideologies included dependence on welfare and other forms of state support that Hong Kong people do not readily associate with their own "self-enterprising" personalities (Ku and Pun 2004). Another motive behind these attempts may have included the desire to "neutralize" the threats posed by mainland immigrants, and mainland immigrant women, in particular. As I have documented throughout this book, the mainland wives who immigrated to Hong Kong for the purpose of family reunion with their Hong Kong husbands were seen as "threatening" to Hong Kong's orderly society for many reasons. These perceptions went well beyond the concern that immigrant wives and their families in Hong Kong would be dependent on social welfare. Other concerns also hinged on women's roles as mothers, wives, and daughters-in-law in their reunited Hong Kong families, where their presence had the effect of challenging local norms of family authority and was perceived as potentially jeopardizing the health and well-being of children and grand-children. Social workers' and governmental officials' concerns about the health and well-being of immigrant children (that linked their health to Hong Kong's future economic, political, and social well-being) targeted immigrant mothers for particular lessons about child development, communication, and "parenting" skills. These efforts to socialize immigrant women into local ideologies of civility and membership were strongly gendered in the sense that immigrant men from the mainland may not have been seen as threats to Hong Kong society in these same ways. Nevertheless, these concerns and efforts reflected the generally negative perceptions about mainlanders held by their Hong Kong Chinese compatriots, who continue to articulate these perceptions of difference that stem from the different political pasts and contemporary political realities of these two regions of the PRC.

EIGHT

Uneasy Reunions

I began this book with a quote from A-Chun, one of the mainland immi-grant wives I got to know over the course of my research on family reunion migration to Hong Kong. Thus, it seems only fitting to return to her words in concluding this book. Reflecting on her immigration experiences, in-cluding her decade of separation from her husband, her reunion with her husband and children in Hong Kong, and her transition to lower-class liv-ing conditions once there, A-Chun cast her move in a positive light. In early summer 2002, about a year and a half after she had legally immigrated to Hong Kong, she told me:

> I've already adjusted well to living in Hong Kong. The year we first came—
> that year was difficult—where we lived, getting kids situated in schools . . .
> But since I've come I've done better than many others. At least, I've adjusted
> well, I'm happy to be with my husband, our family is reunited . . . These
> simple things are enough to satisfy me—perhaps it's because my personality

is like that. Since I was young, my personality has always been this way. I'm not like others who will ask, "How much money? How much money?" . . . I see the kids are healthy, and that's already really good.

My most recent visit with A-Chun and her daughters, in January 2007, confirmed that she still had a positive outlook on her move to Hong Kong and that she and her family were still healthy and doing well. Like A-Chun, many other mainland immigrants to Hong Kong, who have weathered the difficult processes of split-family life and adjustment to Hong Kong's densely inhabited, nervous but orderly, postcolonial yet cosmopolitan, neo-liberal and rights-focused society, have also adjusted well and do not regret the moves and choices they made. Nonetheless, many mainland wives were less successful than A-Chun in negotiating the complex family relationships produced through their cross-border marriages and in adapting to life in Hong Kong once there.

While waiting to immigrate to Hong Kong, women experienced the stress associated with raising children alone and often felt emotionally distant from husbands. Although wives enjoyed relatively comfortable living standards on the mainland during this time, wives' and husbands' relationships often deteriorated as a result of the long years spent living separately, and wives' adaptations to Hong Kong were made more difficult by the downward mobility that they experienced as well as by the intense conflicts that often resulted from living together with unfamiliar in-laws in their tiny (and often decrepit) Hong Kong homes. These tensions, together with the strong social prejudice and economic marginalization that immigrant wives faced in Hong Kong, reinforced their needs to turn to other sources of information in adapting to Hong Kong's hectic pace of life and rational and "orderly" culture of work and interpersonal relations. As a result, many wives turned to social work organizations, which were often directly subsidized by the Hong Kong government, for these sources of information. Through their interactions with both family members and social workers, immigrant women and children were introduced to the normative ideologies of belonging in Hong Kong, which have resulted from Hong Kong's historical status as a British colony as well as from Hong Kong people's unease at being "reunited" with the PRC after more than one hundred and fifty years of colonial rule.

I think it is fair to say that many immigrants had not expected their transitions to Hong Kong life to be as difficult as they were. Of course, the fact that my fieldwork targeted women who had just arrived in Hong Kong meant that my informants were grappling with the onslaught of Hong Kong's many sights and sounds—some exciting, some horrifying, and many overwhelming—for the first time. As a result, their feelings of difficulty, upset, and anger may have been particularly intense. Most wives had not visited Hong Kong for more than a few weeks during the many years they had waited to immigrate there, and the media images of comfortable, middle-class Hong Kong life that they had seen on satellite TV programs while waiting to migrate, combined with their relatively well-off situations on the mainland, may have led them to imagine similar lifestyles for themselves once in Hong Kong. In contrast, wives often found themselves living in crowded, dirty tenements or tiny public housing units with husbands and in-laws. They struggled to find jobs and to communicate their needs to social workers, employers, and government officials, and they continued to hope that, perhaps through their children, they would one day benefit from the cosmopolitan advantages offered by living in Hong Kong rather than on the mainland. Hong Kong's legacies from its colonial past—its international orientation, global status, transnational ways of life—were the qualities that had driven wives' desires to immigrate to Hong Kong and to stay there despite the conflicts and tensions they experienced with family members, social workers, and other Hong Kong people who shaped their periods of transition to Hong Kong life. Nonetheless, many of my informants had been taken off-guard not only by the actual differences between Hong Kong and the mainland but also by the strong rhetoric of difference between themselves and mainlanders perpetuated by Hong Kong people, whose (often unfriendly) actions toward immigrants served as concrete and constant reminders both of the power inherent in abstract conceptions of people and places and also of the ways in which discursive ideologies of membership and belonging have real effects on the lives of immigrants and citizens.

In this way, the situations of mainland immigrants in Hong Kong share strong resonances with the experiences of immigrants—both legal and illegal—throughout the world, whose experiences of inclusion in and exclusion from national or community membership at both actual and discursive levels remains a fundamental aspect of their process of immigration. In the United States, debates over immigrant rights and attempts to "shore up" the borders are ongoing, but they have been particularly intense in recent years, focusing on issues of both political and economic "security" since September 11, 2001. In many European countries, where immigration has strong links to colonialism but has also been facilitated by the formation of the supranational European Union (as once difficult-to-cross borders have become easier to traverse), racial tensions are widespread and reports of immigrant-related violence have become increasingly common (see, for example, Silverstein 2004 and Wikan 2002). In these cases—and in many others—immigration is a socially and politically charged issue because the presence of immigrants—whether or not they are deemed to belong to the communities in which they live—challenges the ideal qualities of civility that define membership in particular locations through the everyday interactions that take place among immigrants and other members of the societies in which they live. Nevertheless, as I explained in the introduction, the case of the family reunion migration that takes place across the Hong Kong/mainland border presents a particularly compelling window for examining these processes of immigration, citizenship, membership, and belonging, because of the strong tensions of similarity that exist among mainland immigrants and the Hong Kong people who seek to exclude them from membership status in the Hong Kong polity.

Mainland Chinese wives and their Hong Kong Chinese husbands, like other Hong Kong people, are all citizens of the PRC. Mainland wives and Hong Kong people also share similar racial and cultural backgrounds and a long historical past, characterized by intensive familial and economic interaction between residents of Hong Kong and Southeast China. Although there were real barriers to interaction among the people of Hong Kong and Guangdong during the PRC's Cultural Revolution, since the late 1970s, the two areas have once again been increasingly interconnected through business, media, and travel. Thousands of Hong Kong people go to the mainland every day for either work or pleasure, and the rapid economic development taking place in the areas of Southeast China bordering on Hong Kong has significantly raised standards of living, created a culture of consumption, and encouraged the development of service-based industry. Furthermore, the majority of Hong Kong citizens are first, second, or third generation immigrants from the mainland. In other words, the mainland wives who immigrated to Hong Kong to join their husbands came to Hong Kong secure in the belief of strong similarities between them and their husbands. In particular, they focused on the fact that they and their husbands were all Chinese, and therefore placed strong emphasis on "traditionally Chinese" family values, which included the importance of family reunion. These beliefs had been reinforced by the PRC nationalist rhetoric deployed throughout the educational system and at key historical moments, such as Hong Kong's return to mainland Chinese sovereignty on July 1, 1997, which also emphasized the similarities between Hong Kong people and mainlanders, who were described as one "family" by the PRC party-state apparatus (Pan et al. 2001).

Why, then, did many of the immigrant wives I got to know during my research in Hong Kong feel as if they did not "belong" in Hong Kong? Almost one year after first arriving in Hong Kong, one informant told me:

> I don't really have any feeling of sense of belonging (Cantonese: *guisuhk-gam*) to Hong Kong. It's like I'm not really a Hong Kong person—that's my feeling. I don't feel like I'm a Hong Kong resident (Cantonese: *guimahn*; Mandarin: *jumin*) or a part of Hong Kong. I don't have any sense of warmth or closeness here . . . It may be because I find it difficult to communicate with Hong Kong people, or also because I think many Hong Kong people look down on people who come from the mainland. That's an obstacle . . . There's nothing about Hong Kong that makes it my place.

Differences in culture, language, nationality, ethnicity—these are the usual suspects that are cited in studies focusing on problems of immigrant incorporation to host societies, and certainly mainland immigrant wives and children in Hong Kong did experience some of these differences. What they had not reckoned on, however, were the ways in which the political differences between the two regions of the PRC would influence their experiences of adjustment to Hong Kong. To be sure, the political difference that separates Hong Kong from the mainland does not exist as an arena that is entirely separate from culture, economics, or social life more generally. Hong Kong's prominence as a global financial center; its cosmopolitanism and international orientation; and its educational, housing, and social welfare systems are all rooted in its specific status as a former British colony and the particular policies of governance that fostered Hong Kong's economic growth and its unique identity separate from that of the mainland. Furthermore, the ways of life—including the relative freedom of civil and political rights; access to foreign travel; socialization into Hong Kong's busy, bureaucratically driven work environment; and subordination as colonial subjects—experienced by Hong Kong people under British colonial rule have led to very different ways of thinking about space, place, time, and personal relations from the mainland Chinese residents who have been influenced by China's socialist and postsocialist systems of governance. It is not my task here to judge whether the intentions and outcomes of the colonial policies that have helped to shape Hong Kong's contemporary economic, social, political, and cultural life are either positive or negative; indeed, there is plenty of local commentary on this subject. It is simply my role to point out that these policies have indeed led to real differences between the everyday ways of life on Hong Kong and the mainland, where the pace of life is still slower than in Hong Kong, where wives are not "required" to work and have larger living spaces than in Hong Kong, where access to social welfare—which was taken for granted in the past—is becoming increasingly difficult, and where citizens still lack particular civil and political rights available to Hong Kong people. Hong Kong people's assumptions about these different ways of life on the mainland have been crystallized in public perception and deployed in particular ways that have affected the incorporation of mainland wives (and other mainland immigrants) into Hong Kong life.

Social workers' lessons taught to mainland immigrants on adapting and integrating to life in Hong Kong were rooted in these perceptions of difference and focused on the daily, mundane interactions that took place between immigrant women and the various Hong Kong social actors they encountered both in their homes and also outside their homes as they sought to get children situated in schools, locate housing, and earn money to support the family. For example, Hong Kong social workers and government employees worked to teach mainland immigrants the importance of their views on the rule of law—that principle of modern, Hong Kong–style "democratic" life that was assumed to be foreign to mainlanders. Hong Kong people, as mainlanders were taught, wait their turns in line; they do not bribe government

Figure 8.1   Hong Kong people waiting in line for the bus (January 2007)

officials; and they cross the street in an orderly fashion, respecting traffic laws. As parents, Hong Kong people are encouraged to be "open" and "empathetic" parents, so that they can develop positive and mutually supportive relationships with their children and develop the strong family bonds that will contribute to Hong Kong's continued economic security and social stability. Most important, Hong Kong people show that they are "civilized" by acting "responsibly" as individuals, citizens, and family members. They do not rely on government welfare; if they do, they still contribute to the greater social well-being by volunteering their unpaid services in exchange for any state support. These ideologies of belonging in Hong Kong, which focus on law-abiding behavior, "family life education," "self-help," and "entrepreneurship" (Ku and Pun 2004) were all begun through British colonial policy aimed at creating a stable and prosperous Hong Kong society. In post-1997 Hong Kong, these discourses continue to be deployed through government policy as well as through social work programs directly subsidized by the Hong Kong government, but they have also gained wide currency among Hong Kong people in general and are inextricably linked to the social imaginary of belonging in the Hong Kong polity.

As I discussed in the introduction, the key tenets in the social imaginary of Hong Kong social and political life all focus around the idea of maintaining and sustaining social stability in Hong Kong. This discourse, which first derived from Hong Kong colonial policy during the Cold War, was rooted in the need for Hong Kong's colonial government to prevent the spillover of political chaos from the mainland to Hong Kong and to manage Hong Kong's ever-growing refugee population, whose social welfare needs were urgent (Lam 2004; Goodstadt 2005; Smart 2006). Over the past few decades, the ethos of a Hong Kong identity separate from that of the Chinese mainland has continued to crystallize, and the attributes of Hong Kong life that support and contribute to this ideal continue to predominate in the social imaginary of Hong Kong people, who link this ideal to goals for Hong Kong's continued economic prosperity and dominance in global financial practices. Mainland immigrants, both legal and illegal, have been seen—and continue to be seen—as threats to this social imaginary of belonging in Hong Kong. This threat stems not only from their status as "mainlanders," who have been socialized with different goals and privileges for relating to state and society than "Hong Kong people," but also because the majority of these immigrants are women, whose roles as wives (will mainland wives be "passive" and "dependent" on their husbands or "independent" and "modern" career women?), daughters-in-law (will mainland daughters-in-law help support their mothers- and fathers-in-law in old age, or will they try to subvert the power of parents-in-law in their Hong Kong homes?), mothers (will mainland mothers foster "healthy," "independent," and "communicative" children or will their "traditional" patriarchal values ultimately limit the possibilities for family cohesion?), and potential members of Hong Kong's labor force (will mainland women's low levels of education and unfamiliarity with Hong Kong's nervous and orderly pace of life compromise Hong Kong's continued economic dominance in the Asia-Pacific region?) also challenge many of the ideal qualities of civility associated with membership in the Hong Kong polity. Thus, despite the many commonalities among mainland immigrants and Hong Kong people, and despite the fact that both groups of individuals are citizens of the

PRC, immigrant wives were seen by many Hong Kong people as a threat to Hong Kong's present and future well-being. As a result, it is not surprising that immigrant wives became the targets for education aimed at socializing them with a Hong Kong-based ethos of belonging.

These interactions between mainland immigrant wives and other members of the Hong Kong polity that I describe throughout this book highlight the fact that social imaginaries of membership and belonging do not exist as unified discursive realms. Instead, these imaginaries are plagued with fault-lines of alliances that sometimes result in strong contradictions between how people idealize qualities of membership and how these qualities are enacted through the empirical experiences of everyday life. Thus, just as mainland immigrants' engagements with Hong Kong people demonstrate the power of localized ideologies of belonging on their migration experiences, these engagements also expose the rifts that exist in Hong Kong's social and cultural landscape of membership and belonging. These rifts are many and widespread. For example, Hong Kong people, despite their focus on rational and law-abiding social norms, do sometimes break the law. Immigrants, social workers, and even one government official at the Labor Department all told stories of employees being refused mandatory rest days by employers, of being fined by employers when ill, and of not being paid wages over periods of many months. Similarly, Hong Kong people champion neoliberal ideologies of "self-help" and vilify mainlanders who are seen as overly dependent on social welfare; nevertheless, almost one-half of Hong Kong's population lives in state-subsidized public housing, and Hong Kong people enjoy many other important social rights, such as subsidized health care and education, which are becoming increasingly expensive or difficult to obtain on the mainland. Furthermore, many Hong Kong people embrace the idea that their family relationships are less patriarchal and thus more "modern" than those of mainland Chinese; at the same time, however, they may also insist that their family relationships are more "authentically" Chinese than those of mainlanders who have lived through PRC state-sponsored attacks on "traditional" family life. In this way, Hong Kong people identify their family life as "traditionally" Chinese while simultaneously disparaging the "traditionally patriarchal" family ideologies they assume mainlanders to hold. Finally, despite Hong Kong people's investment in their path to democracy, and the concomitant focus on sustaining and increasing Hong Kong people's access to the civil and political rights enjoyed by individuals in liberal-democratic societies around the world, the refusal to grant legal membership rights to abode-seekers, coupled with the decade-long periods of waiting imposed on individuals who marry across the Hong Kong/mainland border, fails to recognize citizens' right to family reunion—one of the major human rights tenets recognized by liberal democracies worldwide (Carens 2003; Kofman 2005).

These rifts in the social imaginary of belonging in Hong Kong not only demonstrate the powerful roles played by positionality (that is, class, gender, marital status, educational background, employment, and so forth) in voicing competing claims to membership but also remind us that even among citizens, family members', social workers', and government representatives' visions of incorporating immigrants may not always coincide. On a return visit to Hong Kong in early 2005, I learned that the social service center where the bulk of my research for this book took place had closed after more than thirty years of providing adjustment services to mainland immigrants in Hong Kong. The closure was a result of larger processes requiring the restructuring of family-related social service provision in Hong Kong, but it was also related to the changing priorities of Hong Kong government policy makers in reaction to negative public opinion about mainland immigrants in the wake of the 2000 arson attack and other repeated protests by illegal mainland immigrants seeking the right of abode in Hong Kong. With the center's closure, the social work team that oversaw the provision of services for Chinese immigrants during the period of my fieldwork had been dismantled, and the center's employees had scattered throughout Hong Kong and, in one case, to Taiwan. Recent mainland immigrants were still eligible to receive social services through the newly formed "family welfare center" that the center's governing organization had opened in another location nearby.

I was, of course, disappointed to learn that my fieldsite had "disappeared." But I was not actually surprised to learn of the center's closing; indeed, its existence had seemed uniquely perilous—primarily because of funding issues—even during the period of my fieldwork, when this reorganization of service provision was already being discussed. A family-based framework was thought, by both the center's employees and government representatives, to be more effective in meeting the needs of immigrant clients whose problems were intimately related to the family tensions and other difficulties involved with reuniting with family members in Hong Kong after years of living as split-families on both sides of the mainland/Hong Kong border. On the one hand, this reorganization meant that immigrants could no longer be singled out as specific members of Hong Kong's population made subject to particular kinds of education about local social and economic norms. On the other hand, it also implicated immigrants' family members, and, in particular, their husbands, as targets for some of the same educational lessons about integrating to Hong Kong ideologies of membership that had previously targeted only immigrant women. One could argue that such a move could be seen as positive for Hong Kong's newest immigrant populations, whose problems associated with incorporating into Hong Kong life were deemed serious enough to address through a comprehensive family service framework that could provide social service intervention for much longer than the limited one-year period stipulated by past funding requirements. Furthermore, this new framework acknowledged the difficulty of "defining" who is local (and who is not) in Hong Kong's sociohistorical context of complex interpersonal, cultural, and economic interaction between Hong Kong and mainland China. By no longer singling out New Arrivals as one particular category of Hong Kong people who would enjoy certain welfare benefits while being limited from others, Hong Kong government representatives might have hoped to curb the animosity directed toward this group of Hong Kong people by long-term residents who resented the fact that the government would supply welfare aid to "immigrants" who, legally resident or not, were still not seen as "Hong Kong people."

The previous social service provision for immigrants, which I have described in this book, was not without significant faults. In particular, the competition to ensure adequate program funding often forced social workers into the uncomfortable situation of opting for "quantity" over "quality" service provision, even as immigrants manipulated this same system to "pick" and "choose" the resources they would use from different centers. As a result, immigrants often had limited, rather than in-depth, contact with social workers. Nevertheless, I incline toward a cynical interpretation of the immigrant social service provision reorganization, which I see as reflecting a lessening commitment on the part of the Hong Kong government to provide funds to aid immigrants in their adjustment processes—processes that have been aimed at teaching immigrants both the rights *and* the responsibilities involved in becoming members of the Hong Kong polity. While funding for service provision in Hong Kong has always been highly susceptible to public and media pressure, the refusal to continue support for this much-needed sector of Hong Kong's population signifies an end to the state-supported rhetoric of "going together," in which Hong Kong residents were encouraged to work together with recent mainland immigrants to foster greater social harmony and cohesion. It is true that it is difficult to know at this point what effect this change in service provision will have for the incorporation of immigrant wives to Hong Kong over time. Nevertheless, one can surmise that while some immigrant wives and their families may benefit from long-term mediation, many others will suffer from the decreased access to social rights available to immigrant wives as individuals separate from—but not always equal to—Hong Kong citizens.

In this book, I have highlighted the way in which Hong Kong's reunification with the rest of the PRC has created a rather unique phenomenon in which wives, husbands, and children who are all citizens of one country experience years of waiting to "reunite" with each other—within that same country. Yet in thinking about the shifting and reshaping of borders throughout the world in recent decades, and, in particular, with the recent emphasis on creating regional economic spheres of influence that are nonetheless still demarcated with borders that are impermeable to many individuals desiring to cross those borders, Hong Kong's unusual relationship with the PRC begins to look somewhat less unique. In North America, for example, the North American Free Trade Agreement (NAFTA) has created a situation in which flows of goods and services and U.S. citizens over the border between Mexico and the United States stand in stark contrast to the very solid, ever-growing fence being built along that same border aimed at keeping non–U.S. citizens—even those who have close family members in the United States—out (Massey et al. 2002; Heyman 2004). The fear associated with excluding these "south of the border" "others" from the U.S. polity is ironic, since in 2004 14 percent of the total U.S. population, and 26 percent of the Western U.S. population, was of Hispanic origin (www.census .gov/population/www/socdemo/hispanic/cps2004.html). In other words, the U.S. border shares interesting parallels with the Hong Kong/mainland border, which controls the movement of some members of the PRC polity and not others. At both of these borders, there is a strong history of shared culture along with strong social, familial, and business interconnections. Nevertheless, already existing tensions over supposed "influxes" of economically less-developed immigrants into areas of higher economic development are exacerbated by the conflict between increasing economic ties and financial interdependence of the two regions on each side of the border (which have resulted in a sharp increase of travel of all kinds over the U.S./Mexico border [Massey et al. 2002: 80–83]) coupled with the restrictions on movement by some citizens of those regions to cross those borders. Furthermore, both cases demonstrate the continued salience of citizenship not just as an analytical category but also as an influence on the daily lives of individuals who are citizens of particular polities and who seek to cross (or make less permeable) borders between (and within) spheres of economic cooperation. Framed in this way, both the Hong Kong/mainland border and the U.S./Mexico border become productive sites for thinking about questions of membership more generally because crossing borders has serious implications in terms of access to rights and resources for all citizens of the countries involved.

In Europe, the formation of the European Union has also exacerbated tensions associated with membership rights and contested ideologies of belonging in the national (and supranational) polity. Outbreaks of violence among immigrant youth in Parisian suburban areas, debates over the rights of Muslim girls to wear headscarves in schools, and cases where immigrant parents force their citizen daughters to submit to arranged marriages highlight the ways in which ideologies of membership have concrete repercussions on the socioeconomic status, culture, and daily life of both immigrants and citizens. In other words, as borders throughout the world are reconfigured, simultaneously becoming easier to cross in some ways but more difficult to cross in others, they will continue to contribute to the production of serious social and cultural inequalities among individuals who both strive to cross, and who have succeeded in crossing, those borders. People in the nations defined by those borders—whether citizens, immigrants, or some category of belonging or nonbelonging in between—live side by side, yet they have different access to rights and resources and may also be held to different standards of upholding the responsibilities associated with community membership (see, for example, Wikan 2002). Thus, these interactions highlight the ways in which migration across political difference—in which immigrants and citizens who have been socialized with different goals of relating to state and society around them—affects ideologies of membership and belonging, as individuals continue to struggle with defining the meaning and content of community membership and with negotiating conflicting views of rights and responsibilities for immigrants and citizens. These interactions also focus attention on the many difficulties produced when political and economic entities are formed without taking into account the problems that may result when inequalities of membership are woven into the everyday fabric of human relationships.

The blurring of social, cultural, and political boundaries created through these actual cases of movement back and forth over border areas, and through the creation of "new" and "different" kinds of borders both through the formation of supranational regional areas, such as the European Union and NAFTA, and the "reunification" of Hong Kong with the PRC, can certainly be unsettling for citizens and residents of these areas. These changes also have the potential to be exciting for immigrants (and sometimes for citizens), whose subjectivities may be altered through new possibilities of social, political, and economic engagement engendered by this movement. For many mainland wives who immigrated to Hong Kong, the potential to experience a new lifestyle in "modern," "cosmopolitan" Hong Kong, where children could be educated in English, where wives would have the right to cross freely back and forth over the Hong Kong/ mainland border, and where they could imagine travel to places beyond Hong Kong, created the desire to stay in Hong Kong despite the hardships they experienced there. May, one of the immigrant wives whose experiences figure prominently throughout this book, told me:

> The longer I live in Hong Kong, the more I understand it. But the place I like is where I was born (*jihgei chutsai godouh*). But that's not to say that Hong Kong is bad. That is, to be a woman and marry a man—wherever he is and to follow him—whether it's in Hong Kong or someplace else . . . to follow your husband to the place he was born. Is that good or bad? It depends on the person. I'm not in a hurry to go back to the mainland.

For May, and for many other mainland immigrant wives in Hong Kong, the perceived benefits gained from residence in Hong Kong reinforced their desires to embrace some aspects of the Hong Kong-based ideologies of belonging to which they were introduced through their everyday interactions with family members, social workers, employers, government officials, and other Hong Kong people. Nevertheless, because of their social and economic marginalization in Hong Kong, and the discrimination they faced despite their many moral and legal ties to the Hong Kong polity, many immigrants also challenged these same ideologies by threatening to leave unhappy family situations, by (at times) refusing to work so they could raise children at home, by disappearing from social workers' spheres of influence, and by questioning why they did not have equal rights and status with other Hong Kong people, including their immediate family members. These challenges, combined with immigrants' actual and potential presence in Hong Kong, caused a deep-seated unease among Hong Kong citizens, who remain ever more concerned about the political and cultural implications of their reunification with the mainland—not only for their future economic vitality and social stability, but also for the continuation of their own ways of life as "different" (and, by implication, "better") than those on the mainland. Rather than lessening the social distance between Hong Kong people and mainlanders, the return of Hong Kong to PRC sovereignty served to reinforce the already substantial social prejudice against mainland immigrants in Hong Kong. As a result, immigrant wives entering Hong Kong in the coming years are likely to face many of the same problems that have accompanied the transitions of my immigrant informants in their adaptations to Hong Kong life. In this way, the case of family reunion migration from mainland China to Hong Kong lays bare the extent to which "difference" gets made, even in contexts where underlying assumptions of unity prevail.

Notes

CHAPTER ONE

1. Historically, the numbers of Hong Kong women marrying mainland men have been much smaller than those of Hong Kong men marrying mainland women. In 2006, 18,000 marriages were registered in Hong Kong between Hong Kong men and mainland women, but only 3,400 marriages were recorded between Hong Kong women and mainland men (Xinhua General News Service, 2/24/2007).

2. While the physical presence of the People's Liberation Army (PLA) in Hong Kong has been largely symbolic (and the source of many cartoons) since July 1, 1997, local residents still have concerns about the gradual erosion of the political and civil rights to which they were guaranteed pre-1997. The government of the PRC has "intervened" in at least one important Hong Kong court decision, and many Hong Kong people remain concerned that this ruling has affected the political autonomy of the Hong Kong government and its people (see Chapter Two for a more complete discussion of this topic). At the time of my fieldwork, Hong Kong people were uncertain whether the PRC government would adhere to pre-1997 agreements that would allow Hong Kong people to directly elect their own chief executive in 2007. Their concerns were justified in 2005, when the mainland government refused to indicate a timetable for universal suffrage in Hong Kong, and struggles continued to take place between pro-Beijing and pro-democracy lawmakers in Hong Kong over this and other related issues. In the past few years, Hong Kong people have actively shown their concern at Beijing's attempts to limit increased democratization in the region through several major political protests, at least one of which—on July 1, 2004—numbered up to one million participants, or one-seventh of Hong Kong's total population.

3. The term *floating population* is used to describe the increasingly large numbers of Chinese migrants who leave their place of permanent household residency to pursue work in other cities or areas of China. For a more complete discussion of this topic, see, for example, Solinger (1999) and Zhang (2001).

4. The United Nations World Population Index lists the percentage of female migrants worldwide in mid-year 2005 as 49.6 percent. This represents a steady

increase from 46.8 percent in 1960, but a significant total number increase since 1960, when there were only 75,463,352 migrants recorded compared to 190,633,564 in 2005 (http//esa.un.org/migration/index.asp?panel=1).

5. Technically, there is no such legal category as "Hong Kong citizen," only PRC citizens. Nevertheless, Hong Kong people frequently use the term *citizen* (Cantonese: *simahn*, Mandarin: *shimin*, literally "city people") to refer to themselves in a collective sense (also see Goldman and Perry 2002:5).

6. At the time of this writing, Hong Kong people are still waiting for universal suffrage, which has yet to be granted to them despite promises made otherwise pre-1997.

7. Officially defined as having been legally resident in Hong Kong for less than seven years.

8. In respect of the confidentiality requirements between social workers and their clients, I never had, nor did I ever request, access to the case files of immigrant clients at the center at any time during or after my fieldwork.

9. Because the employees at the center were primarily women, and the wives in my English class were my closest and best immigrant informants, my research data includes little information about Hong Kong men—either in terms of their experiences as husbands of immigrants or as immigrants themselves. Immigrant wives who were content in their spousal relationships were generally happy to introduce me to their husbands, but I only met and had significant time to talk with one husband whose wife was profoundly unhappy with her marital situation. Although many wives introduced me to their husbands at least once, we rarely spent more than a few hours together. Most husbands worked long hours and were therefore not easily accessible. Furthermore, few husbands participated in any of the center's educational or recreational programs, even when programs were billed as "family activities." I could have encouraged my informants to allow me more in-depth interaction with their husbands, but I consciously decided not to force this issue. Since much of the talk that I shared with my informants focused on the relationship difficulties that these wives were having with their husbands and their husbands' family members, I felt that pushing to spend more time with husbands would have been damaging to the relationships that I had already formed.

CHAPTER TWO

1. The legal terminology designating those individuals who are deemed eligible for Hong Kong membership status is "Right of Abode" (Cantonese: *gueilauhkun*). In other words, "Right of Abode" determines which Chinese citizens can legally enter, live, and work in Hong Kong without being deported.

2. Since 1997, ethnically Chinese Hong Kong permanent residents have, of course, been citizens of the PRC, but with special privileges, such as foreign travel, not available to PRC citizens who live on the mainland. Individuals who are Hong

Kong permanent residents enjoy a status that includes many of the rights outlined by classic political science definitions of "citizens" of a nation-state. "Hong Kong residents," now defined as those members of the population with the right to live and work in the region, may apply for permanent residency after having demonstrated that they have been "settled" in a law-abiding fashion in Hong Kong for seven years and that they will continue to claim Hong Kong as their place of primary residence.

3. That this was not an isolated case of corruption was confirmed to me through personal interviews with immigrants who had also been told by mainland officials that their families could only bring one child with them to Hong Kong, even when all children were equally eligible for Hong Kong residency status. Furthermore, this evidence was confirmed by an informant who had worked with Chinese immigrants in Hong Kong throughout the 1990s. Officials in Hong Kong's Immigration Department would not, however, confirm for me that this "illegal" practice by PRC officials had been common prior to 1997.

4. Mainland residents' *hukou* (household residency) were cancelled once they received Hong Kong ID cards.

5. The one exception to this history of unregulated movement over the border was during the anti-Japanese War (from 1942 to 1945), during which time the occupying Japanese forces sealed off Hong Kong, sent many Hong Kong residents over the border to live in China, and did not allow immigration into the area (Ko 1994).

6. "Other provinces of South China" included Fujian, Jiangxi, Hunan, Guizhou, Yunnan, and Guangxi. The "elsewhere in China" group included a "small number of natives of Macao, Singapore, etc." (Hambro 1955:151).

7. During the People's Republic of China's Great Proletarian Cultural Revolution, which began in 1966, youths from China's urban areas were "sent down" to the countryside to perform manual labor and learn about peasant life. Many of these youths were not able to return to China's urban areas until the mid- or late-1970s, by which time they had already become adults.

8. Iam Cheong Ip argues that Hong Kong's public housing program was not developed as a form of social welfare, but rather as out of a larger discourse of sanitation and hygiene that characterized "citizenship" in the colonial period (2004).

9. The process of legal entrance of mainland Chinese residents to Hong Kong remains substantially different from that of other foreign nationals. Entry visas for Hong Kong residents' spouses of other nationalities, according to immigration officials, are processed within four to six weeks, so that the time of separation of family members is kept to a minimum. Intriguingly, if one's spouse is a mainland Chinese citizen who has been living outside the PRC for at least one or two years, there is a "relaxed" immigration scheme that allows the Hong Kong person to sponsor his or her spouse on a dependent visa, without waiting in the "queue" to which all other mainlanders remain subject. In this case, the application for entry will be processed in the same four- to six-week process as that of other foreign nationals (Tam interview, 5/31/2002).

10. "Settled" was defined as being ordinarily resident, not subject under immigration laws to any condition of stay (including imprisonment).

11. Certain individuals are, for legal purposes, not considered to be "resident" in Hong Kong, thus denying them the right of ever qualifying for permanent resident status. These exclusions from residency include large numbers of Hong Kong's nonethnically Chinese population, such as the Filipina, Thai, and Indonesian women who may have lived and worked as domestic helpers in Hong Kong for most of their adult lives, as well as Vietnamese refugees who fled to Hong Kong in the 1970s and 1980s.

12. The Hong Kong government's justification for this questionable means of legal recourse was the result of an oddly constructed survey, which ended up concluding that the judgment would "open a floodgate to 1.67 million mainlanders" who previously would not have been eligible to live in Hong Kong (Chow 5/29/01). Scholars and prodemocracy legislators strongly contested the survey results, with some arguing instead that as few as 130,000 mainlanders would come to live in the region (ibid.).

13. On a return visit to Hong Kong in 2005, I learned that she had been granted Hong Kong residency status. At the time of this writing, she is now legally working and living with her family in Hong Kong.

14. In 2001 and 2002, one could apply for CSSA after legally residing in Hong Kong for one year, and in some cases demonstrating particular hardship, one might be able to receive CSSA even earlier. By mid-2002, however, SAR government officials had begun discussing five years' residency as a more acceptable period of time to apply for CSSA (*Ming Pao* 4/11/02).

CHAPTER THREE

1. As I explained in Chapter Two, prior to 1980, when the "touch-base" policy was abolished, this was the easiest way for mainlanders to immigrate to Hong Kong.

2. See Zhang (2001:33) for the "dangerous" semantic roots of "floating" in Chinese.

3. Because of their rural backgrounds and low levels of education, many of the women in this demographic group often spoke rural dialects other than Cantonese. Alternatively, their Cantonese was so heavily accented that I could not understand them well; they also had more difficultly understanding my accented Cantonese.

4. During the last quarter of 2001, the median family monthly income for mainland immigrants and their families was HK$5,900 (US$756) (Home Affairs Department 2002).

CHAPTER FOUR

1. See Ikels (1996:78–94) for a more detailed description of urban housing spaces in Guangzhou in the early 1990s.

2. For a concise description of the meaning and importance of filial piety in the traditional Chinese context, see Ikels (2004:2–4).

3. Wang (2004: 20) provides an example of a contemporary folk lyric that describes the duties a filial daughter-in-law should provide to her parents-in-law. These duties include consulting parents on the dishes you cook them, setting the table, and serving parents-in-law their food both "elegantly" and respectfully.

4. Over the course of my research, I only had the opportunity to meet several mothers-in-law. At those meetings, mothers-in-laws were invariably polite to their daughters-in-law. In one case, the mother-in-law gave an expensive gift to her daughter-in-law in my presence.

5. Whyte (2004) confirms a similar finding in his research on filial piety in contemporary families in Taipei, Taiwan, and in Baoding, PRC. In comparing attitudes and aspects of "traditional" family life between the two locations, he writes that "the complex set of institutions and practices developed in the PRC after the 1950s helped to preserve strong filial obligations and intergenerational exchanges even as it altered the patterning of these exchanges into more modern forms. Taiwan, despite being a richer society, retained family-based microinstitutions that tended to pattern intergenerational exchanges along more traditional lines emphasizing patrilineal kinship and co-residence" (ibid. 125).

6. The 1976 Hong Kong Census recorded for the first time that a majority of Hong Kong's residents had been born in the colony rather than elsewhere (Hong Kong Government 1976).

7. Smart (2006) explains that Hong Kong's unique Cold War historical status, as a British colony situated next to Communist China, provided part of the impetus for the colonial government to work to solve the housing problem caused by Hong Kong's overcrowding.

8. By the mid-1980s, many squatter areas were no longer inhabited only by recent arrivals. In many cases, these areas had become comfortable living areas of middle-class inhabitants, many of whom may have been hoping to qualify for resettlement to new public housing units. For more on the desirability of those units, see below.

9. Alan Smart has recently provided significant evidence that this fire was not in fact the origin of the public housing program. Instead, he argues that the program developed as a pragmatic response by the colonial government to a number of devastating fires in the region, beginning with the Tung Tau fire in 1951, and as a result of Hong Kong's precarious political situation during the Cold War. For his full argument, see Smart 2006.

10. These privately owned public housing flats were built identically to the newest public units and were offered by lottery at subsidized prices to families meeting certain income requirements as part of the Home Ownership Scheme run by the Hong Kong Housing Authority from 1978 through 2003 (www.housingauthority .gov.hk).

11. While still long, these waits were a substantial improvement over past times, in which the average wait for a public housing unit might have been anywhere from seven years on up.

12. Articles that describe in detail advertising campaigns and the marketing of homes in Hong Kong and the mainland include Fraser 2000 and Cheung and Ma 1999.

13. Bonnie Adrian (2003) also demonstrates that Taiwanese adult children who live with their parents may feel similarly constrained by the lack of "private" space in their homes.

14. See Bosco 2001 for a detailed account of the "Snoopy Craze" during September and October 1998.

CHAPTER FIVE

1. In the literature on immigrant incorporation in the United States (and other areas that have traditionally received large numbers of immigrants from various backgrounds), scholars have generally identified three main forms of "support" to help the adjustment of newly arrived immigrants: ethnic "enclaves," family members, and other forms of social networks (see, for example, Portes and Rumbaut 1996; Constable 1997, 2003; Parreñas 2001; Alba and Nee 2003; Choy 2003). Yet the similarities in cultural and ethnic backgrounds between Hong Kong people and mainland immigrants, along with the fact that the majority of immigrants were wives and children who were incorporated into local households, meant that in Hong Kong there were no "ethnic enclaves" to which mainland immigrants could turn for help.

2. Few of my mainland immigrant informants were able to "pass" for Hong Kong people when I knew them just after they had arrived in Hong Kong; but two years later, when I visited them again, many of the women had adopted new wardrobes, had faddish hairstyles, and were wearing makeup that they had not worn before.

3. On the mainland, Mandarin is the standard dialect that is taught in schools in spoken and written form. Cantonese, the dialect of Chinese spoken in Hong Kong, shares a formal written language with Mandarin Chinese, although the written form that is used is the more "traditional" complex form and also employs characters and phrases of Cantonese dialect that are not understandable to someone who does not speak Cantonese.

4. Sometimes these loan words appear in their correct native pronunciation as one word in an otherwise completely Cantonese sentence, such as the word *keep* in the following Cantonese sentence, *"mgoi neih bong ngoh keepjuh li bun shu,"* which means, "can you please keep (or hold) this book for me?" In other situations, English words have been localized in their pronunciation and are used to express a concept or lifestyle practice that may be common in Hong Kong although not on the mainland, such as "eating at a buffet," approximately localized as *"sihk bouffee."*

5. In the past, the Social Welfare Department had granted funds only to support specific programs or services, which had inhibited the creative use of funds to meet different kinds of clients' needs. Overall, the lump-sum funding process, combined with the social service center's structural flexibility, resulted in center staff members having a considerable role in designing the content and exact activities of the different programs they organized for immigrants. These programs often had as their basis the individual interests of social workers as well as social workers' personal philosophies of how best to interact and provide services to clients.

6. In describing Hong Kong as more ethnically "homogeneous" than many other cosmopolitan, urban centers in the developed world, it is not my intent to deny the rich and varied ethnic diversity that exists among Hong Kong's many different Chinese populations, which include Cantonese, Fujianese, Shanghainese, Chaozhou, and Hakka, among others. For more information on the many different Chinese ethnicities that make up Hong Kong's "Chinese" population, see Guldin 1997.

CHAPTER SIX

1. See Yan (2003:3) for an explanation of the term Chinese *corporate* family model.

2. In this section, as with other parts of this chapter, I use the word *Western* as I encountered the use of this term in Hong Kong, where it referred to particular local conceptions of a white, upper-middle-class, English-speaking ideal rather than representing the full range of social, cultural, economic, and political diversity that exists in the "Western" world.

3. Hong Kong parents have refused to endorse measures that would require schools to teach in Cantonese, a move supported by many specialists in education who argue that "mother-tongue" teaching would lead to better standards of written Chinese among Hong Kong students as well as in greater overall intellectual achievement (Lau 1997:113–16; see also E. Chan 2002).

4. Similar to the mainland Chinese reactions to her children described by Ann Anagnost (1995, 1997a), I found that the attention focused on my son usually focused on these qualities as "positive" compared to the less well-developed attributes of similarly aged local children. Of course, the interpretative focus on his "creative" tendencies was more culturally complex. See discussion below.

5. As Andrew Kipnis notes, "no single English term fully catches the nuances of *suzhi*," which is generally defined as "quality" in English (2006:296). The term refers to a discursive ideology of civility in the PRC—focusing on education, bodily practices, and consumer habits—that is intimately linked to the strength of the Chinese nation, PRC population practices, and the "quality" of its citizens. For in-depth discussion of the meaning of *suzhi*, see ibid. and Anagnost 2004.

6. The other four are "physical and psychological development of children," "effective parenting skills," "emotion and stress management for parents," and "dealing with children's behavioral problems" (www.family-land.org/life/ser_brief,htm).

CHAPTER SEVEN

1. The educational system in Hong Kong is still heavily based on English as well as Chinese instruction, with the result that ordinary Cantonese spoken in Hong Kong is peppered with English words, often inserted as nouns or verbs in the middle of an otherwise "Cantonese" sentence. In this quote, Emily used English for the word *irresponsible*, so I have placed quotes around this word in my translation.

2. For a discussion of Chinese educational campaigns encouraging mothers to breastfeed, see Gottschang 2001.

3. They trace this emphasis in "responsible" citizenship through the three different Chinese words—*guomin, gongmin, and shimin*—which are all translated as "citizen" in English. The term *guomin* refers to the idea of a "national citizen." Although first used over 2,000 years ago "to refer to members of rival warring states," this term was borrowed from Japan and reintroduced to China at the beginning of the twentieth century when the Qing dynasty was overthrown and China became a republic (ibid.). *Gongmin*, literally translated as "public people," is much more commonly used today. Goldman and Perry explain: "Over the course of the twentieth century, the term *gongmin* largely replaced *guomin* in both official and popular parlance as the accepted designation to refer to those persons who are legally recognized as members of a state. The origins of the term *gongmin* lie in the Confucian celebration of public service" (ibid.). In contrast to *guomin* and *gongmin*, the term *shimin*, literally meaning "city people," refers to the rights and responsibilities of urban residents "to maintain social stability and uphold civic virtue" (ibid. 7). Hong Kong people use the term *shimin* (Cantonese *Sihmahn*) to refer to themselves but not *guomin* or *gongmin*.

4. Like models that generalize about "the West," this model is problematic in its sweeping claim that seeks to attribute the same state methods and goals for achieving modernization among communist, colonial, and emerging democratic regimes. Furthermore, it ignores important cases of social protest aimed at challenging these models (such as the Tiananmen uprising in 1989) and obscures major cases of government-initiated atrocities, such as the Great Proletarian Cultural Revolution and the Great Leap Forward, which resulted in the devastation and death of millions of Chinese citizens.

5. The local Hong Kong word for "uncivilized," *yehmaahn*, is one of many locally used words without a written form understandable in Mandarin Chinese.

6. The word *quality* (Cantonese: *jaahtsou*) was also frequently used to distinguish these less educated clients from those who were better educated and with a better grasp of the "commonly" accepted social and behavioral norms—norms that, in Hong Kong, have been heavily influenced by access to Western-based education and media images, as well as by British colonial government advertising. I understood the local Hong Kong use of this word, *jaahtsou*, or *quality* to refer to an immigrant's education level and general ability to "fit into" local Hong Kong norms

of social comportment. As with the discourse on "quality" (Mandarin: *suzhi*) on the mainland, there is a clear link between the perceived poor "quality" of these immigrants and a general concern about the "quality" of the general population. (See Anagnost 2004 and Kipnis 2006 for more on the use of the word *quality* in the PRC.)

7. Both Siu-saan and Emily, however, noted that the Hong Kong government may contribute to attracting these immigrants of "lesser quality" to Hong Kong. By providing as much aid as they do to New Arrivals, the Hong Kong government may be encouraging immigrants who come for the express purpose of making use of such aid.

8. See Chapter Five for more information about immigrant wives' views on working.

9. The types of welfare available to residents of Hong Kong are less comprehensive than the social security and other systems we take for granted as part of the Western welfare state model. See Chapter Two for a more comprehensive discussion of the kinds of welfare available to Hong Kong people.

10. *Triad* refers to members of Chinese organized crime gangs.

11. Both in personal interviews and in media sources, the head of the blamed organization denied any involvement in the attacks.

Works Cited

Abbas, Ackbar. 1997. *Hong Kong: Culture and the Politics of Disappearance.* Hong Kong: Hong Kong University Press.

Adrian, Bonnie. 2003. *Framing the Bride: Globalizing Beauty and Romance in Taiwan's Bridal Industry.* Berkeley: University of California Press.

Alba, Richard, and Victor Nee. 2003. *Remaking the American Mainstream: Assimilation and Contemporary Immigration.* Cambridge, MA: Harvard University Press.

Anagnost, Ann. 1995. "A Surfeit of Bodies: Population and the Rationality of the State in Post-Mao China." In *Conceiving the New World Order: The Global Politics of Reproduction,* ed. by Faye Ginsburg and Rayna Rapp. Berkeley: University of California Press.

———. 1997a. *National Past-Times: Narrative, Representation, and Power in Modern China.* Durham, NC: Duke University Press.

———. 1997b. "Children and National Transcendence in China." In *Constructing China: The Interaction of Culture and Economics,* ed. by Kenneth Lieberthal, Shuen-fu Lin, and Ernest Young. Ann Arbor: Center for Chinese Studies, University of Michigan.

———. 2004. "The Corporeal Politics of Quality (*Suzhi*)." *Public Culture* 16(2):189–208.

Anderson, Benedict. 1983. *Imagined Communities: Reflections of the Origin and Spread of Nationalism.* New York: Verso.

Aretxaga, Begoña. 1997. *Shattering Silence: Women, Nationalism, and Political Subjectivity in Northern Ireland.* Princeton, NJ: Princeton University Press.

The Basic Law of the Hong Kong Special Administrative Region of the People's Republic of China. 1996. Hong Kong: Hong Kong Government Printer.

Berdahl, Daphne. 1999. *Where the World Ended: Re-Unification and Identity in the German Borderland.* Berkeley: University of California Press.

Borneman, John. 1998. *Subversions of International Order: Studies in the Political Anthropology of Culture.* Albany: State University of New York Press.

277

Bosco, Joseph. 2001. "The McDonald's Snoopy Craze in Hong Kong." In *Consuming Hong Kong*, ed. by Gordon Mathews and Tai-lok Lui. Hong Kong: Hong Kong University Press.

Bosniak, Linda. 1998. "The Citizenship of Aliens." *Social Text 56* 16(3):29–35.

Bradford, Sara. September 27, 2001. "IIs 'not classed as foreigners in court.'" *South China Morning Post*.

———. December 12, 2001. "Foreigner sentence ruling overturned." *South China Morning Post*.

Brownell, Susan. 2001. "Making Dream Bodies in Beijing: Athletes, Fashion Models, and Urban Mystique in China." In *China Urban: Ethnographies of Urban China*, ed. by Nancy Chen, Constance Clark, Suzanne Gottschang, and Lyn Jeffrey. Durham, NC: Duke University Press.

Burns, John P. 1987. "Immigration from China and the Future of Hong Kong." *Asian Survey* 27(6):661–82.

Carens, Joseph. 2003. "Who Should Get In? The Ethics of Immigration Admissions." *Ethics and International Affairs* 17(1):95–110.

Census and Statistics Department. 1996. *1996 Population By-Census Main Report*. Hong Kong: Hong Kong Government Press.

———. 2002. *2001 Population Census Main Tables*. Kowloon: Hong Kong Census and Statistics Department.

Chakrabarty, Dipesh. 2002. *Habitations of Modernity: Essays in the Wake of Subaltern Studies*. Chicago: University of Chicago Press.

Chan, Elaine. 2002. "Beyond Pedagogy: Language and Identity in Post-Colonial Hong Kong." *British Journal of Sociology and Education* 23(2):271–85.

Chan, Ming K. 2002. "Introduction: the Hong Kong SAR in Flux." In *Crisis and Transformation in China's Hong Kong*, ed. by Ming K. Chan and Alvin Y. So. Armonk, NY: M. E. Sharpe.

———. 2003. "Different Roads to Home: The Retrocession of Hong Kong and Macau to Chinese Sovereignty." *Journal of Contemporary China* 12(36):493–518.

Chan, Quinton, and Patsy Moy. April 29, 2002. "18pc of migrants on welfare." *South China Morning Post*, p. 1.

Cheah, Charissa S. L., and Kenneth H. Rubin. 2003. "European American and Mainland Chinese Mothers' Socialization Beliefs Regarding Preschoolers' Social Skills." *Parenting: Science and Practice* 3(1):1–22.

Cheung, Gary. April 24, 2002. "Support for ending unskilled migration." *South China Morning Post*, p. 4.

———. July 4, 2002. "Mainland migrants may face education screening." *South China Morning Post*, p. 6.

Cheung, Sidney, and Eric K. W. Ma. 1999. *Advertising Modernity: "Home," Space, and Privacy*. Hong Kong Institute of Asia-Pacific Studies Monograph.

Chow, Chung-yan. October 26, 2001. "Tears of joy as Agnes finally gets to call Hong Kong 'home.'" *South China Morning Post*, p. 1.

Chow, Magdalen. May 29, 2001. "Tung 'misled' abode claimants." *South China Morning Post*, p. 1.

———. January 11, 2002. "Abode seekers to appeal to UN." *South China Morning Post*, p. 1.

Chow, Magdalen, and Shirley Lau. July 21, 2001. "Boy wins landmark abode battle." *South China Morning Post*, p. 1.

Choy, Catherine Ceniza. 2003. *Empire of Care: Nursing and Migration in Filipino American History*. Durham, NC: Duke University Press.

Clark, Constance. 2001. "Foreign Marriage, 'Tradition,' and the Politics of Border Crossings." In *China Urban: Ethnographies of Urban China*, ed. by Nancy Chen, Constance Clark, Suzanne Gottschang, and Lyn Jeffrey. Durham, NC: Duke University Press.

Clarke, W. S. 1986. "Hong Kong Immigration Control: The Law and the Bureaucratic Maze." *Hong Kong Law Journal* 16(3):342–68.

Clifford, James, and George Marcus, eds. 1986. *Writing Culture: The Poetics and Politics of Ethnography*. Berkeley: University of California Press.

Cohen, Myron. 1976. *House United, House Divided: The Chinese Family in Taiwan*. New York: Columbia University Press.

———. 1994. "Being Chinese: The Peripheralization of Traditional Identity." In *The Living Tree: The Changing Meaning of Being Chinese Today*, ed. by Tu Wei-ming. Stanford, CA: Stanford University Press.

Connolly, Norma, and Martin Wong. February 23, 2007. "Scales tip as women outnumber men; census also shows fewer weddings, more females in workplace and more men taking mainland wives." *South China Morning Post*, p. 3.

Cook, Richard. 1998. "Barking mad?" *Postmagazine, Sunday Morning Post*. December 20, pp. 14–15.

Constable, Nicole. 1997. *Maid to Order in Hong Kong: Stories of Filipina Workers*. Ithaca, NY: Cornell University Press.

———. 1999. "At Home but Not at Home: Filipina Narratives of Ambivalent Returns." *Cultural Anthropology* 14(2):203–28.

———. 2003. *Romance on the Global Stage: Pen Pals, Virtual Ethnography, and "Mail Order" Marriages*. Berkeley: University of California Press.

Croll, Elisabeth. 1995. *Changing Identities of Chinese Women: Rhetoric, Experience, and Self-Perception in Twentieth Century China*. Hong Kong: Hong Kong University Press.

———. 1999. "Social Welfare Reform: Trends and Tensions." *China Quarterly* 159: 684–99.

Cruikshank, Barbara. 1999. *The Will to Empower: Democratic Citizens and Other Subjects*. Ithaca, NY: Cornell University Press.

Cunningham, Hilary, and Josiah McC. Heyman. 2004. "Introduction: Mobilities and Enclosures at Borders." *Identities: Global Studies in Culture and Power* 11:289–302.

Davin, Delia. 1999. *Internal Migration in Contemporary China*. New York: St. Martin's Press.

Davis, Deborah. 1989. "My Mother's House." In *Unofficial China: Popular Culture and Thought in the People's Republic*, ed. by Perry Link, Richard Madsen, and Paul Pickowicz. Boulder, CO: Westview Press.

Davis, Deborah, ed. 2000. *The Consumer Revolution in Urban China*. Berkeley: University of California Press.

Draft White Paper. September 1990. "Social Welfare into the 1990's and Beyond." Hong Kong: Working Party on Social Welfare Policies and Services.

Evans, Harriet. 2002. "Past, Perfect or Imperfect: Changing Images of the Ideal Wife." In *Chinese Femininities/Chinese Masculinities: A Reader*, ed. by Susan Brownell and Jeffrey N. Wasserstrom. Berkeley: University of California Press.

Flores, William. 1997. "Citizens vs. Citizenry: Undocumented Immigrants and Latino Cultural Citizenship." In *Latino Cultural Citizenship: Claiming Identity, Space, and Rights*, ed. by William Flores and Rina Benmayor. Boston: Beacon Press.

Flores, William and Rina Benmayor. 1997. *Latino Cultural Citizenship: Claiming Identity, Space, and Rights*. Boston: Beacon Press.

Fong, Vanessa. 2004a. *Only Hope: Coming of Age under China's One-Child Policy*. Stanford, CA: Stanford University Press.

———. 2004b. "Filial Nationalism Among Chinese Teenagers with Global Identities." *American Ethnologist* 31(4):629–47.

———. 2006. "Chinese Youth Between the Margins of China and the First World." In *Chinese Citizenship: Views from the Margins*, ed. by Vanessa L. Fong and Rachel Murphy. London: Routledge.

———. 2007. "Parent Child Communication Problems and the Perceived Inadequacies of Chinese Only Children." *Ethos* 35(1):85–127.

Foucault, Michel. 1979. *Discipline and Punish: The Birth of the Prison*. New York: Vintage.

Fraser, David. 2000. "Inventing Oasis: Luxury Housing Advertisements and Reconfiguring Domestic Space in Shanghai." In *The Consumer Revolution in Urban China*, ed. by Deborah Davis. Berkeley: University of California Press.

Freeman, Caren. 2005. "Marrying Up and Marrying Down: The Paradoxes of Marital Mobility for Chosonjok Brides in South Korea." In *Cross-Border Marriages: Gender and Mobility in Transnational Asia*, ed. by Nicole Constable. Philadelphia: University of Pennsylvania Press.

Friedman, Sara. 2006. *Intimate Politics: Marriage, the Market, and State Power in Southeastern China*. Cambridge, MA: Harvard University Press.

Fung, Heidi. 1999. "Becoming a Moral Child: The Socialization of Shame among Young Chinese Children." *Ethos* 27(2):180–209.

Gaetano, Arianne, and Tamara Jacka, eds. 2004. *On the Move: Women in Rural-to-Urban Migration in Contemporary China*. New York: Columbia University Press.

Glick-Schiller, Nina. 2003. "The Centrality of Ethnography in the Study of Transnational Migration: Seeing the Wetlands Instead of the Swamp." In *American Arrivals: Anthropology Engages the New Immigration*, ed. by Nancy Foner. Santa Fe, NM: The School of American Research Press.

Glick-Schiller, Nina, N. Basch, and L. Szanton-Blanc. 1992. *Towards a Transnational Perspective on Migration*. New York: New York Academy of Science.

Glosser, Susan. 2003. *Chinese Visions of Family and State, 1915–1953*. Berkeley: University of California Press.

Goldman, Merle, and Elizabeth Perry. 2002. "Introduction: Political Citizenship in Modern China." In *Changing Meanings of Citizenship in Modern China*, ed. by Merle Goldman and Elizabeth Perry. Cambridge, MA: Harvard University Press.

Goodstadt, Leo F. 2005. *Uneasy Partners: The Conflict Between Public Interest and Private Profit in Hong Kong*. Hong Kong: Hong Kong University Press.

Gottschang, Suzanne. 2001. "The Consuming Mother: Infant Feeding and the Feminine Body in Urban China." In *China Urban: Ethnographies of Urban China*, ed. by Nancy Chen, Constance Clark, Suzanne Gottschang, and Lyn Jeffrey. Durham, NC: Duke University Press.

Grant, Jonathan S. 2001. "Cultural Formation in Postwar Hong Kong." In *Hong Kong Reintegrating with China: Political, Cultural and Social Dimensions*, ed. by Lee Pui-tak. Hong Kong: The Hong Kong University Press.

Greenhalgh, Susan. 1994. "De-Orientalizing the Chinese Family Firm." *American Ethnologist* 21(4): 746–75.

Greenhouse, Carol. 2002. "Citizenship, Agency, and the Dream of Time." In *Looking Back at Law's Century*, ed. by Austin Sarat, Bryant Garth, and Robert Kagan. Ithaca, NY: Cornell University Press.

Guldin, Gregory. 1997. "Hong Kong Ethnicity: Of Folk Models and Change." In *Hong Kong: The Anthropology of a Chinese Metropolis*, ed. by Grant Evans and Maria Tam. Honolulu: University of Hawaii Press.

Hambro, Edvard. 1955. *The Problem of Chinese Refugees in Hong Kong: Report Submitted to the United Nations High Commissioner for Refugees*. Leyden, Netherlands: A. W. Sijthoff.

Hamilton, Gary, ed. 1999. *Cosmopolitan Capitalists: Hong Kong and the Chinese Diaspora at the End of the 20th Century*. Seattle: University of Washington Press.

Hampshire, James. 2005. *Citizenship and Belonging: Immigration and the Politics of Democratic Governance in Postwar Britain*. New York: Palgrave Macmillan.

Harvey, David. 1990. *The Condition of Postmodernity: An Enquiry into the Origins of Cultural Change*. Cambridge, MA: Blackwell.

Hayes, James. 1996. *Friends and Teachers: Hong Kong and its People 1953–87*. Hong Kong: Hong Kong University Press.

Heaton, William. 1970. "Maoist Revolutionary Strategy and Modern Colonialism: The Cultural Revolution in Hong Kong." *Asian Survey* 10(9):840–57.

Herzfeld, Michael. 1992. *The Social Production of Indifference: Exploring the Symbolic Roots of Western Bureaucracy.* New York: Berg.

———. 2004. *The Body Impolitic: Artisans and Artifice in the Global Hierarchy of Value.* Chicago: Chicago University Press.

Heyman, Josiah. 2004. "Ports of Entry as Nodes in the World System." *Identities: Global Studies in Culture and Power* 11:303–27.

———. 2002. "U.S. Immigration Officers of Mexican Ancestry as Mexican Americans, Citizens, and Immigration Police." *Current Anthropology* 43(3): 479–507.

Ho, Kit-mui (Juanita), Linda Fung Kit Ling, and Tong Choi Ying. 2000. *Practice Manual of Parallel Adjustment Group For New Arrival Families II Effective Parenting Group.* Hong Kong: Hong Kong Family Welfare Society Integrated Family Services for New Arrivals and The University of Hong Kong Department of Social Work and Social Administration.

Home Affairs Department. 2002. "Survey on New Arrivals from the Mainland (Fourth Quarter of 2001)." Hong Kong: Hong Kong Government Printer.

Hong Kong Annual Report 1953. Hong Kong: Hong Kong Government Printer.

Hong Kong Government. 1966. *Hong Kong: Report on the 1966 By-Census.* Hong Kong: Hong Kong Government Press.

Hong Kong Government. 1976. *Report on the 1976 By-Census.* Hong Kong: Hong Kong Government Press.

Hyatt, Susan. 2001. "From Citizen to Volunteer: Neoliberal Governance and the Erasure of Poverty." In *The New Poverty Studies: The Ethnography of Power, Politics, and Impoverished People in the United States,* ed. by Judith Goode and Jeff Maskovsky. New York: New York University Press.

ICAC (*Hong Kong: The Facts: ICAC*). 2000/01. Hong Kong: Information Services Department, Hong Kong Special Administrative Region Government.

IDAR (*Immigration Department Annual Report*). 1970. Hong Kong: Hong Kong Government Press.

IDAR (*Immigration Department Annual Report*). 1971–2. Hong Kong: Hong Kong Government Press.

IDYEB (*Immigration Department Year-End Briefing*). 2006. (www.info.gov.hk/gia/general/200702/08/P200702080211.htm) Retrieved on 2/11/2007.

Ikels, Charlotte. 1996. *The Return of the God of Wealth: The Transition to a Market Economy in Urban China.* Stanford, CA: Stanford University Press.

———. 2004. "Introduction." In *Filial Piety: Practice and Discourse in Contemporary East Asia,* ed. by Charlotte Ikels. Stanford, CA: Stanford University Press.

Ip, Iam-Cheong. 2004. "Welfare or Colonial Citizenship? A Case Study of Early Resettlement Housing." In *Remaking Citizenship in Hong Kong: Community, Nation, and the Global City,* eds. Agnes Ku and Ngai Pun. London: Routledge-Curzon.

Jankowiak, William. 1995. "Romantic Passion in the People's Republic of China." In *Romantic Passion: A Universal Experience?* ed. by William Jankowiak. New York: Columbia University Press.

Judge, Joan. 2002. "Citizens or Mothers of Citizens?: Gender and the Meaning of Modern Chinese Citizenship." In *Changing Meanings of Citizenship in Modern China*, ed. by Merle Goldman and Elizabeth Perry. Cambridge, MA: Harvard University Press.

Kelsky, Karen. 2001. *Women on the Verge: Japanese Women, Western Dreams.* Durham, NC: Duke University Press.

Kipnis, Andrew. 2006. "*Suzhi*: A Keyword Approach." *China Quarterly* 186:295–313.

Ko, Tim-keung, ed. 1994. *Heunggong Gamsik.* (Hong Kong Present and Past). Hong Kong: Joint Publishing Co., Ltd.

Kofman, Eleonore. 2005. "Citizenship, Migration, and the Reassertion of National Identity." *Citizenship Studies* 9(5):453–67.

———. 2004. "Family-Related Migration: A Critical Review of European Studies." *Journal of Ethnic and Migration Studies* 30(2):243–62.

Kondo, Dorinne. 1990. *Crafting Selves: Power, Gender, and Discourses of Identity in a Japanese Workplace.* Chicago: University of Chicago Press.

Ku, Agnes. 2001. "Hegemonic Construction, Negotiation and Displacement." *International Journal of Cultural Studies* 4(3):259–78.

———. 2004. "Immigration Policies, Discourses, and the Politics of Local Belonging in Hong Kong (1950–1980)." *Modern China* 30(3):326–60.

Ku, Agnes, and Ngai Pun. 2004. "Introduction: Remaking Citizenship in Hong Kong." In *Remaking Citizenship in Hong Kong: Community, Nation, and the Global City*, ed. by Agnes Ku and Ngai Pun. London: RoutledgeCurzon.

Kwok, Reginald Yin-Wang, and Roger T. Ames. 1995. "A Framework for Exploring the Hong Kong-Guangdong Link." In *The Hong Kong-Guangdong Link: Partnership in Flux*, ed. by Reginald Yin-Wang Kwok and Alvin Y. So. Armonk, NY: M. E. Sharpe.

Lam, Wai-man. 2004. *Understanding the Political Culture of Hong Kong: The Paradox of Activism and Depoliticization.* Armonk, NY: M. E. Sharpe Press.

Lang, Graeme, and Josephine Smart. 2002. "Migration and the 'Second Wife' Phenomenon in South China: Towards Cross-Border Polygyny." *International Migration Review* 36(2):546–69.

Latham, Kevin. 2000. "Nothing but the Truth: News Media, Power and Hegemony in South China." *The China Quarterly* 163:633–54.

Lau, Chi Kuen. 1997. *Hong Kong's Colonial Legacy.* Hong Kong: The Chinese University Press.

Law, Chi-kwong, Cecilia Chan Lai-wan, Katherine Young, Ko Lau Po-chi, Wong Yu-cheung, Toni Mehrani, Cheng Kai-chi, and Li Wai-ling. 1995. *Contemporary Hong Kong Families in Transition.* Hong Kong: Hong Kong Women Foundation Ltd. and The Department of Social Work and Social Administration at the University of Hong Kong.

Lee, M. K. and S. H. Lu. 1997. "The Marriage Institution in Decline?" In *Indicators of Social Development: Hong Kong 1995*, ed. by S. K. Lau, M. K. Lee,

P. S. Wan, and S. L. Wong. Hong Kong: Hong Kong Institute of Asia Pacific Studies, the Chinese University of Hong Kong, pp. 183–201.

Lee, Mary. 1979. "Ill Winds Over Fragrant Harbour." *Far Eastern Economic Review.* May 25, 1979.

———. March 23, 2002. "Return or face penalty, abode 'rats' are warned by official." *South China Morning Post*, p. 2.

Leung, Ambrose, and Chung-yan Chow. July 21, 2001. "Decision 'disrespectful' to China's Law." South China Morning Post, p. 2.

Levitt, Peggy. 2001. *The Transnational Villagers.* Berkeley: University of California Press.

Li, Wai-ki Viki. 2001. *Seeking an Ideal Wife: Why Hong Kong Men Pursue Mainland Chinese Spouses.* Chinese University of Hong Kong M. Phil. Thesis.

Linde, Charlotte. 1993. *Life Stories: The Creation of Coherence.* Oxford, UK: Oxford University Press.

Lloyd-Smith, Jake. April 23, 2002. "Rowse attacks immigrant 'madness.'" *South China Morning Post*, p. 1.

Luk, Victor. 1995. *Estate Reminiscence (Nguk Chyun Nan Mohng).* Hong Kong: Breakthrough.

Lui, Tai-lok. 2001. "The Malling of Hong Kong." In *Consuming Hong Kong*, ed. by Gordon Mathews and Tai-lok Lui. Hong Kong: Hong Kong University Press.

Ma, Eric Kit-wai. 1999. *Culture, Politics, and Television in Hong Kong.* London: Routledge.

Mahler, Sarah J. 2001. "Transnational Relationships: The Struggle to Communicate Across Borders." *Identities: Global Studies in Culture and Power* 7(4):583–619.

Mamdani, Mahmood. 1996. *Citizen and Subject: Contemporary Africa and the Legacy of Late Colonialism.* Princeton, NJ: Princeton University Press.

Marshall, T. H. 1992. "Citizenship and Social Class." In *Citizenship and Social Class* by T. H. Marshall and Tom Bottomore. London: Pluto.

Massey, Doreen. 1994. *Space, Place, and Gender.* Minneapolis: University of Minnesota Press.

Massey, Douglas S., J. Durand, and N. J. Malone. 2002. *Beyond Smoke and Mirrors: Mexican Immigration in an Era of Economic Integration.* New York: Russell Sage Foundation.

Mathews, Gordon. 1996. "Names and Identities in the Hong Kong Cultural Supermarket." *Dialectical Anthropology* 21(3/4):399–419.

———. 1997. "*Heunggongyahn*: On the Past, Present, and Future of Hong Kong Identity." *Bulletin of Concerned Asian Scholars* 29(3):3–13.

———. 2001. "Cultural Identity and Consumption in Post-Colonial Hong Kong." In *Consuming Hong Kong*, ed. by Gordon Mathews and Tai-lok Lui. Hong Kong: Hong Kong University Press.

"Migrant solutions." *South China Morning Post*, April 29, 2002, p. 15.

Mills, Mary Beth. 1999. *Thai Women in the Global Labor Force: Consuming Desires, Contested Selves.* Piscataway, NJ: Rutgers University Press.

Ming Pao. November 4, 2002. *"Yimin laigang shouwunian bude ling zongyuan."* ("Immigrants should not receive welfare for the first five years in Hong Kong.")

Moy, Patsy. April 29, 2002. "Warning over migrant influx: Lower education and earning capacity make mainland intake a 'threat to development.' " *South China Morning Post*, p. 2.

Moy, Patsy, and Susan Schwartz. January 30, 2002. "Returning abode seekers 'detained and beaten.' " *South China Morning Post*, p. 1.

Murphy, Rachel. 2002. *How Migrant Labor is Changing Rural China.* Cambridge, U.K.: Cambridge University Press.

Nakano, Lynne. 2000. "Volunteering as a Lifestyle Choice: Negotiating Self-Identities in Japan." *Ethnology* 39(2):93–109.

Narayan, Uma. 1997. "Towards a Feminist Vision of Citizenship: Rethinking the Implications of Dignity, Political Participation, and Nationality." In *Reconstructing Political Theory: Feminist Perspectives*, ed. by Mary Lyndon Shanley and Uma Narayan. Cambridge, UK: Polity Press.

Ngai, Mae M. 2004. *Impossible Subjects: Illegal Aliens and the Making of Modern America.* Princeton, NJ: Princeton University Press.

Ong, Aihwa. 1996. "Cultural Citizenship as Subject Making: Immigrants Negotiate Racial and Cultural Boundaries in the United States." *Current Anthropology* 37(5):737–62.

———. 1999. *Flexible Citizenship: The Cultural Logics of Transnationality.* Durham, NC: Duke University Press.

———. 2003. *Buddha is Hiding: Refugees, Citizenship, and the New America.* Berkeley: University of California Press.

Pan, Zhongdang, Chin-Chuan Lee, Joseph Man Chan, and Clement K. Y. So. 2001. "Orchestrating the Family-Nation Chorus: Chinese Media and Nationalism in the Hong Kong Handover." *Mass Communication and Society* 4(3):331–47.

Parreñas, Rhacel. 2001. *Servants of Globalization: Women, Migration, and Domestic Work.* Stanford, CA: Stanford University Press.

———. 2005. *Children of Global Migration: Transnational Families and Gendered Woes.* Stanford, CA: Stanford University Press.

Pessar, Patricia, and Sarah J. Mahler. 2003. "Transnational Migration: Bringing Gender In." *International Migration Review* 37(3):812–46.

Pieke, Frank, Pal Nyiri, Mette Thuno, and Antonella Ceccagno. 2004. *Transnational Chinese: Fujianese Migrants in Europe.* Stanford, CA: Stanford University Press.

Portes, Alejandro, and Ruben Rumbaut. 1996. *Immigrant America: A Portrait.* 2nd ed. Berkeley: University of California Press.

A Problem of People. 1960. Hong Kong: Hong Kong Government Information Pamphlet.

Right of Abode in the Hong Kong Special Administrative Region. 2000. Hong Kong: Immigration Department, the Government of the Hong Kong Special Administrative Region.

Rooney, Nuala. 2001. "Making House into Home: Interior Design in Hong Kong Public Housing." In Gordon Mathews and Tai-lok Lui, eds. *Consuming Hong Kong.* Hong Kong: Hong Kong University Press.

———. 2003. *At Home with Density.* Hong Kong: Hong Kong University Press.

Rosenthal, Elisabeth. July 2, 2002. "Migrants to Chinese boom town find hard lives." *New York Times,* p. A3.

Sassen, Saskia. 2005. "The Repositioning of Citizenship and Alienage: Emergent Subjects and Spaces for Politics." *Globalizations* 2(1):79–94.

Sassen-Koob, Saskia. 1996. "Notes on the Incorporation of Third World Women into Wage-Labor through Immigration and Off-shore Production." In *The Sociology of Migration,* ed. by R. Cohen. Cheltenham, UK: Edward Elgar Publishing Company.

Seller, Maxine S. 1984. "Historical Perspectives on American Immigration Policy: Case Studies and Current Implications." In *U.S. Immigration Policy,* ed. by Richard Hofstetter. Durham, NC: Duke University Press.

Shih, Shu-mei. 1998. "Gender and a New Geopolitics of Desire: The Seduction of Mainland Women in Taiwan and Hong Kong Media." *Signs* 23(2):287–319.

Silverstein, Paul. 2004. *Algeria in France: Transpolitics, Race, and Nation.* Bloomington: Indiana University Press.

Siu, Helen. 1988. "Immigrants and Social Ethos: Hong Kong in the Nineteen-Eighties." *Journal of the Hong Kong Branch of the Royal Asiatic Society* 26:1–16.

Skeldon, Ronald. 1994a. "Reluctant Exiles or Bold Pioneers: An Introduction to Migration from Hong Kong." In *Reluctant Exiles?: Migration from Hong Kong and the New Overseas Chinese,* ed. by Ronald Skeldon. Armonk, NY: M. E. Sharpe.

———. 1994b. "Immigration and Emigration: Current Trends, Dilemmas, and Policies." In *The Other Hong Kong Report 1994,* ed. by Donald McMillen and Man Si-wai. Hong Kong: The Chinese University Press.

———. 1994c. "Hong Kong in an International Migration System." In *Reluctant Exiles? Migration from Hong Kong and the New Overseas Chinese,* ed. by Ronald Skeldon. Armonk, NY: M. E. Sharpe.

Smart, Alan. 1992. *Making Room: Squatter Clearance in Hong Kong.* Hong Kong: University of Hong Kong, Centre of Asian Studies.

———. 2002. "Agents of Eviction: The Squatter Control and Clearance Division of Hong Kong's Housing Department." *Singapore Journal of Tropical Geography* 23(3):333–47.

———. 2003. "Sharp Edges, Fuzzy Categories and Transborder Networks: Managing and Housing New Arrivals in Hong Kong." *Ethnic and Racial Studies* 26(2):218–33.

———. 2006. *The Shek Kip Mei Myth: Squatters, Fires, and Colonial Rule in Hong Kong, 1950–1963.* Hong Kong: Hong Kong University Press.

Smart, Alan, and Josephine Smart. 2001. "Local Citizenship: Welfare Reform, Urban/Rural Status, and Exclusion in China." *Environment and Planning A* 33:1853–69.

Solinger, Dorothy. 1999. *Contesting Citizenship in Urban China: Peasant Migrants, the State, and the Logic of the Market*. Berkeley: University of California Press.

Soysal, Yasmine Nuhoglu. 1994. *Limits of Citizenship: Migrants and Postnational Membership in Europe*. Chicago: University of Chicago Press.

———. 2000. "Citizenship and Identity: Living in Diasporas in Post-War Europe?" *Ethnic and Racial Studies* 23(1):1–16.

Stafford, Charles. 2000. *Separation and Reunion in Modern China*. Cambridge, UK: Cambridge University Press.

Steinberg, Stephen. 1989. *The Ethnic Myth: Race, Ethnicity, and Class in America*. Boston: Beacon Press.

Stewart, Kathleen. 1996. *A Space on the Side of the Road*. Princeton, NJ: Princeton University Press.

Tam, M. S. M. 1996. "Normalization of 'Second Wives'": Gender Contestation in Hong Kong." *Asian Journal of Women's Studies* 2:113–32.

Tse, Thomas Kwan-Choi. 2004. "Civic Education and the Making of Deformed Citizenry: From British Colony to Chinese SAR." In *Remaking Citizenship in Hong Kong: Community, Nation, and the Global City*, eds. Agnes Ku and Ngai Pun. London: RoutledgeCurzon.

Tu, Wei-ming. 1994. "Cultural China: The Periphery as the Center." In *The Living Tree: The Changing Meaning of Being Chinese Today*, ed. by Tu Wei-ming. Stanford, CA: Stanford University Press.

Turner, Bryan S. 1993. "Contemporary Problems in the Theory of Citizenship." In *Citizenship and Social Theory*, ed. Bryan S. Turner. Thousand Oaks, CA: Sage Publications.

———. 2001. "The Erosion of Citizenship." *British Journal of Sociology* 52(2): 198–209.

———. 2004. Forward: Making and Unmaking Citizenship in Neo-liberal Times." In *Remaking Citizenship in Hong Kong: Community, Nation, and the Global City*, eds. Agnes Ku and Ngai Pun. London: RoutledgeCurzon.

Verdery, Katherine. 1998. "Transnationalism, Nationalism, Citizenship, and Property: Eastern Europe since 1989." *American Ethnologist* 25(2):291–306.

Walzer, Michael. 1983. *Spheres of Justice: A Defense of Pluralism and Equality*. New York: Basic Books.

Wang, Danyu. 2004. "Ritualistic Coresidence and the Weakening of Filial Practice in Rural China." In *Filial Piety: Practice and Discourse in Contemporary East Asia*, ed. by Charlotte Ikels. Stanford, CA: Stanford University Press.

Wang, Lu. 2006. "The Urban Chinese Educational System and the Marginality of Migrant Children." In *Chinese Citizenship: Views from the Margins*, ed. by Vanessa L. Fong and Rachel Murphy. London: Routledge.

Watson, James L. 1975. *Emigration and the Chinese Lineage: The Mans in Hong Kong and London*. Berkeley: University of California Press.

———. 1988. "The Structure of Chinese Funerary Rites: Elementary Forms, Ritual Sequence, and the Primacy of Performance." In *Death Ritual in Late*

Imperial and Modern China, ed. by James L. Watson and Evelyn Rawski. Berkeley: University of California Press.

———. 1997. *Golden Arches East: McDonald's in East Asia*. Stanford, CA: Stanford University Press.

Watson, Rubie. 1985. *Inequality among Brothers, Class and Kinship in South China*. Cambridge: Cambridge University Press.

———. 2004. "Chinese Bridal Laments: The Claims of a Dutiful Daughter." In *Village Life in Hong Kong*, by James L. Watson and Rubie S. Watson. Hong Kong: The Chinese University Press.

Whyte, Martin King. 2004. "Filial Obligations in Chinese Families: Paradoxes of Modernization." In *Filial Piety: Practice and Discourse in Contemporary East Asia*, ed. by Charlotte Ikels. Stanford, CA: Stanford University Press.

Wikan, Unni. 2002. *Generous Betrayal: Politics of Culture in the New Europe*. Chicago: University of Chicago Press.

Wolf, Margery. 1972. *Women and the Family in Rural Taiwan*. Stanford, CA: Stanford University Press.

Wong, C. K., and N. S. P. Lee. 2000. "Popular Belief in State Intervention for Social Protection in China." *Journal of Social Policy* 29:109–16.

Wong, Siu-lun. 1988. *Emigrant Entrepreneurs: Shanghai Industrialists in Hong Kong*. Hong Kong: Oxford University Press.

Wu, David Yen-ho. 1994. "The Construction of Chinese and Non-Chinese Identities." In *The Living Tree: The Changing Meaning of Being Chinese Today*, ed. by Tu Wei-ming. Stanford, CA: Stanford University Press.

Wu, Ka-ming. 2003. "Discourse on *Baau Yih Naai* (Keeping Concubines): Questions of Citizenship and Identity in Postcolonial Hong Kong." In *Gender and Change in Hong Kong: Globalization, Postcolonialism, and Chinese Patriarchy*, ed. by Eliza W. Y. Lee. Honolulu: University of Hawaii Press.

Xinhua General News Service. February 24, 2007. "35 Percent Hong Kong Men Marry Mainland Women in 2006: Statistics." Xinhua News Agency.

Yan, Yunxiang. 1996. *The Flow of Gifts: Reciprocity and Social Networks in a Chinese Village*. Stanford, CA: Stanford University Press.

———. 2003. *Private Life Under Socialism: Love, Intimacy, and Family Change in a Chinese Village 1949–1999*. Stanford, CA: Stanford University Press.

Yang, Mayfair. 1994. *Gifts, Favors, and Banquets: The Art of Social Relationships in China*. Ithaca, NY: Cornell University Press.

Yeung, Yue-man, and D. W. Drakakis-Smith. 1982. "Public Housing in the city states of Hong Kong and Singapore." In *Urban Planning Practice in Developing Countries*, ed. by John Taylor and David Williams. Oxford, UK: Pergamon Press.

Yoon, Suh-kyung. 2002. "Crisis of Confidence." *Far Eastern Economic Review*, August 29:43.

Yu, Xinzhong. 2002. "Citizenship, Ideology, and the PRC Constitution." In *Changing Meanings of Citizenship in Modern China*, ed. by Merle Goldman and Elizabeth Perry. Cambridge, MA: Harvard University Press.

Yuval-Davis, Nira, and Pnina Werbner, eds. 1999. *Women, Citizenship, and Difference.* London: Zed Books.

Zhang, Li. 2001. *Strangers in the City: Reconfigurations of Space, Power, and Social Networks Within China's Floating Population.* Stanford, CA: Stanford University Press.

Index

Abbas, Ackbar, 118–19, 127
adopted children, 43, 54–56, 184
Adrian, Bonnie, 80, 112, 272n13
age of immigrants, 76, 77
Alba, Richard, 18, 19, 272n1
Ames, Roger T., 10, 40
Anagnost, Ann, 194, 206, 222, 273n4, 275n6
Anderson, Benedict, 20
Aretxaga, Begona, 19–20
Asian financial crisis of 1997, 5, 99, 227–28, 238
attitudes of Hong Kong people (*heung-gong yahn*) toward mainlanders, 11, 52, 59, 166, 186; and ID cards, 61–64; as negative/antagonistic, 6, 7, 12, 14, 22, 32–33, 45–46, 47–48, 57, 58, 61–65, 64, 67, 72, 77, 80, 113, 137–38, 140, 151–52, 162, 165, 172, 197, 217–19, 223–24, 225–28, 235–38, 248–49, 253–54, 258–59, 260, 261, 265, 275n7; and pan-Chinese identity, 211–12, 255; social worker attitudes, 217–19, 224–49. *See also* cultural differences between HKSAR and PRC; family relationships; Hong Kong discourses of membership/belonging; immigration policies; political difference between HKSAR and PRC

Basch, N., 15
Basic Law of HKSAR, 50–56
Beijing, 76
Benmayor, Rina, 19
Berdahl, Daphne, 20

Borneman, John, 20
Bosco, Joseph, 128, 272n14
Bosniak, Linda, 34
Bradford, Sara, 38
British colonial government, 188, 189, 252, 274n6; and citizens' rights, 21, 22, 35, 220–21; City District Officer Scheme, 195; during Cold War, 43, 45, 258, 271n7; economic policies, 29, 146, 154, 256, 257–58; Family Life Education (FLE) programs, 195–96; housing policies, 107, 114, 115–17, 119, 127–28, 271n7; ID cards, 48; immigration policies, 29, 35, 40–46, 48–51, 270n1; Mutual Aid Committees (MACs), 195; and Opium Wars, 9
British Nationality Act of 1981, 50
Brownell, Susan, 77
Burns, John P., 41, 42, 46, 49

cage dwellers, 247
Canada: citizenship in, 35; immigration to, 23
Cantonese, 7, 19, 28, 41, 84, 99, 190, 270n3, 272n3; English loan words in, 272n4, 274n1; *heunggong yahn*, 14, 61; in Hong Kong vs. Guangdong Province, 83, 152, 192; *jaahtsou*, 274n6; key terms in, 14, 47, 72, 75, 79, 105, 143, 145, 152–53, 156, 162, 169, 219, 225, 241, 244, 255, 268nn5,1, 274n3,5,6; learning of, 87, 91, 150, 152–53, 167, 171, 179
Cantonese cuisine, 133–36